Be My Disciples

Peter M. Esposito
President

Jo Rotunno, MA
Publisher

Susan Smith
Director of Project Development

Program Advisors
Michael P. Horan, PhD
Elizabeth Nagel, SSD

GRADE FIVE

PARISH EDITION

The Subcommittee on the Catechism, United States Conference of Catholic Bishops, has found this catechetical series, copyright 2013, to be in conformity with the *Catechism of the Catholic Church*.

NIHIL OBSTAT
Rev. Msgr. Robert Coerver
Censor Librorum

IMPRIMATUR
† Most Reverend Kevin J. Farrell, DD
Bishop of Dallas
August 22, 2011

The *Nihil Obstat and Imprimatur* are official declarations that the material reviewed is free of doctrinal or moral error. No implication is contained therein that those granting the *Nihil Obstat and Imprimatur* agree with the contents, opinions, or statements expressed.

Acknowledgments

Excerpts are taken and adapted from the *New American Bible* with Revised New Testament and Revised Psalms ©1991, 1986, 1970, Confraternity of Christian Doctrine, Washington, D.C., and are used by permission. All Rights Reserved. No part of the *New American Bible* may be reproduced in any form without permission in writing from the copyright owner.

Excerpts are taken or adapted from the English translation of the *Rite of Baptism for Children*, ©1969, International Committee on English in the Liturgy, Inc. (ICEL). All rights reserved.

Excerpts are taken and adapted from the English translation of the *Roman Missal*, ©2010, International Commission on English in the Liturgy, Inc. (ICEL). All rights reserved

Toll Free   877-275-4725
Fax   800-688-8356

Visit us at RCLBenziger.com
and ByMyDisciples.com

20705 ISBN 978-0-7829-1574-7 (Student Edition)
20715 ISBN 978-0-7829-1580-8 (Catechist Edition)

5th Printing.
January 2016.

Contents

Welcome to Be My †Disciples

Jesus invites you to be his **disciple**. He wants you to know him better, to understand his message, and to follow his way of life. During this year, you will learn more about Jesus and what he asks of you. You will learn about virtues, habits, and qualities that are the marks of a disciple. And you will learn that Catholics who follow Jesus don't keep it to themselves. Jesus' message is such Good News that you just have to share it!

Solve the Puzzle

On the next page, you will be invited to search through your student book to get a preview of what you will be learning this year. The puzzle below is a little bit like a crossword puzzle. Begin by solving the six clues in the boxes on page 7. Then transfer the letters of your answers onto the puzzle squares below that have the corresponding numbers. The solution is a sentence that tells the main theme of the Gospel.

	9	14		20	8	5		16	1	19	3	8	1	12
13	25	19	20	5	18	25		10	5	19	21	19		
16	1	19	19	5	4		6	18	15	13		12	9	6	5
	20	8	18	15	21	7	8		4	5	1	20	8	
	9	14	20	15		1		14	5	23		1	14	4
	7	12	15	18	9	15	21	19		12	9	6	5	

1. We Believe, Part One

This year in Unit 1, you will learn how the __ __ __ __ God speaks to us

    23 15 18 4

through creation, people, and himself. God speaking to us

is called __ __ v __ __ __ __ __ v __ __ __ __ __ __ __.

          4 9   9 14 5 18 5 5 12 1 20 9 15 14

(See pages 13–14.)

2. We Believe, Part Two

This year in Unit 2, you will learn about the section of the Gospel
that tells about the Suffering and Death of __ __ __ __ __. The

                                           10 5 19 21 19

section is called the __ __ __ __ __ __ __ narrative. *(See page 56.)*

                      16 1 19 19 9 15 14

3. We Worship, Part One

In Unit 3, you will learn more about the Church's __ __ __ __ __ __ __,

                                                 12 9 20 21 18 7 25

the "work of the people" that we do when we worship God. The
yearly cycle of the Church's celebration of the liturgy is called the

__ __ __ __ __ __ __ __ __ __ year. *(See pages 85–86.)*

12 9 20 21 18 7 9 3 1 12

4. We Worship, Part Two

In Unit 4, you will learn about how Sacraments celebrate
God's love for us. The Sacraments of __ __ __ __ __ __ __

                                      8 5 1 12 9 14 7

forgive us our sins and reconcile us to God. *(See page 122.)*

5. We Live, Part One

In Unit 5, you will learn that God always keeps his promise.

__ __ __ __, __ __ __ __ __ __ __ __ __ __ __ __

7 15 4 19   6 1 9 20 8 6 21 12 14 5 19 19

is everlasting. *(See pages 172–173.)*

6. We Live, Part Two

In Unit 6, you will learn about the __ __ __ __ __

                                    7 18 5 1 20

__ __ __ __ __ __ __ __ __ __ __. We are to love God and

3 15 13 13 1 14 4 13 5 14 20

we are to __ __ v __ __ __ __ __ __ __ __ __ b __ __ __

          12 15 5 15 21 18 14 5 9 7 8 15 18 19

as we love ourselves. *(See page 189.)*

Do Whatever He Tells You!

The leader leads a procession to the prayer space, holding the Bible high for all to see. He/she places the Bible in a place of honor on the prayer table. All follow and gather around the prayer table and make the Sign of the Cross together.

Leader: Lord, we gather today to honor you and thank you for the gift of your Word. We want to follow the example of Mary, your Mother, and be your disciples in all we say and do.

All: **We will do whatever you tell us to do.**

Leader: A reading from the Gospel according the John.

All: **Glory to you, O Lord.**

Leader: *Proclaim John 2:1-10.*
The Gospel of the Lord.

All: **Praise to you, Lord Jesus Christ.**

Leader: Lord Jesus, your mother, Mary, was your first and best disciple. We want to be your disciples too. Help us to follow you as we learn of your words and deeds in the Gospels. We will do whatever you tell us to do.

All: **Amen! We will do whatever you tell us to do!**

All exchange a sign of peace.

We Believe
Part One

The Trinity

Jesus went to see his cousin John who was baptizing people at the River Jordan. Jesus asked John to baptize him.

After Jesus was baptized, he came up from the water and behold, the heavens were opened [for him], and he saw the Spirit of God descending like a dove [and] coming upon him. And a voice came from the heavens, saying, "This is my beloved Son, with whom I am well pleased."

MATTHEW 3:16–17

What I Have Learned

What is something you already know about these faith terms?

Divine Revelation

_____

_____

_____

The Old Testament

Bible stories before Jesus was born

The Holy Trinity

Father, son and holy spirit

Faith Terms to Know

Put an X next to the faith terms you know. Put a ? next to faith terms you need to learn more about.

- X faith
- X Gospel
- X Lord
- ? Annunciation
- ? Evangelists
- X Abba
- ? inspiration of the Bible

The Bible

What do you know about how to find passages in the Bible?

Look at names at tops.

_____

The Church

What is one thing you could tell a friend about what the Church believes?

That God created everything.

_____

Questions I Have

What questions would you like to ask about the mystery of God?

_____

_____

Looking Ahead

In this chapter, the Holy Spirit invites you to ▶

 **EXPLORE** how Blessed John XXIII helped us live as followers of Christ.

 **DISCOVER** the different ways that God reveals himself to us.

 **DECIDE** how you will come to know God better.

CHAPTER

1

Speak, Lord

? What are some of the ways you come to know people better?

We learn about others through many different ways. One of the ways we can learn about people is through those who know and love others. God the Father sent his Son, Jesus, so that we could know God and his love more deeply.

For God so loved the world that he gave his only Son. JOHN 3:16

? What is God saying to you in this passage? What are some other ways we might come to know God better?

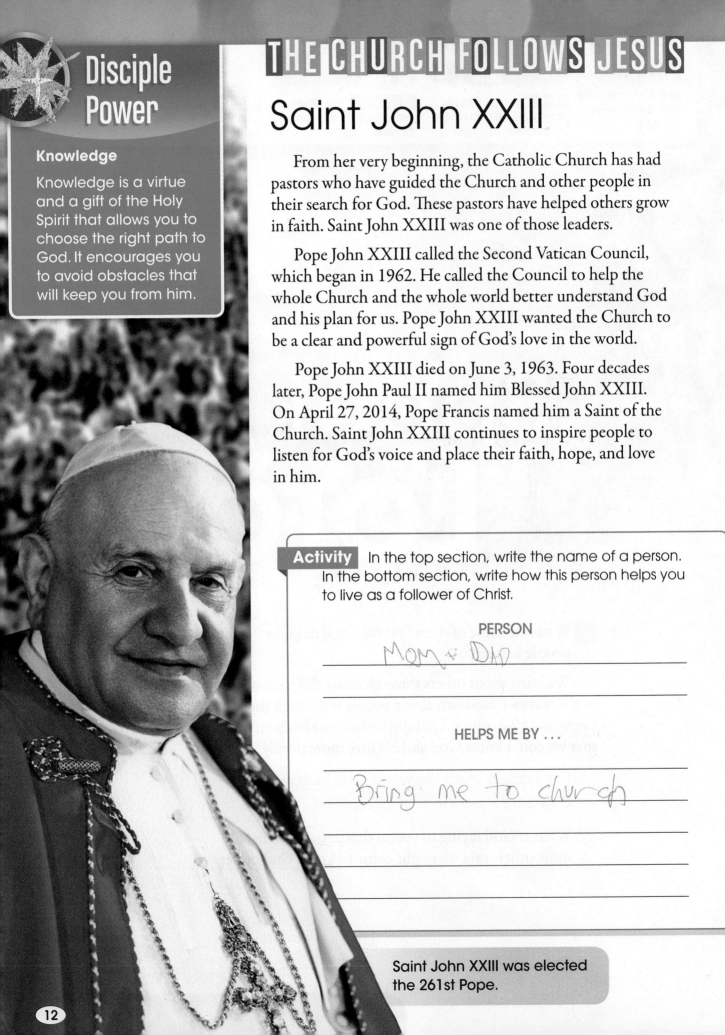

Disciple Power

Knowledge

Knowledge is a virtue and a gift of the Holy Spirit that allows you to choose the right path to God. It encourages you to avoid obstacles that will keep you from him.

Saint John XXIII

From her very beginning, the Catholic Church has had pastors who have guided the Church and other people in their search for God. These pastors have helped others grow in faith. Saint John XXIII was one of those leaders.

Pope John XXIII called the Second Vatican Council, which began in 1962. He called the Council to help the whole Church and the whole world better understand God and his plan for us. Pope John XXIII wanted the Church to be a clear and powerful sign of God's love in the world.

Pope John XXIII died on June 3, 1963. Four decades later, Pope John Paul II named him Blessed John XXIII. On April 27, 2014, Pope Francis named him a Saint of the Church. Saint John XXIII continues to inspire people to listen for God's voice and place their faith, hope, and love in him.

Activity In the top section, write the name of a person. In the bottom section, write how this person helps you to live as a follower of Christ.

PERSON

MOM & DAD

HELPS ME BY . . .

Bring me to church

Saint John XXIII was elected the 261st Pope.

Divine Revelation

Every one of us is born with a desire within us. This desire makes us realize there is someone who is much greater than we are. That someone is God. This desire is part of who we are as human beings. Each of us is looking for God, and he is looking for us.

Saint Augustine, a bishop in Africa in the fourth century, summarized our desire and our search for God. Augustine wrote, "You, O God, have made us for yourself, and our hearts are restless until they rest in you" (FROM *CONFESSIONS*).

God's love for us is so great that he comes to us and invites us to know him, to have hope in him, and to love him. This is the reason God created us.

God Reveals Himself

How does God help us get to know him? The answer is: God reveals himself to us.

We cannot see God. We cannot know what is in God's mind. We cannot, on our own, come to know who God is and his plan of goodness for us and for the world. So God, out of love, revealed himself to us. **Divine Revelation** is God making himself and his plan of creation and Salvation known.

God has revealed that he has created us. He is always inviting us to share in his life and love. Making God part of our lives, learning about him, and knowing him bring us happiness. God wants us to be completely happy with him, not only forever in Heaven but also now on Earth. That is why God created us.

How does God's revelation show us that he loves us?

FAITH FOCUS
In what ways has God revealed himself?

FAITH VOCABULARY
Divine Revelation
God making known over time the mystery of himself and his divine plan of creation and Salvation.

faith
One of the three Theological Virtues. A supernatural gift and power from God inviting us to know and believe in him, and our free response to that invitation.

Saint Anselm of Canterbury

Anselm was the archbishop of Canterbury, England. He is honored as one of the great theologians of the Church. A theologian is a person who studies and explains the faith so we can better understand what God has revealed. Anselm described his work as "faith seeking understanding." His feast day is April 21.

God Speaks Through Creation

One way God speaks to us is through his creation. God is the Creator who tells us about himself through the world we live in. When we look at creation, we realize how wonderful God is.

The sky, the stars, and the galaxies sing of God's love. The beauty of horses galloping through a field, dolphins gliding through the ocean, and eagles soaring in the skies all reflect God's goodness and beauty. All creation gives honor and glory to God.

God Speaks Through People

One of the best ways God helps us know him is through people. Throughout the ages, God has chosen special people through whom he has revealed himself. In the Bible, God tells us that the Israelites were the first people he chose. They would be his people, and he would be their God. The writer of the Book of Deuteronomy, the fifth book of the Bible, reminded the Israelites:

[The Lord] has chosen you from all the nations on the face of the earth to be a people peculiarly his own. DEUTERONOMY 7:6

God was no stranger to his people. He was always present with them.

Activity Design a sticker to give praise to God.

God Is Fully Revealed in Jesus

God revealed himself most fully in his only Son, Jesus Christ. Jesus is the Word of God. He is the Son of God, who became one of us and lived among us. Jesus spent his whole life on Earth revealing God and God's love. Through all of his actions and words, we come to know God.

The Gift of Faith

God is always inviting us to come to know him and believe in him. He gives us the gift of **faith**. God helps us listen to and say yes to that invitation. Faith is a supernatural gift and power that helps us respond to God's invitation with all our heart, mind, soul, and strength.

The Holy Spirit helps us accept the gift of faith. When we accept and live the gift of faith, God works through us to help others come to know, love, and serve him. We are people of faith. We are the community of believers in Jesus Christ. We are the Church.

Catholics Believe

Created for Happiness

God created us to share in his life and love and to be completely happy with him, not only forever in Heaven but also now on Earth.

Activity A cinquain is a five-line verse. Follow the directions and write a cinquain about Jesus.

Jesus, the Word of God

Write two words that describe Jesus.

loving   forgiving

Write three action words that describe Jesus.

outgoing   trustful   healing

Write four words that describe a feeling about Jesus.

humble   caring
helpful   happy

Write another word for Jesus.

God's Son

I FOLLOW JESUS

Every day, the Holy Spirit is helping you come to know, love, and serve God better. Learning what the Catholic Church teaches will help you understand and live what God has revealed. The Holy Spirit will help you grow as a child of God and as a disciple of Jesus Christ.

LEARNING MORE ABOUT GOD

Place a check in the box next to the things you do to grow in your faith. Then write down other things you can do to come to know God better.

- ☑ Reading the Bible
- ☐ Learning the teachings of the Church
- ☑ Praying to the Holy Spirit
- ☐ Thinking about God's gift of creation

Other things I can do to know God better include:

Pray

Go to church more

Some people who can help me grow in my faith are:

priests

teachers

parents + sister

MY FAITH CHOICE

This week, I will try to know God better. I will

read a Bible story

 Pray, thanking God for the gift of knowledge, and ask the Holy Spirit to continue to help you grow in knowing and living your faith.

Chapter Review

Choose three of the faith terms in the word bank. Use each term in a sentence to describe how you come to know God.

creation	people	Jesus Christ	faith	Church

1. Jesus Christ is Gods only son.

2. God made people.

3. God made all of creation.

TO HELP YOU REMEMBER

1. Divine Revelation is God making himself and his plan of creation and Salvation known.

2. We can come to know God through creation, especially through people.

3. God most fully reveals himself in Jesus Christ, the Son of God, who became one of us and lived among us.

Lord, Help Us Believe

Pray this act of faith. Ask God to help you come to know and believe in him better.

Leader: "Speak, LORD, for your servant is listening."

All: **"Speak, LORD, for your servant is listening."**

Leader: Lord, help me come to know you better.

All: **"Speak, LORD, for your servant is listening."**

Leader: LORD, help me listen and say yes to your gift of faith.

All: **"Speak, LORD, for your servant is listening."**
Amen.

1 SAMUEL 3:9

With My Family

This Week . . .

In Chapter 1, "Speak, Lord," your child learned:

▶ Every person has been created with an innate longing and a desire for God.

▶ God has revealed himself and gives us the gift of faith to know and respond to that desire.

▶ Creation points to the existence of a wise, loving, and all-powerful God.

▶ In Jesus Christ, the Son of God, who became one of us and lived among us, God has revealed himself most fully.

▶ The virtue of knowledge is a gift of the Holy Spirit that allows us to choose the right path that will lead us to God. It encourages us to avoid obstacles that will keep us from him.

For more about related teachings of the Church, see the *Catechism of the Catholic Church*, 50–67, 142–175, 185–197, and the *United States Catholic Catechism for Adults*, pages 11–19 and 35–47.

◼ Sharing God's Word

Invite all family members to share their favorite Bible stories. Then talk about what each story tells us about God. Emphasize that the Holy Spirit helps us know and believe in God.

◼ We Live as Disciples

The Christian home and family is a school of discipleship. Choose one of the following activities to help the members of your family follow Jesus:

▶ Invite family members to share the names of people who have helped them know about God. Share how these people have helped.

▶ Watch TV or look through magazines. Talk about what the commercials and advertisements tell us about happiness. How does this compare to the happiness God created us to have?

◼ Our Spiritual Journey

Daily prayer is vital to the Christian life. Through prayer we converse with God. He is our companion on our earthly journey. In this chapter, your child prayed an act of faith. Read and pray together this prayer on page 17.

For more ideas on ways your family can live as disciples of Jesus, visit **www.BeMyDisciples.com**

The Word of God

[?] What is your favorite book to read?

The Bible is the most widely read book in the world. In the Bible, God tells us about his love for us. God most especially tells us about his love through the words and actions of Jesus, the Son of God. In one Gospel story, Jesus calms a storm and calls on his disciples to have faith.

> [Jesus] woke up, rebuked the wind, and said to the sea, "Quiet! Be still!" The wind ceased and there was a great calm. Then he asked [his disciples], "Why are you terrified? Do you not yet have faith?"
> They were filled with great awe and said to one another, "Who then is this whom even wind and sea obey?"
>
> MARK 4:39–41

[?] What can you learn about faith from this story?

Reverence for the Bible

Christians are strengthened by hearing and listening reverently to the Word of God. Saint Jerome reminded us of the importance of the Bible. He wrote, "Ignorance of the Scriptures is ignorance of Christ."

Before the printing press was invented in the sixteenth century, scribes copied the Bible by hand. Artists painted pages of the Bible with colorful images and decorated the edges of the pages with gold.

Many Christian families have a family Bible. They write down the key events of their family's faith story in it. They record Baptisms, marriages, and other important milestones in the faith history of the family.

At every celebration of the Mass, the Word of God is proclaimed aloud. We carry the Book of the Gospels with dignity in the entrance procession and proclaim the Word of God from a place of honor called the *ambo*. This celebration shows the faith of the Church in the Bible as God's own word to us.

When we gather with other members of the Church or as a family to read and listen to the Bible, Jesus is there.

? When does your family and parish hear the Word of God?

Sacred Scripture

Books tell stories of happiness and sadness, successes and failures. The Bible tells the story of God's love for his people and their response to his love. The Bible is God's own word to us. God speaks to us through the Bible.

Sacred Scripture is another name for the Bible. It is a name that means "holy writings." The Bible is a collection of many holy writings. The Church divides the Bible into the Old Testament and the New Testament. The word *testament* means "covenant."

The Holy Spirit inspired, or guided, the human writers of the Bible to faithfully and accurately communicate God's Word. We call this truth of our faith the **Inspiration of the Bible**. Guided by the Holy Spirit, the Church has identified the forty-six books of the Old Testament and the twenty-seven books of the New Testament to be the inspired Word of God. We call this the *canon* of Scripture.

FAITH FOCUS
What kinds of writings are in the Bible?

FAITH VOCABULARY
Inspiration of the Bible
The Holy Spirit guiding the human writers of Sacred Scripture to faithfully and accurately communicate God's Word.

Gospel
The Gospel is the Good News of God's love revealed in the life, suffering, Death, Resurrection, and Ascension of Jesus Christ.

Activity Do you know how to look up a Bible passage? Look up John 8:31–32. First decide whether the passage is in the Old Testament or the New Testament. Then follow the clues below to find the passage.

JOHN = Book of the Bible
(HINT! Look at the top of the Bible page.)

JOHN 8 = Chapter

JOHN 8:31–32 = Verses

Read the passage silently and write in the space what you learned.

_____

_____

_____

Saint Jerome

Saint Jerome (343–420) translated the Bible into Latin. Jerome's translation became known as the Vulgate Bible and was the standard Bible for the Roman Catholic Church for hundreds of years. Saint Jerome is honored as one of the four great Doctors of the Western Church. His feast day is September 30.

The Old Testament

The Old Testament tells the story of the Covenant. The Covenant is the solemn agreement that God and his people entered into. The story of the Covenant begins at creation. It continues with the stories of Noah, Abraham, Moses, and the prophets.

Torah

The Torah is the first five books of the Old Testament. These books are also known as the *Pentateuch*, a word meaning "five containers." The Pentateuch contains the story of the Covenant, the Ten Commandments, and other laws that help God's people live the Covenant.

The Historical Books

There are sixteen historical books. They tell about the struggle of the Israelites to live the Covenant faithfully.

The Wisdom Books

There are seven wisdom books. They teach practical ways to live God's Law.

The Prophetic Books

There are eighteen prophetic books. These books contain the teachings of the prophets. The prophets were people God chose to speak in his name.

? What is the main content of the Torah, the historical books, and the wisdom books of the Bible?

Samuel anointing David as the future King of Israel.

The New Testament

The New Testament reveals that Jesus Christ is the Son of God, the Savior and Redeemer of the world. Jesus is the new and everlasting Covenant. He reveals God and his love for us more fully than anyone else did or ever will do.

The Gospels

The four Gospels of Matthew, Mark, Luke, and John are the heart of the New Testament. Each **Gospel** shares in its own way the story and meaning of Jesus' life, suffering and Passion, Death, Resurrection, and Ascension.

The Acts of the Apostles

The Acts of the Apostles tells the story of the first years of the Church and the work of the Church in the world. Acts gives an account of the Apostles as they spread the Gospel throughout the world.

The Epistles and Letters

These twenty-one letters of Saint Paul the Apostle and other early Christian writers teach about Jesus and how Christians are to live. Longer, formal letters are called *Epistles.*

The Book of Revelation

The Book of Revelation is the last book of the Bible. In it, the Holy Spirit encourages Christians who are suffering to remain faithful to Jesus Christ.

Catholics Believe

Lectionary and Book of the Gospels

The first two readings at Mass on Sunday are proclaimed from the Lectionary. The deacon or priest proclaims the Gospel from the Book of the Gospels.

Table of Contents

Chapter 1

_____

Chapter 2

_____

Chapter 3

_____

Activity The writers of the Bible told the faith story of God's people. You also have a faith story. In the space on the right, write a table of contents for a book that would share your own faith story.

I FOLLOW JESUS

As you listen to the Word of God, the Holy Spirit helps you listen with reverence to what God says to you. His gift of knowledge helps you understand God's Word. His gift of courage gives you strength to put God's Word into practice and to live as a disciple of Jesus.

GOD'S LIVING WORD

Design a poster or Web page using words and images to encourage others to live God's Word.

MY FAITH CHOICE

This week, I will listen to and live God's Word. I will

_____

_____

 Pray, "Come, Holy Spirit, fill my heart with reverence as I listen to your holy Word. Help me live as a disciple of Jesus in my home, at school, and in my neighborhood. Amen."

Chapter Review

Match the faith terms in the left column with the descriptions in the right column.

Terms

_____ **1.** inspiration

_____ **2.** Sacred Scripture

_____ **3.** Pentateuch

_____ **4.** Gospels

_____ **5.** canon of Scripture

Descriptions

a. the first five books of the Old Testament

b. the list of inspired books named by the Church and collected in the Bible

c. the first four books of the New Testament

d. the holy writings of God

e. the help that the Holy Spirit gave to the human writers of the Bible

A Light for My Path

Praying with the Bible is a form of meditation in which we spend quiet time with God. We read and reflect on his Word. We make a decision to live as disciples of Christ. Meditate on God's Word using these steps.

1. Sit quietly. Close your eyes. Breathe slowly.

2. In your mind, picture yourself in a place where you can talk and listen to God.

3. Open your Bible and read John 8:12–16.

4. Take time to talk and listen to God. Say, "Your word, Lord, is a light for my path" (based on Psalm 119:105).

5. After a few quiet moments, ask the Holy Spirit, "What is your word saying to me?" Share your thoughts with a partner.

6. Silently make a faith decision to put God's Word into action.

With My Family

This Week . . .

In Chapter 2, "The Word of God," your child learned:

▶ The Bible contains the holy writings that the Holy Spirit inspired God's people to write.

▶ The list of writings named by the Church is called the canon of Scripture.

▶ The Old Testament tells the first part of the story of the Covenant that God made with his people.

▶ The New Testament tells about the fulfillment of God's promise in the new and everlasting Covenant of Jesus Christ.

▶ The virtue of reverence helps us to have and to show a deep respect for both God and the Church.

For more about related teachings of the Church, see the *Catechism of the Catholic Church*, 50–133, and the *United States Catholic Catechism for Adults*, pages 11–33.

Sharing God's Word

Read together 1 Thessalonians 2:13 and 2 Timothy 3:16–17. Emphasize that the Bible is God's Word to us.

We Live as Disciples

The Christian home and family is a school of discipleship. Choose one of the following activities to do as a family, or design a similar activity of your own:

▶ Talk with each other about how the Bible guides your family to live as disciples of Jesus. Discuss: How is the Bible a light for our path?

▶ Choose a Bible story that you are familiar with. Find it in the Bible and read it together. Pray it as a prayer of meditation.

▶ Invite each person to share the name of a favorite person in the Bible. Share with each other the stories about these people.

Our Spiritual Journey

The prayer of meditation helps us reflect on God's word and ask him to help us understand its meaning for our lives. Such a conversation with God is vital as we live our lives of faith. In this chapter, your child prayed a form of meditation called lectio divina. Read and pray together this prayer on page 25.

For more ideas on ways your family can live as disciples of Jesus, visit **www.BeMyDisciples.com**

Looking Ahead

In this chapter, the Holy Spirit invites you to ▶

EXPLORE how Saint Augustine learned about the mystery of God.

DISCOVER the Church's teaching about the Holy Trinity.

DECIDE how to show love for the Holy Trinity.

The Holy Trinity

[?] What is an example of a mystery you might be able to solve by yourself? What kind would you need the help of others to solve?

The words below are from the Old Testament Book of Psalms. In them, the writer longs to know more about God. Listen reverently to these words from the Bible:

Make known to me your ways, Lord;
  teach me your paths.
Guide me in your truth and teach me,
  for you are God my savior.
  For you I wait all the long day.

PSALM 25:4–5

[?] What else do you know about who God is? What would you like to know?

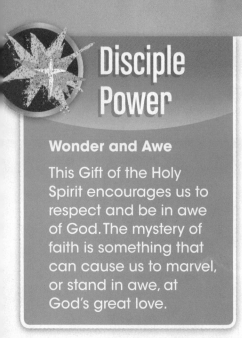

Disciple Power

Wonder and Awe

This Gift of the Holy Spirit encourages us to respect and be in awe of God. The mystery of faith is something that can cause us to marvel, or stand in awe, at God's great love.

Saint Augustine

Many Christians have tried to understand what Jesus meant when he said there is One God who is Father, Son, and Holy Spirit. One of those who tried to understand this mystery of faith was Saint Augustine. You may remember reading about him in Chapter 1.

Did you know there is a famous story about Saint Augustine and his efforts to learn more about God? Whether this story really happened is not as important as the underlying truth it teaches.

One day, Augustine was walking on the beach. The vast ocean inspired him to think about God. As he was walking along, he met a young boy who was taking water from the sea with a small bucket. Augustine watched as the boy kept pouring the water, one bucket at a time, into a hole he had dug in the sand.

Augustine became very curious and asked, "Why do you keep pouring water into the hole?" The boy answered, "Isn't it plain to see? I'm putting the ocean in the hole."

Augustine began to laugh. "That's impossible," he told the boy. "The great sea is much too large for that small hole." The boy looked up and said, "And God is too big for your little mind." Suddenly, the boy disappeared.

In many ways, with the guidance of the Holy Spirit, we can come to know more about the mystery of God the Holy Trinity in whose image we have been created.

? How does this story help your faith in God grow?

The Holy Trinity

Jesus told his disciples,

"Go, therefore, and make disciples of all nations, baptizing them in the name of the Father, and of the Son, and of the holy Spirit." MATTHEW 28:19

The Church follows that command today. Every time the Church baptizes a person, we name the mystery of who God is. We baptize in the name of the One God who is the **Holy Trinity**. We baptize in the name of the One God who is God the Father, God the Son, and God the Holy Spirit. The mystery of the Holy Trinity is the deepest and most central belief of the Christian faith. This is a truth about God we could have never known unless God revealed it to us.

The Old Testament

In the Old Testament, we read the beginning of the story of God's Revelation of himself. God first revealed himself at creation to Adam and Eve. Years later, God came to Abraham and Sarah and revealed that he alone is God. Their descendants, the Israelites, shared through many generations their faith in the One True God.

FAITH FOCUS
What is the mystery of the Holy Trinity?

FAITH VOCABULARY

Holy Trinity
The central belief of the Christian faith; the mystery of One God in Three Divine Persons— God the Father, God the Son, God the Holy Spirit.

Annunciation
The announcement to the Virgin Mary by the angel Gabriel that God had chosen her to be the Mother of Jesus, the Son of God, through the power of the Holy Spirit.

Activity Check (√) the ways you express faith in the Holy Trinity. In the space, name an additional way.

☐ **Bless myself**

☐ **Pray the creeds of the Church**

☐ **Pray the Hail Mary**

_____

_____

Mary, the Mother of Jesus

Many centuries after God revealed himself to Abraham, God invited the Virgin Mary to place her trust in him. God chose the Virgin Mary to be the Mother of Jesus, the Son of God and the Savior he promised to send. She became the Mother of Jesus through the power of the Holy Spirit.

This event, which is recorded in the Gospels of Matthew and Luke, is known as the **Annunciation**. It gives us a glimpse into the mystery of the Holy Trinity. God chose Mary to be the Mother of Jesus, the Son of God. So special is Mary's role in God's plan that she was free from all sin, from the very first moment of her conception and throughout her whole life. We call this Mary's Immaculate Conception.

Jesus Christ

Throughout his life on Earth, Jesus, the Son of God, spoke clearly of the Father and the Holy Spirit. On one occasion, he told Philip the Apostle and the other disciples:

"The Advocate, the holy Spirit that the Father will send in my name—he will teach you everything and remind you of all that [I] told you." JOHN 14:26

Christians have come to believe and understand that Jesus was speaking of One God, who is Father, Son, and Holy Spirit. Many years after his Ascension, or the return of the Risen and Glorified Jesus to his Father in Heaven, the Church named this central mystery of our faith the Holy Trinity.

? What can we learn about the Holy Trinity from Abraham and Sarah, Mary, and Jesus?

"The Annunciation," St. Wilfrid's Church, Burgess Hill, UK

The Nicene Creed

Under the guidance of the Holy Spirit, two early councils, or official meetings of the Church called by the Pope, taught about the great mystery of the Holy Trinity. These were the Council of Nicaea in AD 325 and the Council of Constantinople in AD 381. The Creed, which we profess at Mass, comes from these two councils.

We can never fully understand the mystery of the Holy Trinity. When our life on Earth is completed, we will live forever with God in Heaven. We will see God in a way we have never seen or known him before.

Catholics Believe

Holy Water

Blessing ourselves with holy water and saying, "In the name of the Father, and of the Son, and of the Holy Spirit" is a sacramental of the Church. Each time we bless ourselves, we remember our Baptism and profess our faith in the Holy Trinity.

Activity   Use each letter in the word TRINITY to write seven words or phrases that tell something about the Trinity.

T _____

THREE PERSONS _____

I _____

N _____

I _____

T _____

Y _____

I FOLLOW JESUS

You are becoming a disciple of Jesus Christ. Disciples believe there is One God in Three Divine Persons: God the Father, God the Son, and God the Holy Spirit. Little by little, the Holy Spirit is helping you believe in this wonderful mystery of faith.

THE MYSTERY OF GOD

In the space, create a colorful symbol that expresses your understanding of what you have learned about the Holy Trinity.

MY FAITH CHOICE

This week, I will profess my faith in the Holy Trinity. I will

_____

_____

_____

 Pray, "Come, Holy Spirit, fill my heart with your gift of wonder and awe. Help me come to know, love, and serve you with my whole mind, heart, and soul. Amen."

Chapter Review

Circle whether each statement is true or false.

1. The Holy Spirit is the mystery of One God in Three Divine Persons.

   True   **False**

2. The Annunciation means that Mary was conceived free from all sins.

   True   **False**

3. Jesus spoke to his disciples about the Holy Spirit.

   True   **False**

4. The Book of Revelation is part of the Old Testament.

   True   **False**

5. The Advocate is a name for the Holy Spirit.

   True   **False**

▶ **TO HELP YOU REMEMBER**

1. The Holy Trinity is the central belief of the faith of the Church.

2. The mystery of the Trinity is most fully revealed in Jesus Christ.

3. We profess our belief in the Holy Trinity when we pray the Nicene Creed at Mass.

Renewal of Faith

Let us renew our faith in God now. In this creed, we profess faith in the Holy Trinity. Each year at Easter, people who are baptized renew their faith with these words in which they were baptized.

Leader: Do you believe in God, the Father Almighty?

All: I do.

Leader: Do you believe in Jesus Christ, his only Son our Lord?

All: I do.

Leader: Do you believe in the Holy Spirit?

All: I do.

Leader: This is our faith. This is the faith of the Church. We are proud to profess it.

With My Family

This Week . . .

In Chapter 3, "The Holy Trinity," your child learned:

▶ The Holy Trinity is the mystery of One God in Three Divine Persons—God the Father, God the Son, and God the Holy Spirit.

▶ The mystery of God the Holy Trinity is the central mystery of the Christian faith. It is a truth about God that we could never have known unless God revealed it.

▶ God revealed this mystery over a long period of time.

▶ We profess faith in the Trinity at Baptism.

▶ Each time we pray the Nicene Creed at Mass, we renew and profess our faith in this great mystery.

▶ The gift of wonder and awe encourages us to respect and be in awe of God.

For more about related teachings of the Church, see the *Catechism of the Catholic Church*, 232–260, and the *United States Catholic Catechism for Adults*, pages 49–63.

■ Sharing God's Word

Read together Matthew 28:16–20, the Gospel account of Jesus commissioning the disciples. Emphasize that we profess our faith in the Holy Trinity and remember our Baptism when we pray the Sign of the Cross.

■ We Live as Disciples

The Christian home and family is a school of discipleship. Choose one of the following activities to do as a family, or design a similar activity of your own:

▶ The words of the Nicene Creed can be found on page 258 of this book. Make Nicene Creed puzzle pieces and assemble them with your child to help him or her memorize this important prayer of the Church.

▶ This week, when your family takes part in Sunday Mass, be sure to bless yourself with holy water and pray the Sign of the Cross as you enter and leave the church.

■ Our Spiritual Journey

Our spiritual journey is marked by actions that express our faith in the Trinity. Almsgiving is one of those actions. When we give alms, or share our spiritual and material blessings with others, we profess our faith in God who is the source of all blessings. In this chapter, your child prayed a prayer renewing his or her baptismal profession of faith. Read and pray together this prayer, which is found on page 33.

For more ideas on ways your family can live as disciples of Jesus, visit **www.BeMyDisciples.com**

Looking Ahead

In this chapter, the Holy Spirit invites you to ▶

EXPLORE how the Church uses blessing prayers.

DISCOVER the attributes of God.

DECIDE how to make a quality of God known to others.

CHAPTER

4

Great Is the Lord

? We use images to describe the qualities of people. For example, we might say, "She's as fast as lightning." What is an image you would use to describe yourself?

The prophet Isaiah used many images to describe the relationship between God and his people. In this Scripture passage, Isaiah affirms that we are created by God:

> Yet, O LORD, you are our father;
>> we are the clay and you the potter:
>> we are all the work of your hands. ISAIAH 64:7

? What other images from God's creation tell us something about God's goodness?

Disciple Power

Joy

Joy shows that we are cooperating with the grace of the Holy Spirit. We recognize that true happiness comes, not from money or possessions, but from knowing, trusting, and loving God. Joy is a Fruit of the Holy Spirit.

Blessing Prayers

The Church celebrates her faith in God in many ways. When we pray, we place all our trust and confidence in God. We show that we know that he loves us and will always do what is best for us.

Blessing prayers are one of the five kinds of prayer of the Church. They remind us that God is always with us and blesses us with his love. When we pray a blessing, we are asking for God's power and protection upon a person, a place, an animal such as a pet, an object, or an activity.

Catholics use many blessing prayers. We pray grace before and after meals. We ask God to bless us at the conclusion of Mass. We ask God's blessing on every newly married couple. Some families ask for a blessing when they move into a new home. Catholics also have religious objects such as medals blessed by a priest.

Activity Describe two special blessings you have received.

1. _____

2. _____

Write about a blessing you would like to receive.

_____

_____

Attributes of God

To help us understand who God has revealed himself to be, the inspired writers of the Bible have used certain qualities to describe him. These qualities are called **attributes of God**. They help us get a glimpse into the mystery of God.

One God is One. There is only One God. No one and nothing is like him.

"Hear, O Israel! The LORD is our God, the LORD alone!"

DEUTERONOMY 6:4

Lord God revealed the sacred name YHWH to describe himself. The writers of the Bible used the name *Adonai*, or LORD, in place of the name YHWH.

Almighty God is almighty. This means that God alone can do anything.

"May God Almighty bless you . . . that you may become an assembly of peoples." GENESIS 28:3

Eternal God is eternal. God always has been and always will be. God had no beginning and will have no end.

The LORD is the eternal God. ISAIAH 40:28

Holy God is holy. The word *holy* means "without equal." No one and no thing that God created is equal to him.

"Holy, holy, holy is the LORD of Hosts!" ISAIAH 6:3

Love God is love. God created and saved us to share in that love.

"God is love." 1 JOHN 4:16

Truth God is truth. God is always faithful to his word. He always keeps his promises.

For the LORD's word is true. PSALM 33:4a

❓ Which is your favorite attribute of God? Why?

FAITH VOCABULARY
attributes of God
Qualities of God that help us understand the mystery of God.

Abba
The name Jesus used for God the Father that reveals the love and trust that exist between Jesus, God the Son, and God the Father.

Jesus Teaching by the Seashore, by James J. Tissot

God the Father

God has revealed himself most fully in Jesus Christ. Jesus spoke about God in many ways. Most of all, Jesus spoke about God the Father.

Jesus had a very special name for God the Father. He called God, **Abba**, which means "dear Father" or even "Dad." In Jesus' time, when people used the name *abba,* they show how close they were to their fathers and how much they loved and trusted them. When Jesus called God *Abba*, he revealed how much he loved and trusted his Father.

Jesus invited his disciples to love and trust God the Father as he did. He said,

"This is how you are to pray: Our Father…"   Matthew 6:9

Jesus revealed that his Father is our Father too. God the Father loves us and knows each of us by name. We are his children. When we call God "Father," we are saying that we are his children. We believe, trust, and love God as Abba, our Father.

Activity   Write and decorate your favorite name for God. Use that name today to tell a partner about God. Use this name often in prayer.

God the Creator

Creation shows the great glory of God. God created the whole universe and all creatures, visible and invisible, out of nothing and without any help. Everyone and everything God created is good.

God created people in his image and likeness. He created us with a physical body and a spiritual, immortal soul. Immortal means that our soul will never die.

The writers of the Bible gave the names Adam and Eve to the first humans. No matter the color of our skin, the lives we live, or the languages we speak, we all belong to one family—the family of God.

Original Sin

Sadly, Adam and Eve were not satisfied with God's plan of goodness and holiness for them. They preferred their own way to God's plan. They disobeyed God. The Church calls their decision to live apart from God "Original Sin." It is called Original Sin because it is the first sin and the beginning of all evil and sin in the world.

Original Sin hurts everyone and everything God created. Each person is born sharing in the effects of Original Sin. Despite Original Sin, God invites and helps everyone to share in his goodness and love. He sent Jesus, his only Son, to redeem us and restore our friendship with God.

? What can each person do to overcome the effects of Original Sin?

I FOLLOW JESUS

Disciples of Jesus are people of joy. Your joy comes from your belief that God is always by your side. You can show that you believe in and trust in God the Father, as Jesus did, in many ways. You can pray. You can treat others and the world with respect and kindness.

CREATING A MOVIE

Imagine you are a movie director shooting a movie entitled *"All About God."* In this space, illustrate or write about a scene in that movie.

MY FAITH CHOICE

This week, I will share my faith in God by making known to others one attribute about him. I will show my joy by

_____

_____

_____

 Pray, asking the Holy Spirit to help you live with true happiness in God.

Chapter Review

Unscramble the letters of the words in the word box.
Then match the words with their meanings.

teribusatt	luso	naligOri Sni	gbslseni	lohy
attributes	soul	Original Sin	blessing	holy

1. The qualities of God

   attribute

2. The spiritual dimension of the human person that never dies and lives forever

   soul

3. The sin committed by Adam and Eve

   Origional Sin

4. One of the five kinds of prayer

   blessing

5. A word for God that means "without equal"

   holy

► TO HELP YOU REMEMBER

1. One, almighty, holy, eternal, love, and truth are qualities about himself that God has revealed.

2. God is the Creator of everyone and everything, visible and invisible.

3. Adam and Eve disobeyed God and turned away from his goodness. This sin caused the beginning of all other sin in the world.

Lord, You Alone Are God!

In a prayer of praise, we address God with a title of his greatness.
Praise God using this simple prayer of praise.

Leader: God, you are Abba.

   All: Amen! You alone are God.

Leader: God, you are Most Holy.

   All: Amen! You alone are God.

Leader: God, you are Love.

   All: Amen! You alone are God.

Leader: God, you are One Lord, the Almighty One.

   All: Amen! You alone are God.

With My Family

This Week . . .

In Chapter 4, "Great Is the Lord," your child learned:

▶ The biblical writers used several qualities, or attributes, to describe God.

▶ Jesus loved and trusted his Father, whom he addressed as Abba.

▶ The story of God the Creator and the Fall reveal God's great love for us.

▶ Joy is one of the Fruits of the Holy Spirit.

▶ Joy is a sign that true happiness comes from knowing, trusting, and loving God.

For more about related teachings of the Church, see the *Catechism of the Catholic Church*, 199–227, 268–274, 279–412, and the *United States Catholic Catechism for Adults*, pages 49–75.

■ Sharing God's Word

Read together and quietly think about the Scripture verses on page 37 one at a time. Emphasize that, as amazing as God is, Jesus taught us to call God a simple and familiar name: Father.

■ We Live as Disciples

The Christian home and family is a school of discipleship. Choose one of the following activities to do as a family, or design a similar activity of your own:

▶ Choose one of the Scripture verses on page 37. Make a banner using that verse. Display the banner where it can remind everyone how wonderful God is.

▶ This Sunday, when you take part in Mass, take time to look at the religious statues and other artwork in your church. Talk about how these works of art help you honor and worship God.

■ Our Spiritual Journey

Did you ever notice that people who have very few material possessions, such as Saint Thérèse of the Child Jesus, are people of joy? This joy comes from the recognition that God is always blessing them with his presence. In this chapter, your child prayed a prayer of praise. Read and pray together this prayer on page 41. Praise God for his presence within you.

For more ideas on ways your family can live as disciples of Jesus, visit **www.BeMyDisciples.com**

Unit 1 Review

Name _____

A. Choose the Best Word

Fill in the blanks using the words from the word bank.

Jesus Christ	forty-six	twenty-seven
Mary	attributes of God	faith

1. God revealed himself most fully in _Jesus Christ_

2. There are _46_ books in the Old Testament and _27_ books in the New Testament.

3. God chose _Mary_ to be the Mother of Jesus, the Son of God.

4. The _attributes of God_ help us get a glimpse into the mystery of God.

5. _Faith_ is a supernatural gift and power that helps us respond to God's invitation with all our heart, mind, soul, and strength.

B. Show What You Know

Match the words or phrases in Column A with the words or phrases in Column B.

Column A

1. Divine Revelation

2. Evangelists

3. Torah

4. The mystery of the Holy Trinity

5. Original Sin

Column B

_3_ **a.** the first five books of the Old Testament

_5_ **b.** wounded everyone and everything God created

_4_ **c.** the deepest and central belief of the Christian faith

_1_ **d.** God's making known over time the mystery of God and the divine plan of creation and Salvation

_2_ **e.** the writers of the four Gospels

C. Connect with Scripture

Reread the Scripture passage on page 9.
What connection do you see between this passage and
what you learned in this unit?

Holy Trinity

D. Be a Disciple

1. *Review the four pages in this unit titled The Church Follows*
Jesus. What person or ministry of the Church on these
pages will inspire you to be a better disciple of Jesus?
Explain your answer.

Jesus. He will show me how
to be patient and kind.

2. *Work with a group. Review the four Disciple Power virtues,*
or gifts, you have learned about in this unit. After jotting
down your own ideas, share with the group practical
ways that you will live these virtues day by day.

Hope .. If losing something
I'll try to keep hopeful.

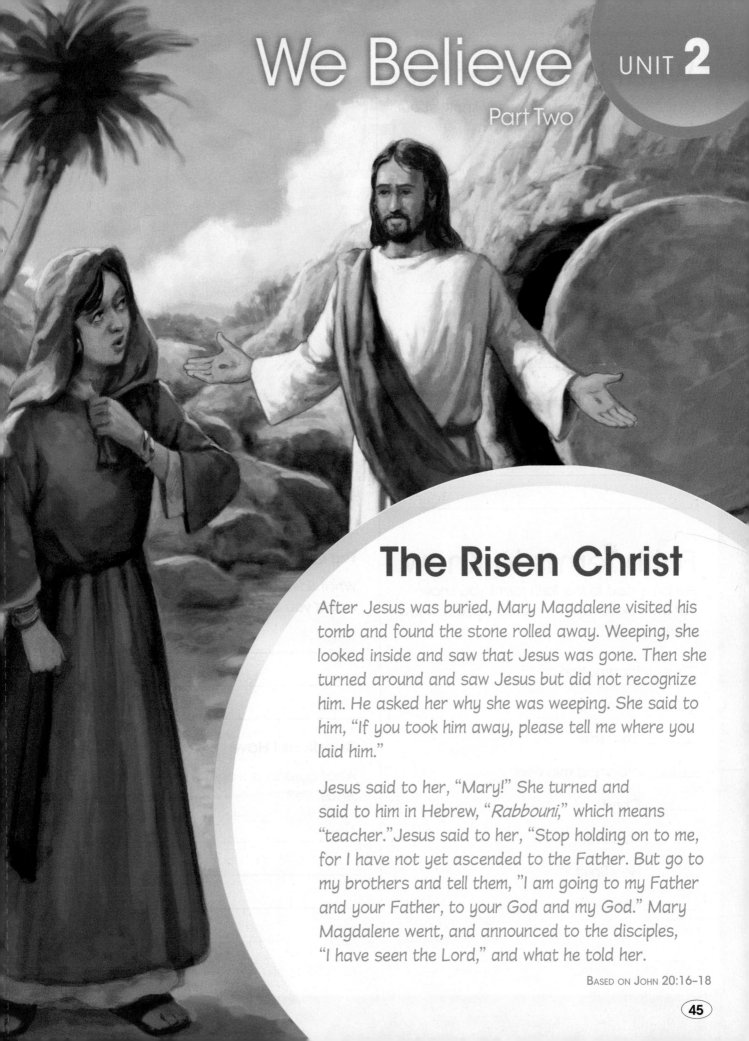

We Believe

Part Two

The Risen Christ

After Jesus was buried, Mary Magdalene visited his tomb and found the stone rolled away. Weeping, she looked inside and saw that Jesus was gone. Then she turned around and saw Jesus but did not recognize him. He asked her why she was weeping. She said to him, "If you took him away, please tell me where you laid him."

Jesus said to her, "Mary!" She turned and said to him in Hebrew, "*Rabbouni*," which means "teacher."Jesus said to her, "Stop holding on to me, for I have not yet ascended to the Father. But go to my brothers and tell them, "I am going to my Father and your Father, to your God and my God." Mary Magdalene went, and announced to the disciples, "I have seen the Lord," and what he told her.

BASED ON JOHN 20:16–18

What I Have Learned

What is something you already know about these faith terms?

The Messiah

_____

_____

_____

The Resurrection

_____

_____

The Marks of the Church

_____

_____

Faith Terms to Know

Put an X next to the faith terms you know. Put a ? next to faith terms you need to know more about.

_____ Incarnation

_____ Ascension

_____ charisms

_____ ordained ministers

_____ Christ

_____ Passover

_____ Holy Spirit

_____ Heaven

The Bible

What do you know about Jesus' birth?

_____

_____

_____

The Church

What Saint or organization of the Church would you like to learn more about?

_____

_____

_____

Questions I Have

What questions would you like to ask about Jesus' life?

_____

_____

_____

Looking Ahead

In this chapter, the Holy Spirit invites you to ▶

EXPLORE what Jesus' name reveals about him.

DISCOVER how art can express belief in Christ.

DECIDE how you will show others that you believe in Jesus.

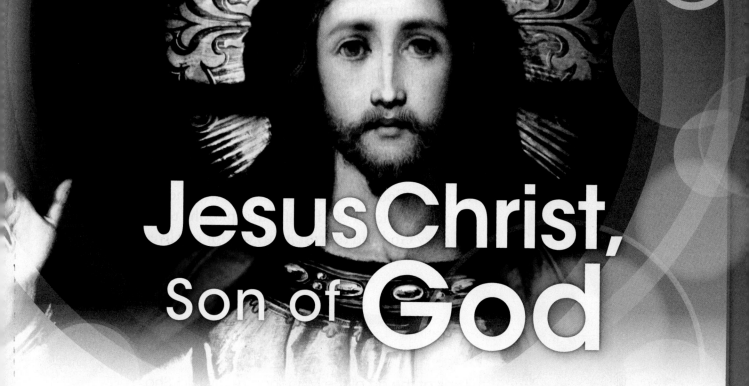

Jesus Christ, Son of God

[?] How was your name chosen? What do you know about the meaning of your name?

Names are very important. They can tell us many things about a person. In the Gospels of Matthew and Luke, we hear the story of an angel announcing the Savior's birth and revealing that he is to be given the name Jesus.

The angel of the Lord appeared [to Joseph] in a dream and said, "[Mary] will bear a son and you are to name him Jesus, because he will save his people from their sins."

BASED ON MATTHEW 1:20–21

[?] What do you think the name Jesus means?

Madonna and Child

From the earliest days of the Church, Christian artists have proclaimed the Nativity. Through painting, sculpture, woodcarvings, and music, Christian artists have retold the story of the birth of Jesus.

The Christian devotion to Mary and her Son, Jesus, is often expressed through the portrayal of Mary holding the Christ Child. These works of art are called "Madonna and Child." The word *madonna* means "my lady."

God asked Mary to be the Mother of his Son, Jesus. Mary trusted in God and said yes to his will with her whole heart. Mary is our model of a faithful disciple. She teaches us to love and obey God and to trust in his will for our lives.

Activity Look at the art of the Madonna and Child. Share what they tell you about the faith of people in Mary and her Child. Check the one you like best. Write a few sentences to explain what it tells you about Mary.

_____

_____

_____

Son of God, Son of Mary

In the Bible, a person's name often describes the role they play in God's plan of Salvation. The Hebrew name for *Jesus* means "God saves." The very name of Jesus reveals that he is the Savior of the world.

All of God's promises in the Bible come true in Jesus. Jesus is the center and heart of God's loving plan of creation and Salvation. Jesus **Christ** is the Messiah, the **Lord,** and the Savior of the world.

Titles for Jesus

There are also several important names or titles for Jesus used in the Gospels. These express the faith of the Church in who Jesus is and the work the Father sent him to do. Three of these titles are Messiah, Christ, and Lord.

Messiah. Throughout the Old Testament, God promised to send a messiah. The title *messiah* means "anointed one." The messiah would be a king who would save, or deliver, God's people from their enemies.

Christ. The English word *Christ* is used for the Hebrew word *messiah* and for the Greek word *kristos*. Jesus is the Christ—the Messiah or Anointed One.

Lord. The Israelites used the word *Lord* for God in place of the name *YHWH*. The letters *YHWH* of the Hebrew alphabet are the letters of the name by which God identified himself to Moses (read Exodus 3:11–15). When we call Jesus "Lord," we are professing the faith of the Church, that Jesus Christ is truly God. He is the Son of God, the Second Divine Person of the Holy Trinity. Jesus is true God and true man.

[?] How do the titles of Jesus help you come to know who Jesus is?

An illustration of the birth of Jesus from an Asian perspective

49

Faith-Filled People

Saint Matthew and Saint Luke, Evangelists

Matthew was a tax collector and one of the first Twelve Apostles. Luke was a physician and a companion of Paul the Apostle. It is only in the Gospels of Matthew and Luke that we read the account of the birth of Jesus.

The Incarnation

The angel Gabriel brought Mary a message telling her that God had chosen her to be the Mother of his Son. Gabriel said to the Virgin Mary that she would conceive and give birth to a son and name him Jesus. When Mary asked how that was possible since she was a virgin, Gabriel replied,

> *"The holy Spirit will come upon you, and the power of the Most High will overshadow you. Therefore the child to be born will be called holy, the Son of God."*
>
> LUKE 1:35

After the birth of Jesus, Luke's Gospel tells us that an angel of God appeared to shepherds, proclaiming the Good News of Jesus' birth. The angel said to them,

> *"[T]oday in the city of David a savior has been born for you who is Messiah and Lord."*
>
> LUKE 2:11

The Church names the mystery of the Son of God becoming man the *Incarnation*. The word incarnation means "putting on flesh." This word names our belief that the Son of God, the Second Person of the Holy Trinity, became fully human without giving up being fully God. Jesus Christ is true God and true man.

Activity Write words that you would use in each setting to express your faith in Jesus Christ.

At Home	At School	In My Community

Mother of God, Mother of All

The four accounts of the Gospel do not tell us much about the childhood life of Jesus. His life was probably very much like the lives of other Jewish children in Nazareth. Mary and Joseph shared their Jewish faith with Jesus. They taught him the customs and practices of their religion.

Mary is truly the Mother of God because Jesus is true God and true man. We remember and celebrate this truth about Mary each year on January 1, the Solemnity of Mary, the Holy Mother of God. This feast of Mary is a holy day of obligation for Catholics in the United States of America.

Mary is our Blessed Mother. She is the Mother of the Church. When Jesus was crucified, Mary, several other women disciples, and John were there with him.

As he was dying on the Cross, Jesus said to Mary, *"Woman, behold your son."* Then he said to John, *"Behold, your mother"* (John 19:26–27). The Church has always seen in these words that Mary is our mother, the Mother of the Church. We trust that Mary cares for us and wants us to grow closer to her Son, Jesus.

? How do Catholics show their devotion to Mary? How can you show Mary your love for her?

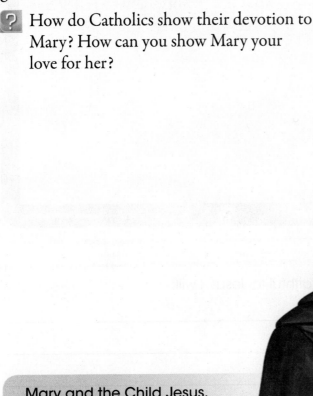

Mary and the Child Jesus, an icon at the Church of Mary Magdalene in Jerusalem, Israel

I FOLLOW JESUS

Each year, the Church celebrates the events of Jesus' life. You can celebrate God's love for you, for your family, and for all people. The Holy Spirit invites you to celebrate that love through living a life of faithfulness and sharing your faith in Jesus with others each and every day.

SHARING THE GOOD NEWS

Create a Web home page. Use words, pictures, or symbols that tell others about your faith in Jesus Christ.

MY FAITH CHOICE

This week, I will show that I am faithful to Jesus. I will:

_____

_____

_____

 Pray, asking God to help you become a more faithful follower of Jesus.

Chapter Review

Choose the correct word from the word bank to complete each sentence.

Madonna	Luke	Annunciation
Christ	Incarnation	John

1. The word _____ is a title for Mary meaning "my lady."

2. The story of Jesus' birth appears in the Gospel of _____.

3. The _____ means the mystery of God becoming man.

4. The title _____ means that Jesus is the Messiah, the Anointed One of God.

5. The announcement of the birth of Jesus to Mary is called the _____.

► **TO HELP YOU REMEMBER**

1. Jesus is the Christ, the Messiah.

2. Jesus Christ is Lord. He is true God, the Second Person of the Holy Trinity, who became true man without giving up being God.

3. The Virgin Mary is the Mother of God.

Jesus' Holy Name

Pray this prayer of petition from the Litany of the Holy Name of Jesus. In this kind of prayer, we ask, or petition, God for his grace to live a life of faithfulness to him.

Leader: Jesus, Son of the living God,

All: have mercy on us.

Leader: Jesus, Son of the Virgin Mary,

All: have mercy on us.

Leader: Jesus, Good Shepherd,

All: have mercy on us.
Amen.

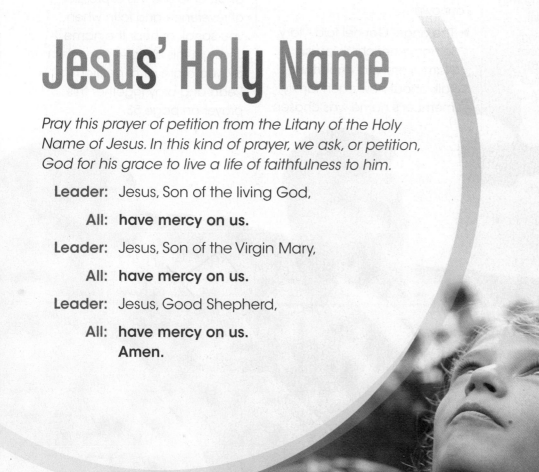

With My Family

This Week . . .

In Chapter 5, "Jesus Christ, Son of God," your child learned:

► Titles for Jesus, such as Christ, Lord, and Messiah help us understand who Jesus is and the work God the Father sent him to do.

► The mystery of the Son of God becoming fully human while remaining fully God is called the Incarnation.

► Mary, the Mother of Jesus, is truly the Mother of God because Jesus is the Son of God.

► Faithfulness is a quality that shows we are cooperating with the grace of the Holy Spirit.

For more about related teachings of the Church, see the *Catechism of the Catholic Church*, 422–451, 456–478, 484–507, and the *United States Catholic Catechism for Adults*, pages 77–87.

■ Sharing God's Word

Read together the Bible story about the birth of Jesus at the beginning of the Gospel according to Matthew and the Gospel according to Luke. Emphasize what the Gospel accounts of Jesus' birth tell us about who he is and the work he was sent to do.

■ We Live as Disciples

The Christian home and family is a school of discipleship. Choose one of the following activities to do as a family, or design a similar activity of your own:

► The angel Gabriel told Mary to name her child Jesus. Names are very important. Talk about how each family member's name was chosen.

► Jesus showed his love for his mother. It is very important to show our love for family members. Be sure to do special things this week to show your love for one another.

■ Our Spiritual Journey

Showing reverence for the name of Jesus is an expression of our faith in him, the Son of God and the Son of Mary. Bowing our heads slightly when we speak or hear the name Jesus is a long tradition of the Church. Encourage one another to use this expression of reverence and faith when you speak or hear the name Jesus. In this chapter, your child prayed a prayer of petition. Read and pray together this prayer on page 53.

For more ideas on ways your family can live as disciples of Jesus, visit **www.BeMyDisciples.com**

Looking Ahead

In this chapter, the Holy Spirit invites you to ▶

EXPLORE the devotion of the Stations of the Cross.

DISCOVER more about the Paschal Mystery.

DECIDE how to share your faith in the Risen Christ with others.

CHAPTER
6

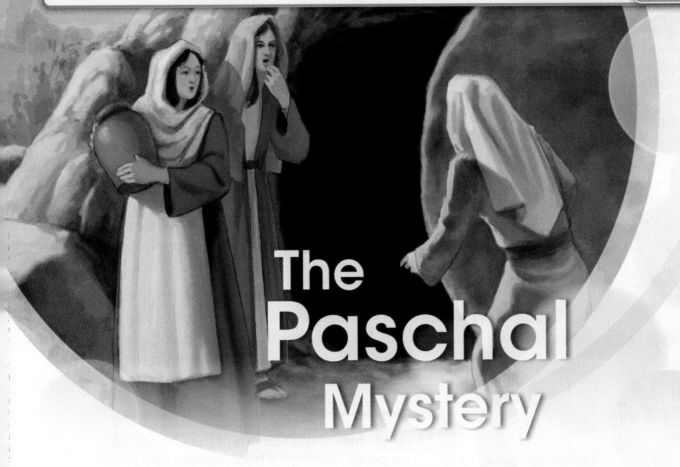

The Paschal Mystery

? What have been some of the key events in the life of your family?

On the third day after the disciples took Jesus' body down from the Cross, wrapped it in linen cloths, and placed it in the tomb, Luke's Gospel tells us:

> [At] daybreak on the first day of the week [the women who had come from Galilee] took the spices they had prepared and went to the tomb. They found the stone rolled away from the tomb; but when they entered, they did not find the body of the Lord Jesus.
>
> LUKE 24:1–3

? What details do you know about the Passion, Resurrection, and Ascension of Jesus? How might you have responded if you had discovered the empty tomb?

Hope

Hope is the virtue that keeps us from discouragement by placing our trust in Jesus and the promise of eternal life.

Stations of the Cross

Ever since the early centuries of Christianity, people have made pilgrimages to the Holy Land to visit the places associated with the life, Death, and Resurrection of Jesus Christ. Because everyone cannot visit the Holy Land, churches built shrines to commemorate the Passion and Death of Christ.

The first of these shrines was probably set up between AD 600 and 700 at the Church of Saint Stephen in Bologna, Italy. By the 1600s, the custom and tradition of praying the Stations of the Cross, or following the Way of Jesus, was widespread. The spreading of this custom is attributed to the Dominicans, Augustinians, and Franciscans.

When we pray the Stations of the Cross, we profess and proclaim our belief in the Passion, the suffering, and the Death of Jesus. We announce that God's plan of Salvation and Redemption for all people of all times is fulfilled in Christ. By his Death, Jesus gained life everlasting for all people.

Activity Turn to the Stations of the Cross on page 263 of your book. Identify which of the Stations are shown here and write the number under each picture.

The Passover of the Lord

God entered into a Covenant with Abraham, choosing him to be the father of God's people. When God's people were suffering from a great famine, Abraham's descendants traveled to Egypt in search of food. Joseph, Abraham's great-grandson, was already living there and was a highly respected leader in Egypt. He recognized his family, fed them, and invited them to stay in Egypt.

One of the most important events in the history of the Israelites, or Hebrews, was God freeing them from slavery in Egypt. Over a period of time, the Egyptians made the Hebrews their slaves. God's people prayed, asking God to deliver, or free, them from slavery. God chose and sent Moses to lead his people to freedom. Moses and his brother Aaron bravely faced Pharaoh, the Egyptian ruler. Over and over they tried to persuade Pharaoh to let the Hebrews leave Egypt.

Again and again Pharaoh refused, despite the signs that God sent. Then something happened. Many young Egyptians were dying in their homes, but the Hebrews and their children were being spared. Death "passed over" the homes of the Hebrews.

Finally, Pharaoh let God's people go. The Jewish people gather each year in the springtime to remember and celebrate this event called **Passover**.

? Look at the Memorial Acclamation we pray at Mass on page 269. What does it have to do with the Paschal Mystery?

page 269

FAITH FOCUS
How does the Jewish feast of Passover help us to understand the Paschal Mystery of Jesus?

FAITH VOCABULARY

Passover
Passover is the Jewish feast celebrating God's sparing of the Hebrew children from death and the passage of his people from slavery to freedom.

Paschal Mystery
The Paschal Mystery is the "passing over" of Jesus from life through death into new and glorious life; the Passion, Death, Resurrection, and glorious Ascension of Jesus.

A Jewish family celebrates Passover.

Faith-Filled People

Saint Veronica

The Church passes on to us the tradition that as Jesus was carrying his Cross he was met by Veronica, one of his disciples. Veronica reached out and wiped the blood and sweat off Jesus' face with her veil. This act of faith and compassion is remembered in the Sixth Station of the Cross. The Church celebrates the feast day of Saint Veronica on July 9.

The Passion of the Lord

When we celebrate the Eucharist, we remember and share in the **Paschal Mystery**. The Paschal Mystery consists of the Passion (the Suffering and Death), Resurrection, and Ascension of Jesus Christ. These key events are the central theme of the Gospel. The part that tells about Jesus' Suffering and Death is called the Passion narrative.

The Passion of the Lord includes these events:

The Last Supper. During the week in which Jesus died, he went to Jerusalem and celebrated Passover. At a Passover meal with his disciples, which Christians have named the Last Supper, Jesus gave the Church the Eucharist.

The Betrayal and Arrest. After the Last Supper, Judas led a group of Jesus' enemies to the Garden of Gethsemane where Jesus was praying. It was there that Judas betrayed Jesus and handed him over to be arrested.

The Trial and Sentencing. Accusing him of blasphemy, Jesus' enemies handed him over to the Romans to be tried. Fearing the Roman emperor and the crowd, the judge, Pontius Pilate, handed Jesus over to be crucified.

Suffering, Death, and Burial. Jesus carried his Cross to Calvary, a hill outside Jerusalem where criminals were crucified. It was there that Jesus died. After Jesus died, Joseph of Arimathea and other disciples of Jesus buried his body in a new tomb.

Activity Imagine you are with the disciples at Jesus' arrest and trial. On this journal page, describe your thoughts and feelings.

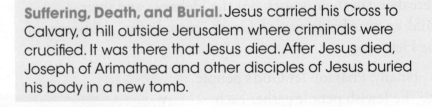

Good Friday procession in Jerusalem, Israel

The Resurrection of the Lord

Three days after Jesus died and was buried, he was raised to a new and glorified life. We call this mighty deed of God the Resurrection.

The Resurrection is the heart of our Christian faith. Writing to the Church in Corinth, Saint Paul taught:

> But if Christ is preached as raised from the dead, how can some among you say there is no resurrection of the dead? If there is no resurrection of the dead then neither has Christ been raised. And if Christ has not been raised, empty [too] is our preaching; empty, too, your faith. . . . If for this life only we have hoped in Christ, we are the most pitiable people of all.
>
> 1 Corinthians 15:12–14, 19

When we profess that Jesus was raised from the dead, we do not mean he simply came back to life again. When the Risen Christ appeared to his disciples, they at first did not recognize him because his body was gloriously changed by the Holy Spirit. God raised Jesus into a new and glorious life.

The Ascension of the Lord

For forty days after the Resurrection, the Risen Jesus met with his disciples and continued to teach them. During one final meeting on the Mount of Olives, which is near Jerusalem, he ascended to his Father. We call this the Ascension.

When we profess our faith in the Ascension, we mean that Jesus has returned in glory and majesty to his Father. He has gone to prepare a place for us. Where Christ has ascended, we hope one day to follow. We are responsible for continuing the mission of Jesus on Earth.

God's plan of Salvation and Redemption is fulfilled in Jesus Christ. Through his Paschal Mystery, Jesus frees us from sin. Joined to Christ in Baptism, we can "pass over" from sin and death to new life with him, his Father, and the Holy Spirit. Raised to new life by the power of the Holy Spirit, we are made sharers in the fullness of life with God.

? Why is the Resurrection the heart of our Christian faith?

I FOLLOW JESUS

Through Baptism, you were made a sharer in the Paschal Mystery of Jesus Christ. You received the gift of the Holy Spirit and the promise and hope of eternal life. You can share joy and hope with people who suffer. You can share love where there is hatred.

NEW LIFE IN CHRIST

In this space, create a symbol or design a banner that announces the Good News of Jesus' Resurrection.

MY FAITH CHOICE

This week, I will proclaim that I am a person of hope. I will share my faith in the Paschal Mystery of Jesus with others. I will

_____

_____

_____

 Pray to the Risen Lord Jesus, who is always with you. Ask him to be a beacon of hope in your family, school, and community.

Chapter Review

Use the clues to discover the events and meaning of the Paschal Mystery.

1. Forty days after Easter we celebrate

    a. the Ascension   **b.** Pentecost

2. The Passover meal Jesus celebrated with his disciples is called

    a. the Last Supper   **b.** the Feast of Harvest

3. We call Jesus being raised from the dead the

    a. Ascension   **b.** Resurrection

4. Jesus was crucified on a hill called

    a. Calvary   **b.** Jerusalem

The Exsultet

The Church sings the Exsultet at the Easter Vigil, the great celebration of the Resurrection. This joyful proclamation announces the Resurrection of Jesus and the gift of hope to the world. Pray together the beginning of this prayer.

All: **Sound aloud our mighty King's triumph!**

Group 1: Exult, let them exult, the hosts of heaven, exult, let Angel ministers of God exult,

Group 2: let the trumpet of salvation sound aloud our mighty King's triumph!

All: **Sound aloud our mighty King's triumph!**

Group 1: Be glad, let earth be glad, as glory floods her, ablaze with light from her eternal King,

Group 2: let all corners of the earth be glad, knowing an end to gloom and darkness.

All: **Sound aloud our mighty King's triumph!**

FROM THE EXSULTET
ROMAN MISSAL

With My Family

This Week . . .

In Chapter 6, "The Paschal Mystery," your child learned:

▶ The Paschal Mystery is Christ's work of redemption through his Passion, Resurrection, and Ascension.

▶ During the week in which he died, Jesus celebrated the "passing over" meal with his disciples.

▶ The Paschal Mystery of Jesus is his "passing over" from suffering and death to new and glorious life.

▶ Hope is the Theological Virtue that keeps us from discouragement by placing our trust in Jesus and the promise of eternal life.

For more about related teachings of the Church, see the *Catechism of the Catholic Church*, 571–664, and the *United States Catholic Catechism for Adults*, pages 89–100.

■ Sharing God's Word

Invite the family to share what they know about the Gospel accounts of Jesus' Passion, Resurrection, and Ascension. Emphasize that each time we celebrate the Eucharist, we are made sharers in the Paschal Mystery.

■ We Live as Disciples

The Christian home and family is a school of discipleship. Choose one of the following activities to do as a family, or design a similar activity of your own:

▶ When you take part in Mass this week, look for the crucifix and the Paschal candle. Talk about how these can remind us of the Paschal Mystery. After Mass, walk the Stations of the Cross. Stop at each Station, and talk about how each Station describes Jesus' Passion.

▶ Imagine that you were present with the disciples when Jesus was arrested and put on trial. Talk about how you would have felt or what you would have thought.

■ Our Spiritual Journey

Life on Earth is a pilgrimage. Christians make this pilgrimage as a people of hope. When faced with the reality of death, our faith in the Paschal Mystery stirs our hearts to proclaim, "Indeed for your faithful, Lord, life is changed and not ended" (*Preface I, for the Dead,* Roman Missal). In this chapter, your child prayed the *Exsultet,* professing his or her faith in the Resurrection. Read and pray together this prayer on page 61.

For more ideas on ways your family can live as disciples of Jesus, visit

www.BeMyDisciples.com

Looking Ahead

In this chapter, the Holy Spirit invites you to ▶

EXPLORE a person who continued the mission of Jesus.

DISCOVER the work of the Holy Spirit.

DECIDE how you will use your gifts to improve the world.

CHAPTER **7**

Many Gifts, One Spirit

? What does it mean to say that a person or group has "spirit"?

Having spirit is an important quality in a person. "Spirit" energizes people to do good works. God has given the Church the gift of the presence of the Holy Spirit. The Holy Spirit is always with the Church. In the Acts of the Apostles we read,

> When the time for Pentecost was fulfilled, they were all in one place together. And suddenly there came from the sky a noise like a strong driving wind, and it filled the entire house in which they were. . . . And they were all filled with the holy Spirit. ACTS 2:1–2, 4

? What evidence do you see that the Holy Spirit is always with the Church?

Disciple Power

Courage

Courage, or fortitude, is one of four Cardinal Virtues and a Gift of the Holy Spirit. Fortitude helps us stand up for our faith in Christ. It helps us overcome obstacles that might keep us from practicing our faith. It helps us continue to choose that which is good.

Saint Katharine Drexel

The Holy Spirit is always at work in the Church. From the time of the Apostles, the Holy Spirit has helped the Church continue the mission of Jesus.

Missionaries leave their families and travel to preach and live the Gospel. Missionaries often encounter hardships. Sometimes it takes great courage to be a missionary.

Katharine Drexel (1868–1955) was a missionary who lived and worked in the United States. She left her home to serve the Church. She used her family's wealth to help Native Americans and African Americans in the United States.

Katharine founded the Sisters of the Blessed Sacrament to work with her. The courageous Sisters spent much of their time traveling across the United States. They founded missions and schools in thirteen states, including Xavier University in New Orleans. Today, the Sisters continue the missionary work Katharine Drexel began.

In 2000, Katharine Drexel was named a Saint of the Church by Pope John Paul II. Her feast day is celebrated on March 3.

Activity   How well did you listen? Fill in the blanks below.

1. The _____ _____ is always at work in the Church.

2. Missionaries travel to preach and live the _____.

3. Katharine _____ was a missionary to _____

   and _____.

The Work of the Holy Spirit

At the Last Supper, Jesus spoke to his disciples about many things. He told them he would soon be leaving them and returning to his Father. He taught them to love each other as he had loved them. Jesus also made this promise:

"But now I am going to the one who sent me, and not one of you asks me, 'Where are you going?' But because I told you this, grief has filled your hearts. But I tell you the truth, it is better for you that I go. For if I do not go, the Advocate will not come to you. But if I go, I will send him to you."

JOHN 16:5–7

The disciples listened to Jesus. But, at that time, they did not fully understand what he was saying. While they were frightened and confused that he would soon leave them and return to his Father, the disciples trusted Jesus. After his Ascension, they returned to Jerusalem and waited for the coming of the Advocate promised by Jesus.

? When do you pray to the Holy Spirit?

FAITH FOCUS
What is the work of the Holy Spirit in the Church?

FAITH VOCABULARY
charisms
Charisms are graces, or gifts, given by the Holy Spirit to build up the Church on Earth for the good of all people and the needs of the world.

Sacred Tradition
Sacred Tradition is the passing on of the teachings of Christ by the Church through the power and guidance of the Holy Spirit.

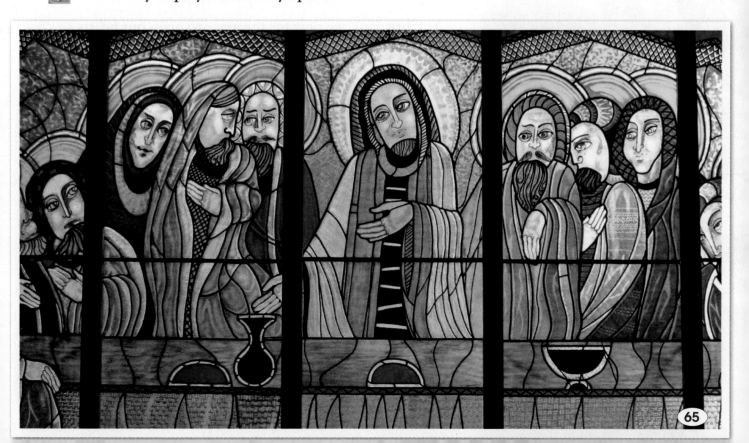

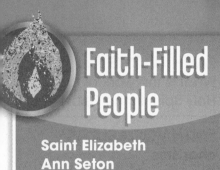

Saint Elizabeth Ann Seton

Saint Elizabeth Ann Seton founded the Sisters of Charity, the first religious community of women in the United States. Guided by the Holy Spirit, they devoted themselves to working in schools, orphanages, and hospitals. Saint Elizabeth Ann is the first native-born American to be named a Saint. Her feast day is January 4.

Jesus Keeps His Promise

The Holy Spirit came upon the disciples as Jesus had promised (read Acts 2:1–2, 4). The Holy Spirit is the Advocate whom Jesus promised would come. An advocate is one who speaks up for someone. The Holy Spirit is always with us and gives us strength and direction to continue the work of Jesus. He gives us the grace to deal with all the hard times in our lives. He gives us the grace to live with courage and confidence. The Holy Spirit never leaves us alone. He is always with the Church and with each and every member of the Church.

The Holy Spirit is always at work in the Church. He is the Teacher who helps the Church understand what Jesus taught. The Holy Spirit is the Advocate who gives the Church the gifts necessary to fulfill Jesus' command:

"Go, therefore, and make disciples of all nations, baptizing them in the name of the Father, and of the Son, and of the holy Spirit, teaching them to observe all that I have commanded you."

MATTHEW 28:19–20

The Holy Spirit is always with us, guiding and strengthening us to live Jesus' command to love one another as he did. He blesses each of us with **charisms**, or special graces, that we are to use to help build up the Church.

As Christians, we pray for the grace to open our hearts and minds to the Holy Spirit. Praying to the Holy Spirit makes all the difference in the way we live each day.

Activity Complete this prayer. Make it your own personal prayer. Keep a copy of your prayer in your Bible or some other place. Pray it each day.

Come, Holy Spirit, _____

_____

_____.

The Holy Spirit Today

The Church is the Temple of the Holy Spirit. The Holy Spirit, our Teacher and Sanctifier, works in many ways to build up the Church: God's Word, the Sacraments, the virtues, and charisms, which are special gifts of the Holy Spirit that build up the Church.

Our Teacher

The Holy Spirit is our Teacher who guides us in understanding and teaching what God has revealed in Jesus Christ. The Holy Spirit helps the Pope and the bishops teach clearly and authentically what God has revealed through Scripture and **Sacred Tradition**. Sacred Tradition is the passing on of the teachings of Christ by the Church through the power and guidance of the Holy Spirit.

Our Sanctifier

The Holy Spirit is our Sanctifier or the One who makes us holy. Through the Holy Spirit, we receive sanctifying grace. This is the gift of holiness that makes us sharers in the very life and love of God. We also receive actual graces that help us to live as Jesus taught.

The Holy Spirit makes us one with Christ and each other. The Holy Spirit continues to help the Church prepare for the coming of the Kingdom of God. At that time, Christ will come again in glory, and his work on Earth will be finished.

? How have you experienced the Holy Spirit active in your life and in your family?

Catholics Believe

Fruits of the Holy Spirit

In Galatians 5:22–23, Saint Paul lists nine signs that show the Holy Spirit is present with and at work in the Church. They are called the Fruits of the Holy Spirit. They are charity, joy, peace, patience, kindness, generosity, faithfulness, gentleness, and self-control. The tradition of the Church also names goodness, modesty, and chastity as the Fruits of the Holy Spirit.

I FOLLOW JESUS

The Holy Spirit gives you gifts, or charisms, to continue the work of Jesus wherever you are.

THE HOLY SPIRIT IS MY HELPER

A magazine has decided to write an article about you. They have learned what you are doing to make your neighborhood a better place. Write the opening paragraph of the article about you.

_____

_____

_____

_____

_____

_____

_____

_____

_____

MY FAITH CHOICE

This week, I will live as a follower of Jesus by working to make the world a better place. I will use the gift of _____

to _____

_____

_____.

 Pray to the Holy Spirit, asking for the gift of courage in order to always choose good and speak up for your faith.

Chapter Review

Use words from this chapter to complete these sentences.

1. The Holy Spirit is the _____ who Jesus promised would always be with the disciples and the Church.

2. The Holy Spirit blesses us with _____ to continue the work of Christ.

3. The Holy Spirit dwells in the _____ today.

4. The Holy Spirit is the _____ , or the One who makes us holy.

5. The Holy Spirit helps the _____ and the _____ to authentically teach what Jesus taught.

▶ **TO HELP YOU REMEMBER**

1. Jesus promised that he would not leave his disciples alone after he returned to his Father.

2. Jesus sent the Holy Spirit to guide the Church as her Advocate, Teacher, and Sanctifier.

3. The Holy Spirit makes the Church holy.

Spread the Gospel

At Baptism, we are joined to Christ, receive the gift of the Holy Spirit, and become members of the Body of Christ, the Church. All the baptized receive the grace and call to spread the Gospel and make people his disciples as he commanded.

Leader: Let us join together and pray that we cooperate with the Holy Spirit and share the Gospel with everyone.

All: **Father, you will your Church to be the sacrament of Salvation for all people. Send the Holy Spirit to inspire the hearts of your people to continue the saving work of Christ everywhere.**

Leader: Grant us this through our Lord Jesus Christ who lives and reigns with you and the Holy Spirit, one God, forever and ever.

All: **Amen.**

With My Family

This Week . . .

In Chapter 7, "Many Gifts, One Spirit," your child learned:

▶ The Church is the Temple of the Holy Spirit, and the Holy Spirit is always at work in the Church.

▶ The Holy Spirit is our Teacher and Advocate. The Holy Spirit is our Sanctifier, the One who makes us holy and gives us the grace to live holy lives.

▶ Each of us is blessed with charisms, or special graces, that we are to use to help build up the Church.

▶ The virtue of courage is one of the seven Gifts of the Holy Spirit. It helps us speak up for our faith and continue the mission of Jesus.

For more about related teachings of the Church, see the *Catechism of the Catholic Church*, 683–741, 797–801, and 1091–1109, and the *United States Catholic Catechism for Adults*, pages 101–123.

▪ Sharing God's Word

Read together 1 Corinthians 12:4–7. Emphasize that the Holy Spirit gives each of the baptized special graces, or charisms, to help them continue the work of Jesus.

▪ We Live as Disciples

The Christian home and family is a school of discipleship. Choose one of the following activities to do as a family, or design a similar activity of your own:

▶ Take turns telling one another what special talents, or gifts, you see in each other. Encourage each other to use his or her gifts to spread the Gospel.

▶ Making good decisions takes practice and the grace of the Holy Spirit. Choose to do one thing this week to help others.

▶ Find out more about Saint Katharine Drexel or another Saint. Talk about how this Saint used his or her gifts to continue the work of Jesus Christ.

▪ Our Spiritual Journey

Saint Francis of Assisi is quoted as saying, "Preach the Gospel and, if necessary, use words." In the earliest days of the Church, the Spirit invited nonbelievers to faith in Christ through the loving actions of the members of the Church. We proclaim the Gospel when we consistently practice the discipline of almsgiving. This is when we share our material and spiritual blessings with others. In this chapter, your child prayed for the spreading of the Gospel. Read and pray together this prayer on page 69.

For more ideas on ways your family can live as disciples of Jesus, visit **www.BeMyDisciples.com.**

Looking Ahead

In this chapter, the Holy Spirit invites you to ▶

EXPLORE one way the Church is continuing the work of Jesus.

DISCOVER the four Marks and the mission of the Church.

DECIDE how you will use your gifts to continue the work of Christ.

CHAPTER 8

Thy Kingdom Come!

[?] Why is it sometimes easier to do a project when people work together as classmates, friends, or family?

We work together as the Body of Christ to continue the work of Jesus Christ until the end of time. Saint Paul reminds us,

> For as in one body we have many parts, and all the parts do not have the same function, so we, though many, are one body in Christ and individually parts of one another.   ROMANS 12:4–5

[?] What does this Scripture passage tell us about the Church?

Disciple Power

Peace

Peace is one of the signs, or Fruits of the Holy Spirit, named in the New Testament. Christians are followers of Christ, the Prince of Peace. As faithful disciples, we cooperate with the grace of the Holy Spirit to create peace throughout the world.

Catholic Relief Services

Peace comes from God. True peace comes by our living as the Body of Christ in the world. God's peace comes from doing just works, like reaching out to people in need. The Catholic Church in the United States works for peace here and throughout the whole world.

In 1943, the Catholic bishops of the United States founded Catholic Relief Services. The people of Catholic Relief Services preach the Gospel by their actions. With the grace and guidance of the Holy Spirit, they live the Gospel of peace and justice among people who are suffering in many places throughout the world.

When people are suffering from poverty, the people of Catholic Relief Services are there. When people are suffering from natural disasters or from wars, the people of Catholic Relief Services are there.

Catholic Relief Services invite people by their words and actions to deepen their faith and trust in God.

Activity Write about or draw a way Catholic Relief Services work to help others. Include a way that you could assist them.

The Body of Christ

The Holy Spirit has invited us to be members of the Church, the Body of Christ. Saint Paul the Apostle used the image of the human body to help us understand what it means to belong to the **Church**. The Church is the Body of Christ. She is the new People of God whom God calls together in Christ by the power of the Holy Spirit.

Christ is the Head of his Body, the Church. All the faithful are her members. Each member of the Church has a different role or responsibility within the Church. The members of the Church belong to three groups, each with specific responsibilities for the work of the Church. These groups include the lay faithful (or laity or laypeople), the ordained, and the consecrated life.

Lay Faithful. Most baptized people are members of the laity. The lay faithful have the responsibility to work together to serve in the world as Jesus did.

Ordained Ministers. The Holy Spirit calls some male members of the Body of Christ to serve the whole Church as bishops, priests, and deacons. They form the clergy. The Pope is the bishop of Rome, the pastor of the Church on Earth.

The Consecrated Life. Some of the laity and ordained consecrate their lives to God in a special way. Most of them live as members of religious communities, which are approved by the Church. Members of religious communities support one another in living their Baptism and serving the Church in many ways.

[?] What other ways do you see the Church living as a sign of God's caring love in the world?

Saint John Paul II

Karol Wojtyla grew up in a small town in Poland. He was elected Pope in 1978 and chose the name John Paul II. As Pope John Paul II, he led the Church in continuing the work of Christ and preparing the way for the coming of the Kingdom of God. On April 27, 2014, Pope John Paul II was named a Saint of the Church.

The Marks of the Church

The Church has four essential characteristics. These characteristics are called the Marks of the Church. The four Marks of the Church identify her as the Church founded by Jesus. The Marks of the Church are one, holy, catholic, and apostolic.

> **The Church is one.** We believe in one faith and one Lord, and we share one Baptism.

> **The Church is holy.** Our sharing in the life of the Holy Trinity is the source of the Church's holiness.

> **The Church is catholic.** The Church reaches out to all people and welcomes them into the family of God.

> **The Church is apostolic.** We trace our faith back to the Apostles. The Pope and other bishops are the successors of the Apostles. They share in the responsibility Jesus gave to the Apostles to teach in his name and make all people disciples of Jesus.

Members of the Church share the faith of the Church and believe what the Church teaches. They pray together and celebrate the Sacraments together with Christ and the Holy Spirit. They serve others by sharing Jesus' healing, forgiveness, and hope with all people.

Activity Create a bookmark to illustrate one of the four Marks of the Church.

Life Everlasting

All the faithful believers in Christ form the *Communion of Saints*. This includes those in Heaven, in Purgatory, and those faithful living on Earth.

The Church continues the work of Christ and prepares the way for the coming of the **Kingdom of God**. Christ proclaimed,

> "This is the time of fulfillment. The kingdom of God is at hand. Repent, and believe in the gospel." MARK 1:15

The Kingdom, or Reign, of God will come about at the end of time when Christ will come again in glory. In the Kingdom, all the faithful will live in communion with God.

> Jesus taught that the Kingdom of God was a place of eternal happiness. It would fully come about at the end of time, and there will be "new heavens and a new earth." 2 PETER 3:13

When we die, life is changed yet not ended. Life after death includes Heaven, Purgatory, and hell.

> **Heaven.** Heaven is everlasting life with God, the angels, and with Mary and the other Saints. All those who have been faithful to God will live with God the Father, Jesus, and the Holy Spirit in happiness forever.

> **Purgatory.** The faithful who are not ready to receive the gift of eternal happiness when they die will have the opportunity to purify their love for God before entering Heaven. This is called Purgatory.

> **Hell.** When people sin seriously and do not ask God for forgiveness, they choose to stay separated from God now and forever. Eternal separation from God is hell.

At the moment of death, our lives will be judged by God. This is called the particular judgment. At the end of time there will be the Final Judgment of all. All who have been faithful to God will be called forth to live in Heaven.

? What is an example of one way you can help prepare the way for the coming of the Kingdom of God?

The Ascension, by Caserta Bazile

I FOLLOW JESUS

The Holy Spirit helps you use your gifts to follow Jesus, the Prince of Peace. The Holy Spirit gives you the grace to be a peacemaker and prepare for the coming of the Kingdom of God.

THY KINGDOM COME

Think about your talents or gifts. List three of your gifts below. Describe how you can use those gifts with others to prepare for the Kingdom of God.

MY FAITH CHOICE

This week, I will try to come to know God better. I will

_____

_____

_____.

 Take a moment now and ask the Holy Spirit to help you live as a peacemaker.

Chapter Review

Two of the three answers under each statement are correct. Circle the letter of the statement that does NOT correctly complete the sentence.

1. The Church is
   a. the Body of Christ
   b. all people in the world
   c. the new People of God

2. Main groups of people who make up the Church include the:
   a. lay faithful
   b. ordained ministers
   c. teachers and doctors

3. Among the four Marks of the Church are
   a. catholic
   b. holy
   c. discipleship

▶ **TO HELP YOU REMEMBER**

1. The Church, the Body of Christ, is made up of the lay faithful, the ordained, and members of the consecrated life.

2. The Church has four Marks. They are one, holy, catholic, and apostolic.

3. All the members of the Church work together to prepare for the coming of the Kingdom of God.

Thy Kingdom Come

In the Our Father, we pray for the coming of the Kingdom of God and for the grace to help prepare the way for it. This prayer is at the center of the Gospel and is prayed every day around the world. Raise your hands, palms up, and pray the Our Father.

Leader: Our Father, who art in heaven,

Group 1: hallowed be thy name;

Group 2: thy kingdom come,

Group 1: thy will be done on earth as it is in heaven.

Group 2: Give us this day our daily bread,

Group 1: and forgive us our trespasses,

Group 2: as we forgive those who trespass against us;

Group 1: and lead us not into temptation

Group 2: but deliver us from evil.

All: **Amen.**

With My Family

This Week . . .

In Chapter 8, "Thy Kingdom Come!" your child learned:

▶ All the members of the Church, the Body of Christ, have different roles and responsibilities to continue the work of Christ.

▶ The Holy Spirit guides the Church to continue that work until the end of time.

▶ The Kingdom of God will be established in its fullness at the end of time.

▶ Followers of Christ are peacemakers. The grace of the Holy Spirit helps us to follow Jesus Christ and to prepare for the coming of the Kingdom of God.

For more about related teachings of the Church, see the *Catechism of the Catholic Church*, 668–679, 787–795, 811–972, and the *United States Catholic Catechism for Adults*, pages 101–113.

■ Sharing God's Word

Read together Saint Paul's teaching on the Church as the Body of Christ in 1 Corinthians 12:12–31. Emphasize that Christ is the Head of his Body, the Church. All of the baptized are members of the Church.

■ We Live as Disciples

The Christian home and family is a school of discipleship. Choose one of the following activities to do as a family, or design a similar activity of your own:

▶ Pray the Our Father this week. Praise God and ask him for grace to strengthen you to prepare the way for the coming of the Kingdom.

▶ Talk about all the ways your family continues the work of Christ. Decide one way you can work as a family with other members of your parish to continue the work of Christ.

■ Our Spiritual Journey

Daily prayer, daily conversation with God, is vital to the Christian life. Praying the Our Father keeps us in the presence of God the Father and in communion with him and his Son. Integrate the ancient tradition of praying the Our Father three times daily in your life as a family. In this chapter, your child prayed the Our Father. Pray the Our Father as a family.

For more ideas on ways your family can live as disciples of Jesus, visit **www.BeMyDisciples.com.**

Unit 2 Review

Name _____

A. Choose the Best Word

Fill in the blanks using the words from the word bank.

Sanctifier	Annunciation	Marks
Resurrection	Teacher	Church

1. One, holy, catholic, and apostolic are known as the

_____ of the Church.

2. The announcement of the birth of Jesus was a special
moment in the life of the Virgin Mary. We call this moment

the _____.

3. The Holy Spirit is our _____ and _____.

4. The _____ is when Jesus was raised to a
new and glorified life.

5. Christ is the Head of his Body, the _____.

B. Show What You Know

Match the items in Column A with those in Column B.

Column A

_____ **1.** Sacred Tradition

_____ **2.** Hell

_____ **3.** Paschal Mystery

_____ **4.** Mary

_____ **5.** the Church

Column B

a. the Body of Christ; the new People of God

b. the passing on of the teachings of Christ
by the Church

c. the "passing over" of Jesus from life
through death into a new and glorious life

d. our Blessed Mother; Mother of the Church

e. eternal separation from God

C. Connect with Scripture

Reread the Scripture passage on page 45.
What connection do you see between this passage and
what you learned in this unit?

_____

_____

_____

D. Be a Disciple

1. *Review the four pages in this unit titled The Church Follows*
Jesus. What person or ministry of the Church on these
pages will inspire you to be a better disciple of Jesus?
Explain your answer.

_____

_____

_____

2. *Work with a group. Review the four Disciple Power virtues,*
or gifts, you have learned about in this unit. After jotting
down your own ideas, share with the group practical
ways that you will live these virtues day by day.

_____

_____

_____

We Worship
Part One

The Bread of Life

Jesus explained to the crowd of people,

"Amen, amen, I say to you, whoever believes has eternal life. I am the bread of life. Your ancestors ate the manna in the desert but they died; this is the bread that comes down from heaven so that one may eat it and not die. I am the living bread that came down from heaven; whoever eats this bread will live forever; and the bread that I will give is my flesh for the life of the world." JOHN 6:47–51

What I Have Learned

What is something you already know about these faith concepts?

Sacraments

_____

_____

_____

grace

_____

_____

Eucharist

_____

_____

Faith Terms to Know

Put an X next to the faith terms you know. Put a ? next to faith terms you need to learn more about.

_____ Triduum

_____ liturgy

_____ holy water

_____ Original Sin

_____ anointed

_____ Chrism

_____ Mass

_____ crucified

The Bible

What do you know about how Jesus announced the beginning of his ministry?

_____

_____

_____

The Church

How and when does the Church celebrate the Resurrection of Jesus?

_____

_____

_____

Questions I Have

What questions would you like to ask about the Mass?

_____

_____

Looking Ahead

In this chapter, the Holy Spirit invites you to ▶

EXPLORE how the Church thanks God for his works.

DISCOVER the importance of the liturgy.

DECIDE how you will worship God in all that you do and say.

CHAPTER
9

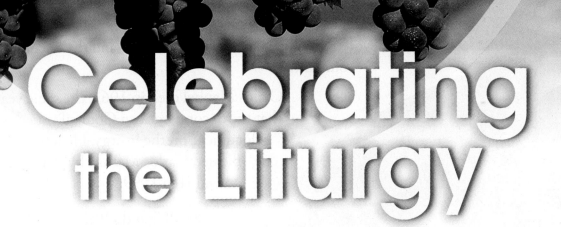

Celebrating the Liturgy

❓ How do you show your thanks to others?

Merci. Gracias. Asante. Cám ón. All of these words mean "thank you." Listen to these words of thanks from Scripture:

> We thank you, God, we give thanks;
>> we call upon your name,
>> declare your wonderful deeds. Psalm 75:2

❓ What are some of the "wonderful deeds" of God for which you are thankful?
Why do you think it is important to show our gratitude to God?

Disciple Power

Perseverance

This is the virtue by which we hold to our faith even through trying events or circumstances. To persevere in faith, we must continually nourish it with the Word of God and the celebration of the Sacraments.

Blessed by God

Not all people are treated fairly by life. Those who are not can become bitter and sad. However, some still are able to do great works for the Kingdom of God. Carlos Manuel Rodriguez Santiago was such a person.

Carlos Manuel was born in 1918 in Puerto Rico. He was a very bright boy, but he had many health problems. He dreamed of becoming a college professor, but his health did not permit him to finish his education. He was a person of very deep faith, and he persevered in spite of his poor health. He decided that he would spend his life telling others about Jesus.

Carlos Manuel especially wanted people to understand the importance of the Paschal Mystery of Jesus Christ. Since that is most fully expressed in the Mass and Sacraments, he devoted his life to helping others understand the celebration of our faith.

Carlos Manuel died in 1963, the same year that the Second Vatican Council issued its document on the liturgy. He was declared Blessed Carlos Manuel by Pope John Paul II in 1999.

? What do Blessed Carlos Manuel's choices in life teach us about how to be disciples of Jesus?

We Worship God

When the Church comes together to worship God, we celebrate the **liturgy**. The word *liturgy* means "work of the people." We gather to pray, honor, thank, and give glory to God for all he has done and continues to do for us. Liturgy includes the celebration of the Seven **Sacraments**, the Liturgy of the Hours, and Benediction of the Most Blessed Sacrament.

The Holy Trinity is present with the Church when we come together to celebrate the liturgy. We worship One God in Three Divine Persons, the Holy Trinity. We pray to the Father, through the Son, and in the Holy Spirit.

Each time the Church celebrates the liturgy, we share more fully in the new life Jesus gained for us. We are changed and become more like Jesus. We find strength to live as Jesus did and to bring his life and love to the world.

When the Church celebrates the liturgy, the whole Church takes part. We remember, celebrate, and are made sharers in the Paschal Mystery.

FAITH FOCUS
Why do we celebrate the liturgy as a community?

FAITH VOCABULARY
liturgy
The liturgy is the work of the Church, the People of God, of worshiping God. Through the liturgy, Christ continues the work of Redemption in, with, and through his Church.

Sacraments
Sacraments are the seven main liturgical signs of the Church given to the Church by Jesus Christ. They make his saving work present and make us sharers in the life of God, the Holy Trinity.

Activity Illustrate one way you have been strengthened by the Church's liturgy to bring Jesus' life and love to the world.

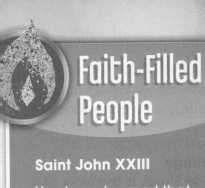

Saint John XXIII

You have learned that Pope John XXIII called all the bishops together in 1962. He and the bishops decided to make several changes in the way the Church celebrates the liturgy. One of the most important changes was to celebrate the Sacraments in the native language of the people.

The Year of the Lord's Grace

The Church celebrates the liturgy every day and all year long. This yearly cycle of the Church's celebration of the liturgy is called the liturgical year. Throughout the year, we celebrate and take part in God's plan of saving love for us.

The liturgical year is a year of the Lord's grace, celebrating the mysteries of Jesus' life. It includes weekly Sunday celebrations and feasts of the Lord, of Mary, and other Saints within seasonal cycles.

 **Advent Season.** The Church celebrates God's coming among us. We get ready to remember Jesus' birth on Christmas Day. We remember Jesus' promise to come again in glory at the end of time.

 Christmas Season. We remember and celebrate that the Son of God, Jesus the Savior, came and lived among us.

 Lenten Season. We strive, with the help of the Holy Spirit, to grow in our life in Christ. We support those preparing to be baptized at Easter. We prepare to renew our own baptismal promises.

 Triduum. This three-day celebration of Holy Thursday, Good Friday, and Easter Vigil/Easter Sunday is the heart and center of the liturgical year.

 Easter Season. For fifty days, we joyfully reflect on the Resurrection and our new life in Christ. On the fortieth day, we celebrate the Ascension of the Lord. On the fiftieth day, we celebrate Pentecost.

 Ordinary Time. Other weeks of the year are called Ordinary Time. We listen to Jesus' teachings and learn ways to live as his followers.

❓ Describe some of the ways you see your parish celebrating the seasons of the liturgical year.

The Seven Sacraments

Before Jesus returned to his Father, he said,

"I am with you always, until the end of the age."

MATTHEW 28:20

Jesus is especially present with his Church when we celebrate the Seven Sacraments he gave us. They are our seven main liturgical celebrations and signs of God's work. They put us in contact with the saving work of Jesus Christ. Through the Sacraments, he transforms us. All of the Sacraments build up the Body of Christ. Through them, our life with the Holy Trinity is strengthened. The Seven Sacraments have three main groups:

Sacraments of Christian Initiation. Through Baptism, Confirmation, and Eucharist, we are joined to Christ and become full members of the Church. We are made sharers in God's life and receive help to live as his children.

Sacraments of Healing. Through Penance and Reconciliation and Anointing of the Sick, we celebrate and share in God's healing love.

Sacraments at the Service of Communion. Through Holy Orders and Matrimony, some members of the Church are consecrated to serve the whole Body of Christ, the Church.

Activity For each of the letters in the word "Sacrament," write a word that tells something that happens in the Sacraments.

S _____

A _____

C _____

R _____

A _____

M _____

E _____

N _____

T _____

I FOLLOW JESUS

You join with Christ and other members of the Church throughout the year to celebrate the liturgy and give thanks to God. Each season of the liturgical year helps you live, grow, and persevere in faith.

CELEBRATING OUR LIFE IN CHRIST

Choose a liturgical season. Create and design a banner to help you celebrate it. Include a message about living the season. Be sure to use the liturgical color for that season.

MY FAITH CHOICE

This week, I will celebrate my faith in Jesus, the Savior. I will

_____

_____

_____

 Pray, "Dear Jesus, help me to always be strong in my faith and nourish me through the Eucharist. Amen."

Chapter Review

Write the letter of the correct description in the right column on the line next to each faith term.

Faith Terms

_____ **1.** Sacraments

_____ **2.** Paschal Mystery

_____ **3.** Lent

_____ **4.** Easter

_____ **5.** Sacraments of Christian Initiation

_____ **6.** liturgy

Descriptions

a. Jesus' suffering, Death, Resurrection, and glorious Ascension

b. a season of the Church year that prepares us for Easter

c. Sacraments by which we are joined to Christ and become full members of the Church

d. work of the People of God

e. seven liturgical celebrations of the Church given to us by Christ

f. a season of the Church during which we rejoice in Christ's Resurrection

TO HELP YOU REMEMBER

1. The liturgy is the Church's work of worshiping God.

2. The liturgical year is the Church's cycle of worship that celebrates God's great plan of saving love for us and for all people.

3. The Sacraments make the saving work of Jesus Christ present to us and make us sharers in the life of God, the Holy Trinity.

Lift Up Your Hearts

Learn to pray this simple prayer of praise and honor to God. We pray or sing these words at Mass. Pray it together with your class and pray it often quietly in your heart.

Leader: Let us lift up our hearts and give thanks and praise to God.

Group 1: Holy, Holy, Holy Lord God of hosts.

Group 2: Heaven and earth are full of your glory.

All: Hosanna in the highest.

Group 1: Blessed is he who comes in the name of the Lord.

Group 2: Blessed is he who comes in the name of the Lord.

All: Hosanna in the highest.

BASED ON PREFACE ACCLAMATION,
ROMAN MISSAL

With My Family

This Week . . .

In Chapter 9, "Celebrating the Liturgy," your child learned:

▶ The liturgy is the Church's work of worshiping God.

▶ The liturgy includes the celebration of the Sacraments, the Liturgy of the Hours, and Benediction of the Most Blessed Sacrament.

▶ The Sacraments are the signs of God's work among us that Jesus gave to the Church.

▶ Like the calendar year, the Church liturgical year of worship is made up of a cycle of seasons and feast days.

▶ Perseverance is the virtue by which we hold to our faith even through trying events or circumstances.

For more about related teachings of the Church, see the *Catechism of the Catholic Church*, 1135–1186, and the *United States Catholic Catechism for Adults*, pages 165–179.

◼ Sharing God's Word

Read Psalm 75:2 together. Share how the psalmist's attitude of thankfulness is expressed in this psalm verse. Emphasize that the whole life of your family should give honor and glory, praise and thanks to God.

◼ We Live as Disciples

The Christian home and family is a school of discipleship. Choose one of the following activities to do as a family, or design a similar activity of your own:

▶ Identify and talk about the season of the liturgical year you are now celebrating with the Church. Invite family members to share which of the liturgical seasons they like best. Talk about how this season helps them give praise and thanks to God.

▶ When your family takes part in the celebration of Mass this weekend, pay close attention to the liturgical colors and decorations. Talk about how the liturgical season helps you remember and share in God's great plan of saving love for the world.

◼ Our Spiritual Journey

Christians are a "thankful people," and the Eucharist is the Church's great prayer of thanksgiving. Regular participation in the celebration of the Mass and frequent reception of Holy Communion are vital for our spiritual journeys as Christians.

For more ideas on ways your family can live as disciples of Jesus, visit **www.BeMyDisciples.com**

Looking Ahead

In this chapter, the Holy Spirit invites you to ▶

EXPLORE how Saint Maximilian Kolbe lived his Baptism.

DISCOVER the celebration and effects of Baptism.

DECIDE how you will live your Baptism.

CHAPTER
10

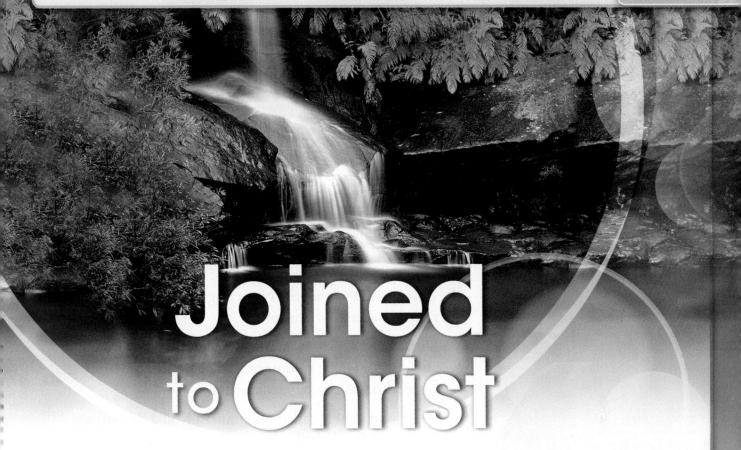

Joined to Christ

[?] What do you think your life would be like without water?

Jesus spoke of the importance of water. In John's account of the Gospel, the Pharisee Nicodemus asked Jesus what he had to do to enter the Kingdom of God. Jesus answered,

> "Amen, amen, I say to you, no one can enter the kingdom of God without being born of water and Spirit."
>
> JOHN 3:5

[?] How do you think water helps us understand the meaning of the Sacrament of Baptism?

Disciple Power

Generosity

Generosity is a Fruit of the Holy Spirit. Practicing generosity helps us serve the Church and the world. With generosity, we share our gifts and our talents with others. We share our material and spiritual blessings.

A Model of Generosity

Raymond Kolbe lived what it means to be "born of water and the Spirit." He was born in Poland in 1894. When he was twelve years old, the Blessed Virgin Mary appeared to him. From then on, Raymond developed a great love and devotion for Mary.

When he grew up, Raymond became a Franciscan priest and took the name Maximilian Mary. Several years later, World War II broke out, and Father Maximilian was arrested and sent to a Nazi concentration camp.

Although he suffered great abuse, Father Maximilian gave spiritual help to the other prisoners. Together, they prayed the Rosary and sang hymns to Mary. Father Maximilian told the other prisoners that the Nazis might kill their bodies, but they could never kill their souls.

Ultimately, Father Maximilian made the greatest sacrifice—his life. He volunteered to take the place of another prisoner who was condemned to death.

Pope John Paul II called Maximilian Kolbe the patron Saint of the difficult 20th century. During a time of war, he brought many people to a deeper faith in God when everything else was lost. He was named a Saint of the Church. He is a model of the type of generosity that Christ calls the baptized to live.

Activity Create a title for a biography of Saint Maximilian Kolbe that describes his importance.

Followers of Christ

Baptism is one of the three Sacraments of Christian Initiation. Here is a summary of the rite of, or way, of celebrating Baptism. Each part of the Rite of Baptism shows that the people being baptized are receiving the gift of new life from God.

The Rite of Baptism

Blessing of the water. After the celebration of the Liturgy of the Word, the priest or deacon says a prayer and anoints the chest of those to be baptized. He greets everyone at the baptismal font or pool. Blessing the water, he retells the story of creation and Salvation.

Renunciation of sin and profession of faith. All present join with those to be baptized and reject sin. All promise to live as God's children. All profess faith in God, the Holy Trinity.

Baptism in water. The person to be baptized now enters, or is immersed in, the water or has water poured on his or her head three times as the celebrant says the words, "(Name), I baptize you in the name of the Father, and of the Son, and of the Holy Spirit."

Anointing with Chrism. The celebrant anoints the top of the head of each of the newly baptized with the holy oil of **Chrism**. This shows that the Holy Spirit is with the baptized to strengthen them to live as members of the Body of Christ, the Church, and take part in the work of Christ the Priest, Prophet, and King.

White garment and lighted candle. The newly baptized receive a white garment and a candle lit from the Easter candle. Clothed in Christ, the baptized are to keep the flame of faith alive in their hearts.

? How do the symbols used in the Rite of Baptism show that the people being baptized are receiving the gift of new life from God? Work with a partner to prepare your response.

FAITH FOCUS
What is the meaning of the Sacrament of Baptism?

FAITH VOCABULARY
Baptism
Baptism is the Sacrament of Christian Initiation in which we are first joined to Jesus Christ, become members of the Church, are reborn as God's adopted children, receive the gift of the Holy Spirit, and by which Original Sin and personal sins are forgiven.

Chrism
Chrism is one of the three oils the Church uses in the celebration of the liturgy. It is used in the Sacraments of Baptism, Confirmation, and Holy Orders. Chrism is also used in the consecration of churches and altars.

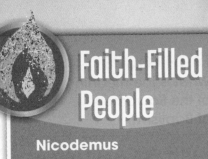
Nicodemus

John's Gospel tells us the story about the Pharisee Nicodemus. He first went to Jesus, asked Jesus many questions, and came to believe in Jesus. Nicodemus' faith in Jesus grew. He defended Jesus when people criticized Jesus. After Jesus died, Nicodemus and Joseph of Arimathea buried Jesus' body in a tomb carved in the side of a mountain.

The Special Graces of Baptism

All the words, actions, and objects used in the Rite of Baptism point to the deeper meaning of what we are seeing and hearing. We call what happens at Baptism the effects, or special graces, of Baptism. The word *graces* tells us that all that happens in Baptism is a gift from God.

Children of the Father. Through Baptism, we receive new life in Jesus Christ. We are born again as adopted children of God the Father. Saint John reminds us,

> See what love the Father has bestowed on us that we may be called the children of God.　1 JOHN 3:1

Members of the Church, the Body of Christ. We are joined to Christ through Baptism. We become members of the Body of Christ, the Church. We become part of a larger family of faith, the Church.

Temples of the Holy Spirit. Saint Paul reminds us,

> Do you not know that you are the temple of God, and that the Spirit of God dwells in you?
>
> 1 CORINTHIANS 3:16

Through Baptism, we receive the gift of the Holy Spirit. The Holy Spirit helps us to live as members of the Body of Christ. Throughout our lives, the Holy Spirit invites and helps us live as children of God and followers of Jesus Christ.

Forgiveness of sin. Baptism frees us from Original Sin that we inherited from the first humans. Baptism also takes away all personal sins that we may have committed. Everything that separates us from God is washed away. We receive the gift of sanctifying grace. We are made sharers in the life of God, the Holy Trinity.

Activity On this candle, describe one thing you might do to live your Baptism.

The Life of Grace

The Sacrament of Baptism welcomes new members into the Church. It is the first Sacrament we receive. It is the "doorway" to the Christian life. It not only *initiates* the believer into the Church. It does much more. Through Baptism, Christians "are reborn of water and the Spirit." They enter into a completely new life that gives them a new and deeper relationship with God.

All people are God's children, but Baptism makes that connection even more special. Baptism makes a person a co-heir with Christ in God's Kingdom. The baptized person is an adopted son or daughter of God. The newly baptized person receives sanctifying grace, the gift of the Holy Spirit, and the gifts of God's love, holiness, and life.

In Baptism, you, or your parents speaking for you, made a decision to respond to God's invitation to live a life of faith. You promised to follow the way of Jesus Christ. Every day of your life, you will continue to make conscious decisions to live your life in Christ.

? What are some ways you are trying to live a life in Christ?

Catholics Believe

Baptismal Garment

At Baptism, the newly baptized are dressed in a white garment. The white garment is a symbol of the gift of new life in Christ the newly baptized have received. The priest or deacon prays, "(Name), you have become a new creation.... See in this white garment the outward sign of your Christian dignity. May you bring it unstained into the everlasting life of heaven" (*Rite of Baptism*).

I FOLLOW JESUS

The Holy Spirit lives within you. He teaches you and gives you the help, or graces, to live the Gospel. The Holy Spirit teaches and helps you to be generous and to become a light in the world.

BEING A LIGHT IN THE WORLD

Illustrate a scene that shows what you and other fifth graders might do to live the Gospel.

MY FAITH CHOICE

This week, I will try to come to know God better. This week, I will try to live my Baptism. I will _____

_____

_____

_____.

 Pray, "Holy Spirit, give me the grace to become more generous with my time and talents, even when it is inconvenient. Amen."

Chapter Review

Circle the Sacrament words hidden in the puzzle. Use the words in one or more sentences that describe what happens in Baptism.

```
E R T Y Y A N O I N T I N G H K E
W M Q F B B A P T I S M Q E R V I
X N F O R G I V E N E S S L Q L S
N H J O P S K A W A T E R D F S Z
```

_____

_____

_____

Do You Believe?

We renew our baptismal promises at Mass on Easter Sunday and whenever we take part in a Baptism liturgy. We can also do this as a class.

Leader: Do you believe in God, the Father almighty, creator of heaven and earth?

All: I do.

Leader: Do you believe in Jesus Christ, his only Son, our Lord, who was born of the Virgin Mary, was crucified, died, and was buried, rose from the dead, and is now seated at the right hand of the Father?

All: I do.

Leader: Do you believe in the Holy Spirit, the holy catholic Church, the communion of saints, the forgiveness of sins, the resurrection of the body, and the life everlasting?

All: I do.

Leader: This is our faith. This is the faith of the Church. We are proud to profess it, in Christ Jesus our Lord.

All: Amen.

BASED ON THE *RITE OF BAPTISM FOR CHILDREN*

TO HELP YOU REMEMBER

1. Baptism, Confirmation, and Eucharist are the three Sacraments of Christian Initiation.

2. Baptism joins us to Christ. We are reborn as God's children. We receive the gift of the Holy Spirit and become members of the Church.

3. In Baptism, Original Sin and all personal sins are forgiven.

With My Family

This Week ...

In Chapter 10, "Joined to Christ," your child learned:

▶ The Sacrament of Baptism is one of the three Sacraments of Christian Initiation and the first Sacrament we receive.

▶ Baptism brings us into new life in Christ and makes us members of the Body of Christ, the Church.

▶ Through Baptism, we receive sanctifying grace and the gift of the Holy Spirit.

▶ By God's gift, through water and the Holy Spirit, Original Sin and everything that separates us from God is washed away.

▶ Generosity helps us live our Baptism by serving the Church and the world.

For more about related teachings of the Church, see the *Catechism of the Catholic Church*, 1210–1284, and the *United States Catholic Catechism for Adults*, pages 181–199.

■ Sharing God's Word

Read Matthew 3:13–17 together. Emphasize that through Baptism, we receive the gift of the Holy Spirit and the graces, or help, of the Holy Spirit to prepare for the Kingdom of God.

■ We Live as Disciples

The Christian home and family is a school of discipleship. Choose one of the following activities to do as a family, or design a similar activity of your own:

▶ When your family participates in Mass this week, go to the ambry after Mass. The ambry is the place where the Chrism and other holy oils used in the celebration of the liturgy are kept. Point out the sacred Chrism with which we are anointed at Baptism and Confirmation.

▶ Look at your family photo albums and find Baptism pictures. Share stories about each person's Baptism. Talk about who was there and why Baptism is an important family day. Talk about all the ways your family lives Baptism.

■ Our Spiritual Journey

God speaks to us through his gifts of creation. We use water throughout the day. Drinking and washing with water are "graced moments." They are moments that can help us make the connection between the visible and invisible. Use these moments to recall that you indeed have been reborn. You are a new creation.

For more ideas on ways your family can live as disciples of Jesus, visit **www.BeMyDisciples.com** ▶

Looking Ahead

In this chapter, the Holy Spirit invites you to ▶

EXPLORE the work that Dorothy Day did to live her faith in Christ.

DISCOVER the effects of the Sacrament of Confirmation.

DECIDE how you will carry on the mission of Christ.

We Celebrate the Holy Spirit

? What does it mean to have a goal or a mission?

One day, Jesus went to the synagogue in Nazareth. The rabbi gave him a scroll on which the writings of Isaiah the prophet were written. Jesus rolled the scroll open and announced to the people his mission. Jesus read aloud,

"'The Spirit of the Lord is upon me,
because he has anointed me
    to bring glad tidings to the poor.
He has sent me to proclaim liberty to captives
    and recovery of sight to the blind,
        to let the oppressed go free,
and to proclaim a year acceptable to the Lord.'"

LUKE 4:18–19

? How does the mission of Jesus continue today?

Disciple Power

Understanding

Understanding is a Gift of the Holy Spirit that helps us know the meaning of the teachings of the Church. It also helps us be sympathetic to others and sense when someone is hurting or in need of compassion.

Good News for the Poor

Dorothy Day worked hard at living her Baptism. She worked hard at her mission of being a "light in the world." She worked hard at bringing "glad tidings to the poor."

When Dorothy Day was eight years old, her father lost his job, and the family moved to a poor neighborhood in Chicago. Soon her father found another job, and the family moved again. Because of this experience, Dorothy never forgot about the needs of people who were poor. Dorothy really understood what it means to be poor.

After Dorothy went to college, she began working as a newspaper reporter in New York City. She had no religious beliefs but became interested in the Catholic faith through a religious sister. After some time, she joined the Catholic Church.

Dorothy wanted to find ways to improve the lives of people who were poor. She met Peter Maurin, who had the same idea. Together they opened a house of hospitality where people who were poor could stay and get food and clothing.

Peter encouraged Dorothy to use her God-given gifts to start a newspaper that would describe what she was doing. Soon Dorothy realized that the articles in her paper were making people aware of the needs of the poor. Her newspaper, *The Catholic Worker*, cost only a penny, just as it does today.

Dorothy and Peter started the Catholic Worker Movement, which opened many houses of hospitality across the United States. For 50 years, Dorothy shared Jesus' concern for the poor and truly lived out the mission given to her in Baptism.

? How does the story of Dorothy Day help you understand your own role in spreading the mission of Jesus Christ?

Confirmed in the Spirit

Dorothy Day exhibited the Holy Spirit's gift of understanding. At Baptism, we receive the seven Gifts of the Holy Spirit. These gifts are strengthened in us at **Confirmation**. They help us live holy lives.

The Gifts of the Holy Spirit

Wisdom helps us know God's will for our lives.

Understanding enables us to know the meaning of the teachings of our Catholic faith. It also helps us sense the need for compassion.

Counsel, or Right Judgment, helps us know what is right and to make good choices.

Fortitude, or Courage, strengthens us to be witnesses of Jesus Christ and to defend our Catholic faith.

Knowledge helps us know that God is more important than anything else in life.

Piety, or Reverence, helps us love and respect God.

Fear of the Lord, or Wonder and Awe, inspires us to be filled with love and reverence for God.

FAITH VOCABULARY
Confirmation
Confirmation is the Sacrament of Christian Initiation that strengthens the graces of Baptism and in which our new life in Christ is sealed by the gift of the Holy Spirit.

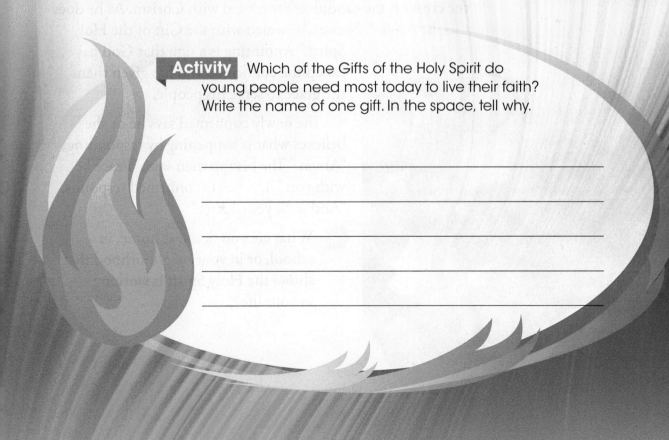

Activity Which of the Gifts of the Holy Spirit do young people need most today to live their faith? Write the name of one gift. In the space, tell why.

_____

_____

_____

_____

_____

Celebrating Confirmation

The bishop is the usual minister of the Sacrament of Confirmation. But sometimes the bishop names a priest to celebrate Confirmation. This usually happens when people are confirmed at the Easter Vigil in their parish church.

There are key words, actions, and objects used in the Rite of Confirmation that show how the Holy Spirit seals, or completes, our Baptism. One of the images that the Bible uses to teach us about the Holy Spirit is fire. Filled with the Holy Spirit, our hearts are "on fire" to live our Baptism. Sealed with the gift of the Holy Spirit, we are strengthened to continue the work of Christ.

The Rite of Confirmation

Laying on of hands. The bishop holds out his hands and extends them over the candidates for Confirmation. He prays, asking God, the Father of our Lord Jesus Christ, to pour out the Holy Spirit upon them to be their helper and guide.

Anointing with Chrism. One by one, the candidates with their sponsors go to the bishop. The sponsor places his or her right hand on the shoulder of the candidate and presents the candidate by name to the bishop. The bishop places his right hand on top of the head of the candidate and makes a sign of the cross on the candidate's forehead with Chrism. As he does this, he prays, "(Name), be sealed with the Gift of the Holy Spirit." Anointing is a sign that God has called the confirmed and has given them the grace to serve his people.

The newly confirmed says he or she believes what is happening by responding, "Amen." The bishop then says, "Peace be with you." The newly confirmed responds, "And with your Spirit."

What are you doing at home, in school, or in your neighborhood that shows the Holy Spirit is working in your life?

Anointed Ones

In the Scriptures, anointing with fragrant oil is a sign of God's special favor. In the Old Testament, we read the account of the anointing of David by Samuel. This anointing showed that David was chosen by God to be king of the Israelites and that the Holy Spirit was with him to fulfill that mission. We read,

> The LORD said, "There—anoint him, for this is he!" Then Samuel, with the horn of oil in hand, anointed him in the midst of his brothers; and from that day on, the spirit of the LORD rushed upon David.
>
> 1 SAMUEL 16:12–13

To be anointed is to be chosen and blessed to do God's work. Priests, prophets, and kings were anointed to show the importance of the work they were to do. The name *Christ* means "the anointed one." In Hebrew, the same word is *Messiah*. Jesus was anointed by God for the work he did, and so are we. As followers of Christ, we are also anointed ones. We are anointed in Baptism and Confirmation to continue the work of Christ, the Priest, Prophet, and King.

At Baptism, we are anointed with sacred Chrism. When we celebrate the Sacrament of Confirmation, we are again anointed with Sacred Chrism. As the bishop anoints us, he says, "Be sealed with the Gift of the Holy Spirit." This seal of Confirmation is a sign that the Holy Spirit is present. We have been marked forever as belonging to Christ.

Activity Design your own seal to show that you belong to Christ. Share your design with others in the group.

103

I FOLLOW JESUS

In Baptism and Confirmation, we receive the Gifts of the Holy Spirit. These seven gifts help us live holy lives, defend the Catholic faith, and carry out the mission that we received at Baptism.

THE GIFTS OF THE HOLY SPIRIT IN ACTION

Choose one of the seven Gifts of the Holy Spirit. Draw a picture or write a brief story or lyrics to a verse of a song of one way you might use that gift in daily life.

MY FAITH CHOICE

This week, I will carry on the mission of Christ by helping others to understand his message. I will

_____

_____

Pray, "Come Holy Spirit, increase the gift of understanding in my life. Amen."

Chapter Review

Decode the faith message.

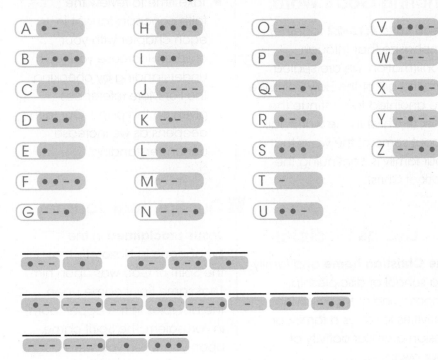

A • −	H • • • •	O − − −	V • • • −
B − • • •	I • •	P • − − •	W • − −
C − • − •	J • − − −	Q − − • −	X − • • −
D − • •	K − • −	R • − •	Y − • − −
E •	L • − • •	S • • •	Z − − • •
F • • − •	M − −	T −	
G − − •	N − •	U • • −	

_____ _____ _____ • _____ • − • − • •

• − − − − − − − − • • − • • − − • • − • •

− − − • − • • • − • • • •

Send Us Your Spirit

Leader: Let us remember that the Holy Spirit dwells within each one of us. He is our helper and teacher. Let us pray:

God, our Father, send us the spirit of wisdom and understanding.

All: Send us your Spirit, Lord.

Leader: Send us the spirit of right judgment and counsel.

All: Send us your Spirit, Lord.

Leader: Send us the spirit of knowledge and reverence.

All: Send us your Spirit, Lord.

Leader: Send us the spirit of wonder and awe.

All: Send us your Spirit, Lord.

With My Family

This Week . . .

In Chapter 11, "We Celebrate the Holy Spirit," your child learned:

- ▶ The Sacrament of Confirmation confirms, or seals, our Baptism.

- ▶ The Holy Spirit strengthens us with his seven gifts to live the Gospel.

- ▶ In the Rite of Confirmation, the candidates are anointed with Sacred Chrism. The name Christ means "the anointed one." As followers of Christ, we are also anointed ones.

- ▶ Understanding is one of the seven Gifts of the Holy Spirit. It helps us know the meaning of Church teaching and helps us be sympathetic to the needs of others.

For more about related teachings of the Church, see the *Catechism of the Catholic Church*, 1285–1321, and the *United States Catholic Catechism for Adults*, pages 201–211.

■ Sharing God's Word

Read Luke 4:16–22 together. Emphasize that through Confirmation, we are sealed with the gift of the Holy Spirit. We are anointed to continue the work of Christ in the world. Talk about some of the ways that your family is continuing the work of Christ.

■ We Live as Disciples

The Christian home and family is a school of discipleship. Choose one of the following activities to do as a family, or design a similar activity of your own:

- ▶ List the years in which family members received the Sacraments of Christian Initiation, namely Baptism, Confirmation, and Eucharist. Then make a time line of other important dates in your family's spiritual history. Display the time line prominently in your home.

▶ Take time to review the faith concepts taught in each chapter with your children. Increase your own understanding by checking the For More references given on this page. Our faith deepens as we increase our understanding.

■ Our Spiritual Journey

Jesus proclaimed in the synagogue in Nazareth that the Spirit of God was upon him. That same Spirit came upon the disciples in the upper room in Jerusalem. The Spirit came upon you when you were baptized and continues with you wherever you are and will be with you wherever you go. We can turn to the Holy Spirit in prayer to give us the gifts we need to follow Christ.

For more ideas on ways your family can live as disciples of Jesus, visit **www.BeMyDisciples.com**

Looking Ahead

In this chapter, the Holy Spirit invites you to ▶

EXPLORE the life of Blessed Mother Teresa.

DISCOVER the effects of the Sacrament of the Eucharist.

DECIDE how you will announce the Gospel in words and actions.

CHAPTER
12

One Bread, One Cup

[?] What elements make up a memorable meal shared with others?

Here is what Jeusus said and did during his last meal with his Apostles:

[He] took bread, said the blessing, broke it and gave it to them saying, "This is my body, which will be given for you; do this in memory of me." And likewise the cup after they had eaten, saying, "This cup is the new covenant in my blood, which will be shed for you."

LUKE 22:19–20

[?] What did Jesus want his disciples to understand?

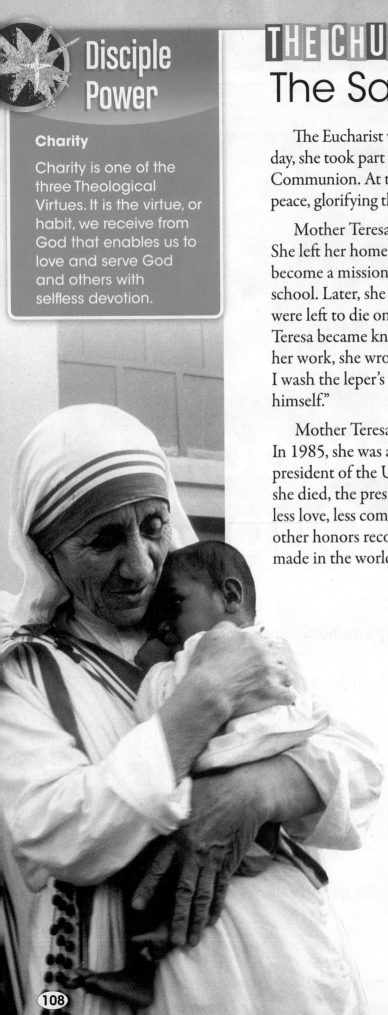

Charity

Charity is one of the three Theological Virtues. It is the virtue, or habit, we receive from God that enables us to love and serve God and others with selfless devotion.

THE CHURCH FOLLOWS JESUS
The Saint of the Gutter

The Eucharist was the center of Mother Teresa's life. Every day, she took part in the celebration of Mass and received Holy Communion. At the conclusion of Mass, she truly went out "in peace, glorifying the Lord by [her] life."

Mother Teresa was born in Albania on August 26, 1910. She left her home in 1928 to join the Sisters of Loreto to become a missionary. In 1929, she arrived in India to teach school. Later, she dedicated her life to serving people who were left to die on the streets. Because of this work, Mother Teresa became known as the "Saint of the Gutter." Describing her work, she wrote, "I see God in every human being. When I wash the leper's wounds, I feel that I am nursing the Lord himself."

Mother Teresa received the Nobel Peace Prize in 1979 In 1985, she was awarded the Medal of Freedom by the president of the United States, Ronald Reagan. On the night she died, the president of France said, "This evening, there is less love, less compassion, less light in the world." These and other honors recognized the difference Mother Teresa's life made in the world.

On October 19, 2003, just six years after she died, Pope John Paul II named Mother Teresa a "Blessed" of the Church. This honor recognizes that Mother Teresa faithfully lived the Gospel and is a model of charity for all Christians to follow. Her life was a living witness to the love of God. "God still loves the world," she wrote, "and he sends you and me to be his love and his compassion to the poor."

? Why could sharing in the Eucharist strengthen you to be a living witness of God's love?

In Memory of Christ

The Sacraments nourish and strengthen us to live as Jesus' followers. At the Last Supper, Jesus gave us the Sacrament of the **Eucharist**. He gave us the gift of his Body and Blood. Jesus said to his disciples, "Do this in memory of me" (Luke 22:19). Each time we celebrate the Eucharist, we do what Jesus did at the Last Supper.

The Sacrifice of the Cross

Jesus freely gave up his life on the Cross to save us from sin. He freely offered himself, or sacrificed his life, to his Father. Through the Eucharist, we join in Jesus' sacrifice of his life for us. Saint Paul reminds us:

> For as often as you eat this bread and drink the cup, you proclaim the death of the Lord until he comes.

1 CORINTHIANS 11:26

When we celebrate the Eucharist, we remember and share in the one sacrifice of Christ. We offer ourselves with Jesus through the power of the Holy Spirit to God the Father.

Activity With a partner, create a skit showing yourselves freely and generously using your gifts and talents to serve God and others as Jesus did. Jot your ideas here.

FAITH FOCUS
Why do we call the Mass a sacrifice?

FAITH VOCABULARY
Eucharist
Eucharist is the Sacrament of Christian Initiation in which we are made sharers in the Paschal Mystery of Christ, we receive the Body and Blood of Christ, and we are joined most fully to Christ and to the Church, the Body of Christ.

Mass
Mass is the main sacramental celebration of the Church at which we gather to listen to God's Word and share in the Eucharist.

Kruzifix (Crucifix), J. P. Hinz, Germany

Óscar Romero

Óscar Romero was the archbishop of San Salvador, El Salvador, which is in Central America. On March 24, 1980, Archbishop Romero was shot through the heart while he was celebrating Mass. He was assassinated because he spoke out, again and again, against people who were unjust to the poor people in his country.

Archbishop Óscar Romero distributing Holy Communion at Mass in El Salvador

The Mystery of the Eucharist

The Eucharist is a great mystery of our faith. By sharing in the Eucharist, we are made sharers in the fullness of life in Jesus. We are more fully joined to Jesus and to one another. We share in the Paschal Mystery of Jesus Christ and the life of the Holy Trinity. The Church uses many names for the Eucharist to help us understand the meaning of this great mystery of God's love.

Names for the Eucharist

The Lord's Supper. The Eucharist is called the Lord's Supper. We join with the Lord, the Head of the Church. We give thanks and praise to the Father as Jesus did with his disciples at the Last Supper.

Breaking of Bread. The Eucharist is the holy meal and banquet Jesus gave to the Church. Through the words of the priest and the power of the Holy Spirit, the unleavened bread and wine made from grapes are changed into the Body and Blood of Christ. In Holy Communion, we receive the gift of Jesus himself, the Bread of Life. The consecrated bread and wine are really and truly Jesus.

The Holy Sacrifice. In the Eucharist, the one sacrifice of Jesus Christ is made present again. The Eucharist does not just remember and celebrate an event that has already taken place. Joined to Christ, we offer ourselves through the power of the Holy Spirit to God the Father.

The Mass. The word *mass* comes from the Latin word "*missio*," which means "mission" or "sending." At the conclusion of **Mass,** we are sent forth on a mission. We are sent forth with the command "Go and announce the Gospel of the Lord."

Activity Work with a partner. Plan a poster that would encourage better attendance at Mass. List your main points here.

The Celebration of Mass

The Church celebrates the Eucharist at Mass. The Mass is the central gathering of the Church. We come together to worship God. We join with Jesus in the power of the Holy Spirit to give thanks and praise to God the Father. We commit ourselves to work with the poor. We look forward to living forever with God and with Mary and all the Saints in Heaven. Every member of the worshiping assembly has an active part in the celebration of Mass.

The Mass

The Introductory Rites. We remember and celebrate that God has called us together to be his people. We gather and form a worshiping community.

The Liturgy of the Word. The Sunday celebration of Mass includes three Scripture readings. We listen and respond to God's Word. The Gospel, which is the third reading, is the center of the Liturgy of the Word. After the proclamation of the Gospel, the priest or deacon preaches a Homily. This helps us understand and live the Word of God. We then pray the Profession of Faith, or Creed, and the Prayer of the Faithful.

The Liturgy of the Eucharist. The Eucharist is the center of the Christian life. In the Eucharistic Prayer, we join with Christ and give thanks and praise to God the Father. By the power of the Holy Spirit and the words of the priest, the bread and wine become the Body and Blood of Christ.

We pray aloud or sing the Our Father and share a sign of peace as we prepare for Holy Communion. We profess our faith in Jesus Christ, the Lamb of God. We walk in procession to receive the Body and Blood of Christ.

The Concluding Rites. The priest asks God's blessing on the assembly. We are sent forth to carry on the work, or mission, of Jesus Christ.

? When you pray the Prayer of the Faithful this week, which needs of the world will you pray for?

I FOLLOW JESUS

The Eucharist is the center of your Christian life. Receiving the Eucharist strengthens you to go and announce the Gospel and give glory to God by your life.

ANNOUNCING THE GOSPEL

Describe how you can love and serve the Lord. Choose an action you are not already doing.

At home: _____
_____
_____
_____

At school: _____
_____
_____
_____

In your neighborhood: _____
_____
_____

MY FAITH CHOICE

This week, I will announce the Gospel and glorify God through my actions and words. I will _____
_____
_____

 Pray to Jesus, asking that you may follow his example and the example of Blessed Mother Teresa and Archbishop Romero, who loved and served God and others through acts of charity.

Chapter Review

Complete this crossword puzzle. Each clue for the puzzle points to the mystery of the Eucharist.

ACROSS

3. The _____ bread, which is the Body of Christ, is called the Blessed Sacrament.

4. When we celebrate the Eucharist, we join in Jesus' _____ of his life for us.

DOWN

1. By sharing in the _____ we share in the fullness of life in Christ.

2. In Holy Communion, we receive the Body and Blood of _____.

Praise God!

This prayer is based on a hymn for the feast of the Body and Blood of Christ on the Second Sunday after Pentecost.

Leader: Let us give thanks and praise to God for the gift of the Eucharist.

Group 1: The cup of blessing that we bless is the Blood of Christ.

All: Bring God all the praise you know.

Group 2: The bread we break is the Body of Christ.

All: Bring God all the praise you know.

Group 3: Whoever eats the bread and drinks from the cup will live forever.

All: Bring God all the praise you know.

BASED ON 1 CORINTHIANS 10:16–17, JOHN 6:51, AND *LAUDA SION*

With My Family

This Week . . .

In Chapter 12, "One Bread, One Cup," your child learned:

▶ The Sacrament of the Eucharist is at the center of the Christian life. The Eucharist is the Sacrament of the Body and Blood of the Lord Jesus Christ.

▶ At the Eucharist, the bread and wine truly become the Body and Blood of Christ through the power of the Holy Spirit and the words of the priest.

▶ When we celebrate the Eucharist, the one sacrifice of Jesus Christ is made present. We are made sharers in the Paschal Mystery and receive the promise of eternal life.

▶ The Theological Virtue of charity is a gift from God. It gives us the ability to love and serve God above all else and others because of our love for God.

For more about related teachings of the Church, see the *Catechism of the Catholic Church*, 1322–1405, and the *United States Catholic Catechism for Adults*, pages 213–232.

■ Sharing God's Word

Read together 1 Corinthians 11:23–26, Saint Paul's account of the institution of the Eucharist. Discuss with your child proper behavior at Mass. Our gestures of respect show our belief that the Lord is really and truly present in the Eucharist.

■ We Live as Disciples

The Christian family and home is a school of discipleship. Choose one of the following activities to do as a family, or design a similar activity of your own.

▶ Spend some time this weekend praying before the tabernacle. You will notice a candle burning next to it. This candle is called a sanctuary lamp. Genuflect before the tabernacle to profess your faith in Jesus, present in the Blessed Sacrament.

▶ At the end of Mass, the assembly is sent forth with these or similar words: "Go and announce the Gospel of the Lord." All respond, "Amen." On the way home, choose one thing each of you can do this week to live and announce the Gospel to one another.

■ Our Spiritual Journey

Fasting is one of the central and traditional spiritual disciplines of the Church. In a Eucharistic fast, Catholics in good health abstain from food or drink (except necessary medicine and water) for at least one hour before receiving Holy Communion. This fasting deepens our spiritual hunger for the food that is vital to living our life in Christ. Pray the "Praise God!" prayer on page 113 this week at a family dinner.

For more ideas on ways your family can live as disciples of Jesus, visit **www.BeMyDisciples.com**

Unit 3 **Review**

A. Choose the Best Word

Fill in the blanks, using the words from the word bank.

Blessed Sacrament	Advent	Baptism	Lent
Confirmation	Christmas	Mass	Easter

1. _____, _____, _____, and

   _____ are liturgical seasons.

2. The Sacrament of _____ seals or

   completes our Baptism.

3. The _____ is the central gathering of the Church.

4. _____ welcomes new members into the Church.
   It is the "doorway to the Christian life."

5. The consecrated bread, which is the Body of Christ, is

   called the _____.

B. Show What You Know

Match the items in Column A with those in Column B.

Column A

1. knowledge

2. sanctifying

3. the liturgical year

4. Sacraments of Christian Initiation

5. the Last Supper

Column B

_____ **a.** when Jesus gave us the Eucharist, the gift of his Body and Blood

_____ **b.** helps us know that God is more important than anything else in life

_____ **c.** grace received at Baptism

_____ **d.** the yearly cycle of the Church's celebration of the liturgy

_____ **e.** Baptism, Confirmation, and Eucharist

C. Connect with Scripture

Reread the Scripture passage on the page 81.
What connection do you see between this passage and
what you learned in this unit?

_____

_____

_____

D. Be a Disciple

1. *Review the four pages in this unit titled The Church Follows*
   Jesus. What person or ministry of the Church on these
   pages will inspire you to be a better disciple of Jesus?
   Explain your answer.

_____

_____

_____

2. *Work with a group. Review the four Disciple Power virtues,*
   or gifts, you have learned about in this unit. After jotting
   down your own ideas, share with the group practical
   ways that you will live these virtues day by day.

_____

_____

_____

We Worship

Part Two

The Forgiving Father

Jesus told the story of a man with two sons. The younger son took his inheritance and spent all of it. Without money, he took a job caring for pigs. He was hungry, so he went back and apologized to his father, who ran up and kissed him. The father planned a feast.

The older brother became angry and jealous. He told his father, "Look, all these years I served you and not once did I disobey your orders; yet you never gave me even a young goat to feast on with my friends."

The father said, "My son, you are here with me always; everything I have is yours. But now we must rejoice, because your brother was dead and has come to life again; he was lost and has been found."

BASED ON LUKE 15:11–32

What I Have Learned

What is something you already know about these faith concepts?

Priesthood

_____

_____

_____

Anointing of the Sick

_____

_____

Penance and Reconciliation

_____

_____

_____

Faith Terms to Know

Put an X next to the faith terms you know. Put a ? next to faith terms you need to learn more about.

_____ forgiveness

_____ sin

_____ healing

_____ ordination

_____ Holy Orders

_____ bishop

_____ consent

The Bible

What do you know about Jesus' healings?

_____

_____

_____

The Church

What Saint or organization of the Church would you like to learn more about?

_____

_____

_____

Questions I Have

What questions would you like to ask about the Sacraments of Healing or the Sacraments at the Service of Communion?

_____

_____

_____

Looking Ahead

In this chapter, the Holy Spirit invites you to ▶

EXPLORE how a young Saint offered forgiveness.

DISCOVER the grace of Penance and Reconciliation.

DECIDE how you will be a person of forgiveness.

CHAPTER

13

Jesus Heals the Sinner

? When have you forgiven someone or asked for forgiveness? How did it feel?

Imagine you are sitting with Jesus and his disciples on the side of a mountain near a large lake. You are listening carefully to Jesus. He is explaining what it means to be one of his disciples. He teaches you the Our Father and then says,

"If you forgive others their transgressions, your heavenly Father will forgive you. But if you do not forgive others, neither will your Father forgive your transgressions." MATTHEW 6:14–15

? What is Jesus inviting you to do?

Mercy

Mercy is one of the Fruits of the Holy Spirit. A person who acts with mercy has a forgiving and understanding heart. "Blessed are the merciful, for they will be shown mercy" (Matthew 5:7).

THE CHURCH FOLLOWS JESUS

Saint Maria Goretti

The disciples of Jesus understood Jesus' command to forgive in the Our Father in light of God's merciful love for all. As God treats us, we are to treat one another.

On July 5, 1902, Maria Goretti, an eleven-year-old Italian girl, was sitting quietly mending a shirt. No one else was home. Alessandro, a nineteen-year-old neighbor, stopped by. He had been bothering Maria for a long time so she was not glad to see him. A while later, Alessandro attacked Maria with a knife, seriously wounding her and then ran away.

Maria was taken to a hospital, but little could be done for her. After twenty hours of suffering from her wounds, she died. Before her death, Maria forgave Alessandro and prayed for him.

Alessandro was sent to prison for thirty years. While he was in prison, he said that Maria had appeared to him in a dream. After this experience, Alessandro fully repented for his sin. He had a conversion and spent the rest of his life doing penance.

Maria Goretti not only listened to Jesus' words, but she lived them. The Church has named her a Saint, and she is a model of Jesus' command to forgive. The Church celebrates the feast of this young Saint on July 6.

? How might Saint Maria Goretti's act of forgiveness challenge you to become a more forgiving person?

The Sacrament of Forgiveness

Everyone needs forgiveness. Everyone needs to forgive. Jesus reminded us and clearly revealed that God forgives. The work of Jesus, the Son of God, was and is a work of forgiveness. Remember Jesus' words as he was near death on the Cross. He had been beaten, scourged, crowned with thorns, nailed to the Cross, and raised up to die a very painful death. As he nears death, he prays aloud for all to hear,

> "Father, forgive them, they know not what they do."
>
> LUKE 23:34

God is always ready to forgive us when we sin. Sin is freely choosing to do or say what we know is against God's will. It is also freely choosing to do or say what we know we have the responsibility to do or say to live as a child of God. Sin shows disrespect for God.

Sin and Forgiveness

When we sin, we harm the person God created us to be. We wound our human dignity. We offend God and damage our relationship with the Church and other people.

The Holy Spirit invites us to ask for and accept God's forgiveness and to accept God's forgiveness for our sins. The Holy Spirit helps us to forgive others.

We need God's help, or grace, not to sin again. God helps us change our ways and live more like children of God and disciples of Jesus. We also need God's grace to avoid temptation. Temptation is all that leads us away from God and his love.

? What is the difference between commiting a sin and making a mistake?

FAITH FOCUS
What do we celebrate in the Sacrament of Penance and Reconciliation?

FAITH VOCABULARY
Sacrament of Penance and Reconciliation
In the Sacrament of Penance and Reconciliation, we receive God's forgiveness, through the ministry of the priest, for the sins we commit after Baptism.

Sacraments of Healing
There are two Sacraments of Healing. They are the Sacrament of Penance and Reconciliation and the Sacrament of the Anointing of the Sick.

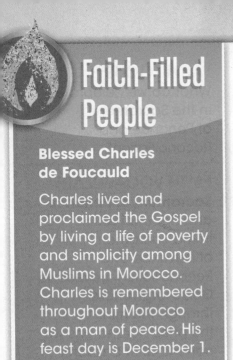

Sacrament of Healing

Jesus gave the Church two **Sacraments of Healing**. They are the **Sacrament of Penance and Reconciliation** and the Sacrament of the Anointing of the Sick.

The Sacrament of Penance and Reconciliation is also sometimes called the Sacrament of Penance, the Sacrament of Reconciliation, the Sacrament of Forgiveness, the Sacrament of Confession, and the Sacrament of Conversion. Through this Sacrament, we receive both God's forgiveness for the sins we commit after Baptism and his grace not to sin.

Sacrament of Peace

In the Gospel according to John, we read about the time that Jesus came to his Apostles after he rose from the dead. The Risen Jesus said to them:

> "Peace be with you. As the Father has sent me, so I send you." And when he had said this, he breathed on them and said to them, "Receive the holy Spirit. Whose sins you forgive are forgiven them, and whose sins you retain are retained."
>
> JOHN 20:21–23

Jesus gave the Church the authority to forgive sins. Today, bishops and priests continue this work. When they speak in the name of Jesus, they offer God's forgiveness. Through the words of the bishop or priest and the power of the Holy Spirit, our sins are forgiven. We receive the gift of God's peace and are reconciled, or made friends again, with God and the Church.

Activity Create a symbol for forgiveness in the space. Share your idea with a partner.

Celebrating the Sacrament

We can celebrate the Sacrament of Penance and Reconciliation alone with the priest, or we can gather as a community and celebrate it. When we celebrate this Sacrament as a community, we always meet alone with the priest to confess our sins and receive absolution. These four parts are always part of the celebration of this Sacrament:

Confession

After we examine our consciences, we meet individually with a priest and confess, or tell, our sins to him. We must always confess any serious sins.

Penance

The priest gives us a penance. He may ask us to say a prayer or do an act of kindness. Accepting and doing our penance shows that we are truly sorry for our sins and that we want to make up for the harm caused by our sins.

Contrition

We pray an act of contrition. In this prayer, we admit we have sinned. We express our sorrow for having offended God. Being truly sorry for our sins means we do not want to sin again. We really want to cooperate with the Holy Spirit to change the way we live.

Absolution

Absolution is the forgiveness that the priest speaks in the name of God. When the priest says, "I absolve you," God speaks through him. "I absolve you" means "I forgive you. You are free from your sins."

When we celebrate the Sacrament of Reconciliation, we receive God's forgiveness and healing love. We are reconciled with God and the Church. We are pardoned from eternal punishment due to mortal sins and from temporary punishment, at least in part, due to our sins. We receive the gift of peace of conscience. And we receive the grace to live as faithful adopted sons and daughters of God and disciples of Jesus.

? How would you describe the benefits of this Sacrament to a friend who is not Catholic?

I FOLLOW JESUS

The Holy Spirit helps you continue the healing work of Jesus. You forgive those who may have offended you. You ask for God's forgiveness when you sin.

GOD'S HEALING LOVE

Design cover art for music about God's forgiveness. Choose a title for the music collection that reminds people of God's healing love.

MY FAITH CHOICE

This week, I will try to show mercy by forgiving someone, or I will ask for forgiveness. I will

_____

_____

Thank the Holy Spirit for helping you forgive those who hurt you and helping you ask for forgiveness from someone you hurt.

Chapter Review

Complete each sentence correctly.

1. Sin is _____

_____

2. Confession is _____

_____

3. Absolution is _____

_____

4. One important thing I learned this week is _____

_____

5. It is important because _____

_____

Lord, Have Mercy

Leader: We are here to ask for God's mercy for the wrong we have done.

Reader 1: Lord, there have been times when we have not been at peace with a family member.

All: Lord, have mercy.

Reader 2: Lord, there have been times when we have hurt others by our words and actions.

All: Lord, have mercy.

Reader 3: Lord, there have been times when we have refused to forgive someone.

All: Lord, have mercy.

Leader: Let us prayer together.

All: Lord, help us change and grow ever closer to you. Amen.

With My Family

This Week . . .

In Chapter 13, "Jesus Heals the Sinner," your child learned:

▶ The Sacrament of Penance and Reconciliation continues the healing ministry of Jesus.

▶ Through Reconciliation, we receive forgiveness for sins we commit after Baptism.

▶ Confession of sins, contrition (sorrow), penance, and absolution are always part of the Rite of Reconciliation.

▶ The virtue of mercy helps us seek and give forgiveness. This mirrors the gift of forgiveness that God offers us.

For more about related teachings of the Church, see the *Catechism of the Catholic Church,* 1420–1498, and the *United States Catholic Catechism for Adults,* pages 233–247.

◼ Sharing God's Word

Read John 20:22–23 together. Emphasize that bishops and priests today speak in the name of Jesus when they offer God's forgiveness in the Sacrament of Penance and Reconciliation.

◼ We Live as Disciples

The Christian family and home is a school of discipleship. Choose one of the following activities to do as a family, or design a similar activity of your own:

▶ Invite family members to share stories, movies, or TV shows about forgiving others and being forgiven. Emphasize that when we forgive, we bring healing to others. When we are forgiven, we receive the gift of healing.

▶ Practice the virtue of mercy within your family. Make a conscious effort to ask forgiveness of your children when necessary and affirm their own efforts to practice this virtue with one another.

◼ Our Spiritual Journey

God's peace is the fruit of living in right relationship with God, with people, and with all creation. This is a goal of our spiritual journey. Discern how you are living as a peacemaker. Teach your children this part of the Prayer of Saint Francis: "Lord, make me an instrument of your peace."

For more ideas on ways your family can live as disciples of Jesus, visit **www.BeMyDisciples.com**

Looking Ahead

In this chapter, the Holy Spirit invites you to ▶

EXPLORE how chaplains continue the healing work of Jesus.

DISCOVER how we celebrate the Sacrament of the Anointing of the Sick.

DECIDE how you will be a person of healing for others.

CHAPTER

14

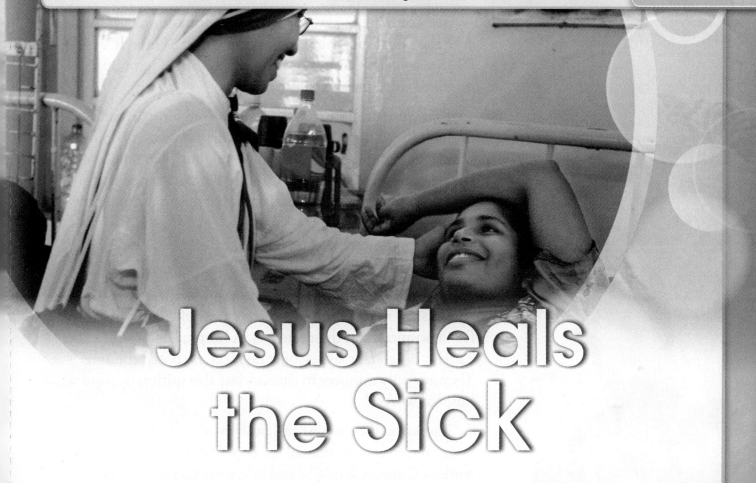

Jesus Heals the Sick

? When you have been sick, who has taken care of you?

Imagine you have been traveling with Jesus since he began his public ministry. One day, you are traveling with him through Galilee. This is what you see:

People brought to Jesus a paralytic lying on a stretcher. When he saw their faith, Jesus said to the paralytic, "Courage, your sins are forgiven." Then Jesus said to the paralytic, "Stand up, pick up your stretcher, and go home." He rose and went home. The crowds were amazed.

BASED ON MATTHEW 9:2, 6–8

? How do you think the man felt after being healed?

Kindness

The English word *kindness* is sometimes used to translate the biblical word for *mercy*. We live the virtue of kindness by generously treating others as we want to be treated. We are called to be as kind to others as God is to us.

THE CHURCH FOLLOWS JESUS

Hospital Chaplains

The Church has always shared the compassion of Jesus with the sick. From the very beginning of the Church, caring for the sick has been one of her central works. Catholic hospitals continue this tradition today.

Each year, millions of patients are cared for in over a thousand Catholic hospitals and health-care centers in the United States of America. The hospitals are often named after Saints, such as Saint Frances Cabrini, who dedicated their lives to caring for the sick. The names of hospitals sometime reflect the healing stories of Jesus, such as Good Samaritan Hospital and Mercy Hospital.

Catholics serve the sick in hospitals in many ways. There are Catholic doctors, nurses, technicians, dieticians, and administrators. Chaplains also serve the sick people cared for in hospitals and their families. A hospital chaplain can be a priest, deacon, or layperson who receives special training. They not only minister to the sick but also spiritually support hospital workers.

The work of chaplains and other workers in Catholic hospitals reminds us that all the baptized share in the healing work of Christ. Chaplains and other workers in Catholic hospitals are symbols that the Church continues the work of Christ the Healer in towns, cities, and countries all over the world.

? What are some of the ways your parish continues Jesus' work of healing with people who are sick?

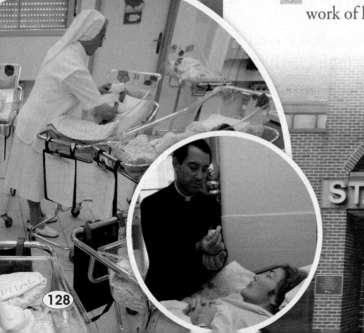

ST. JOSEPH'S HOSPITAL

Anointing of the Sick

Jesus' healing of people who were suffering from illnesses was part of the work of Salvation his Father sent him to do. In the Gospels, there are many accounts of Jesus healing people. (see John 9:1–12; Mark 2:5–11). Jesus' healings were signs of the saving presence of God among his people.

When Jesus healed people who were sick, he healed them physically and spiritually. Jesus not only healed people's bodies but, more importantly, he helped them grow in their faith and love for God.

The Healing Work of Jesus Today

Through the power of the Holy Spirit, Jesus' healing continues today. He gave the Church the **Sacrament of the Anointing of the Sick** to continue his work among the sick in the world. The Church celebrates this Sacrament with members of the Church who are seriously ill or weak because of old age. Through union with Jesus, the sick find strength, peace, and courage. A person may receive this Sacrament more than once.

Only bishops and priests may administer the Anointing of the Sick. Using the Oil of the Sick, the bishop or priest anoints the sick person's forehead and hands as he prays that the sick person receive God's healing grace.

FAITH FOCUS
What does the Church celebrate in the Sacrament of the Anointing of the Sick?

FAITH VOCABULARY
Sacrament of the Anointing of the Sick
The Sacrament of the Anointing of the Sick is the Sacrament of Healing that strengthens our faith, hope, and love for God when we are seriously ill, weakened by old age, or dying.

Activity List ways you might continue Christ's work among the sick.

_____

_____

_____

_____

_____

_____

_____

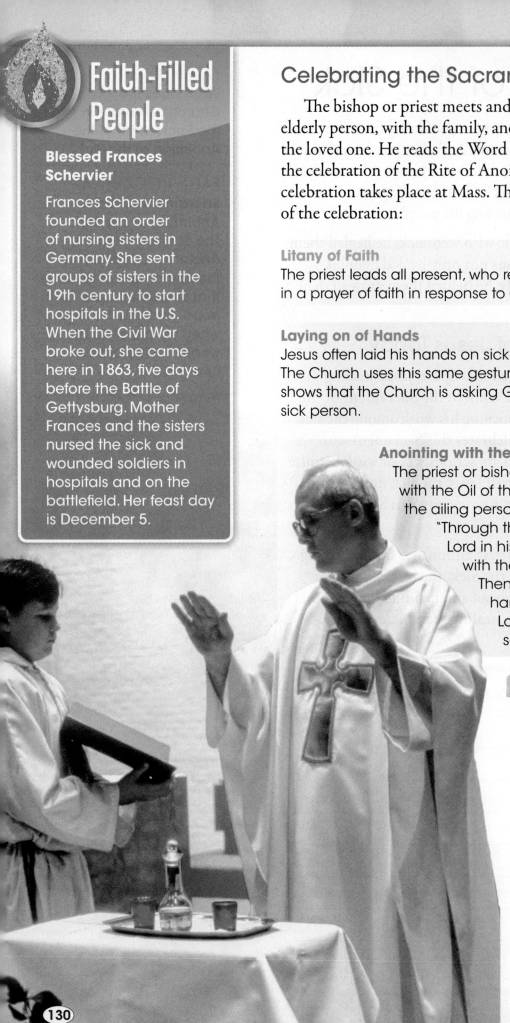

Faith-Filled People

Blessed Frances Schervier

Frances Schervier founded an order of nursing sisters in Germany. She sent groups of sisters in the 19th century to start hospitals in the U.S. When the Civil War broke out, she came here in 1863, five days before the Battle of Gettysburg. Mother Frances and the sisters nursed the sick and wounded soldiers in hospitals and on the battlefield. Her feast day is December 5.

Celebrating the Sacrament

The bishop or priest meets and prays with the sick or elderly person, with the family, and with those caring for the loved one. He reads the Word of God. Then he leads the celebration of the Rite of Anointing. Sometimes this celebration takes place at Mass. These are the three main parts of the celebration:

Litany of Faith

The priest leads all present, who represent the whole Church, in a prayer of faith in response to God's Word.

Laying on of Hands

Jesus often laid his hands on sick people (see Luke 4:40). The Church uses this same gesture in this Sacrament. It shows that the Church is asking God's blessing on the sick person.

Anointing with the Oil of the Sick

The priest or bishop anoints the sick person with the Oil of the Sick. First he anoints the ailing person's forehead as he prays, "Through this holy anointing may the Lord in his love and mercy help you with the grace of the Holy Spirit." Then he anoints the person's hands as he prays, "May the Lord who frees you from sin save you and raise you up."

What is the meaning behind the actions in each part of the Rite of Anointing? Share your ideas with a partner.

The Special Graces of the Sacrament

The Sacrament of the Anointing of the Sick celebrates God's love and healing power. Any members of the Church who are dying, seriously ill, or suffering because of old age may receive this Sacrament.

These are the special graces a person receives in this Sacrament:

▶ The person is united to Christ's suffering on the Cross for his or her own good and the good of the Church.

▶ The person receives the strength, peace, and courage to endure the sufferings of old age or illness.

▶ The person receives forgiveness of sins if unable to receive the Sacrament of Penance and Reconciliation.

▶ The person's health is restored if it is God's will.

▶ If the person is in danger of dying, he or she is prepared for death and the hope of eternal life with God in Heaven.

Activity   In the space below, write the names of anyone you know who is ill or is suffering. Include them in your daily prayers.

_____

_____

_____

_____

I FOLLOW JESUS

Jesus is present with the whole assembly during the celebration of the Anointing of the Sick. He is present in many other ways too. The Holy Spirit helps you continue the healing work of Jesus. When you reach out to family, friends, and neighbors and care for them when they are sick, Jesus is there with you.

JESUS' WORK OF HEALING

Read the following Scripture passages in a Bible. On the lines, tell how Jesus treated each of the people who came to him for healing.

Matthew 9:27–31

_____

_____

_____

Luke 7:11–17

_____

_____

_____

Matthew 8:14–15

_____

_____

_____

MY FAITH CHOICE

This week, I will reach out to others who are sick or suffering. I will

_____

_____.

 Pray to Jesus, asking him to help you continue to grow in kindness, spreading God's love to others, especially to those who are sick or suffering.

Chapter Review

Circle T if the statement is true. Circle F if the statement is false. Tell a partner what will make the false statements true.

1. Reconciliation and Anointing of the Sick are Sacraments of Service. **T   F**

2. The Church celebrates Anointing of the Sick with young people, grown-ups, and elderly people. **T   F**

3. All the baptized can administer the Sacrament of the Anointing of the Sick. **T   F**

4. Christ's suffering can give new meaning to our own suffering. **T   F**

What is the most important thing you learned in this lesson? Why do you think is it the most important?

_____

_____

_____

▶ **TO HELP YOU REMEMBER**

1. Jesus continues his ministry of healing through the Sacrament of the Anointing of the Sick and the Sacrament of Penance and Reconciliation.

2. Through the Anointing of the Sick, those who are seriously ill, weakened because of old age, or dying are joined to the suffering of Christ and receive strength and courage.

3. A person may receive the Sacrament of the Anointing of the Sick more than once.

A Prayer for the Sick

When we pray for other people, we pray a prayer of intercession. Pray this prayer of intercession for people who are sick.

Leader: Jesus showed us God's love for people, who are sick. Let us pray to God for all the members of our families, for our friends, and for all who are sick. (Pause.) Bless those who are sick and fill them with new hope and strength.

All: **Lord, have mercy.**

Leader: Support all those who care for the sick.

All: **Lord, have mercy.**

Leader: Quietly give thanks to God who is full of mercy and kindness.

All: **Amen.**

With My Family

This Week . . .

In Chapter 14, "Jesus Heals the Sick," your child learned:

▶ Throughout his life on Earth, Jesus cured people physically and spiritually.

▶ When Jesus cured people, he was also inviting them to grow in faith, trust, and love for God.

▶ Through the Anointing of the Sick, Christ continues his healing ministry among the sick in the world today.

▶ The virtue of kindness helps us reach out to others and treat them as we would want to be treated.

For more about related teachings of the Church, see the *Catechism of the Catholic Church,* 1499–1532, and the *United States Catholic Catechism for Adults,* pages 249–259.

Sharing God's Word

Read together Matthew 8:1–4, Matthew 9:18–26, Mark 2:1–12, Luke 7:1–10, and Acts of the Apostles 3:1–10. Then discuss how your family reaches out to those who are sick and suffering.

We Live as Disciples

The Christian home and family is a school of discipleship. Choose one of the following activities to do as a family, or design a similar activity of your own:

▶ Keep a "book of the sick" in your home by writing the names of the ill in a special journal. Pray for these people together as a family.

▶ When family members or others are ill, create a card of support made by the whole family. Make sure each family member has contributed in some way.

Our Spiritual Journey

One of the earliest prayers in the Christian tradition is this: "Lord Jesus Christ, Son of God, have mercy on me, a sinner." Encourage all members of your family to memorize this prayer and pray it regularly at bedtime or together at times of shared prayer.

For more ideas on ways your family can live as disciples of Jesus, visit **www.BeMyDisciples.com**

Looking Ahead

In this chapter, the Holy Spirit invites you to ▶

EXPLORE how Father Philip Neri was a leader in the Church.

DISCOVER the meaning of the Sacrament of Holy Orders.

DECIDE how you will work with others to serve the Church.

CHAPTER
15

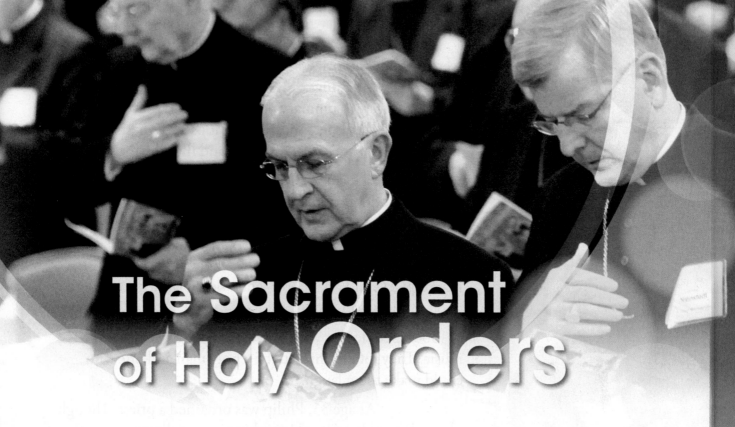

The Sacrament of Holy Orders

❓ Who are some people who serve others in your family, in your school, and in your parish?

Imagine that you are a leader of the Church and you live in Ephesus, a city in what is today the country of Turkey. Paul reminds you of your calling to serve Jesus, saying:

> Keep watch over yourselves and over the whole flock of which the holy Spirit has appointed you overseers, in which you tend the church of God.
>
> ACTS OF THE APOSTLES 20:28

❓ What do you think Paul is telling you about being a leader in the Church?

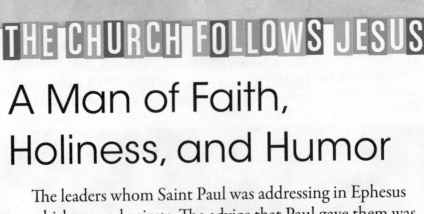

Faith

Faith is one of the three Theological Virtues. It is a gift from God that helps us respond to his invitation to know and believe in him.

A Man of Faith, Holiness, and Humor

The leaders whom Saint Paul was addressing in Ephesus were bishops and priests. The advice that Paul gave them was based on the teachings of Jesus that were passed on to him. His words were a summary of the command that Jesus gave to Peter and the other Apostles. Bishops and priests since the time of the Apostles have followed and lived by those words.

Philip Neri lived in Rome in the sixteenth century. He believed God was calling him to use his serious love of God and his quirky sense of humor to bring people back to God. His two favorite books were the New Testament and a book of jokes and riddles. Some days, Philip would go to the marketplaces and ask people when they planned to do some good in the world.

Soon people met with him for prayer, discussion, and music. They found Philip to be a holy man and one who could make them laugh.

At age 35, Philip was ordained a priest. Though people enjoyed his joking personality, many spoke of his holiness saying he was a living Saint. But Philip did not want to be taken too seriously. When he heard talk of his being a Saint, Father Neri shaved off half of his beard! Who could look at that sight and think of a Saint?

By the time he died at age 80, many people in Rome had been changed by the work and spirit of Saint Philip Neri.

? How does the way you live your life help others know of God's love?

A Sacrament of Service

All Christians are called to be leaders among the people with whom they live. We are called to be lights in the world. All the baptized—laypeople, religious, and ordained ministers—are members of the Body of Christ. Saint Paul reminds us that each member has an important role in the Church (see 1 Corinthians 12:12–30).

All Christians receive this calling and the graces to live it in the Sacrament of Baptism. Baptism joins us to Christ and to all members of the Church. We receive the call, or vocation, and the graces to continue the work of Christ, to build up the Church, and to prepare the way for the coming of the Kingdom of God. In Confirmation, these graces are strengthened. In the Eucharist, we are continually nourished to be lights in the world.

Sacraments at the Service of Communion

Two Sacraments, Holy Orders and Matrimony, set aside some of the baptized for the holy purpose to serve the whole Church. For this reason, they are called **Sacraments at the Service of Communion**. The **Sacrament of Holy Orders** consecrates, or sets aside for a holy purpose, members of the Church to serve the whole Church as bishops, priests, and deacons.

FAITH FOCUS
What does the Sacrament of Holy Orders celebrate?

FAITH VOCABULARY
Sacraments at the Service of Communion
The Sacraments at the Service of Communion are the two Sacraments that set aside members of the Church to serve the whole Church, namely, Holy Orders and Matrimony.

Sacrament of Holy Orders
The Sacrament of Holy Orders is the Sacrament through which a baptized man is consecrated to serve the whole Church as a bishop, priest, or deacon.

Activity Write how you have seen bishops, priests, and deacons serving the Church.

_____

_____

**Joseph Maria
Rubio y Peralta**

Father Joseph was a member of the Society of Jesus, or Jesuits. He served the Church in Spain, becoming well-known as the "Apostle of Madrid" and the "Pastor of the Poor." The Church celebrates his feast day on May 2.

Holy Orders

In the Sacrament of Holy Orders, men are ordained by a bishop to serve the Church as bishops, priests, and deacons. Only men who have been baptized and who are considered by the Church to have a vocation to Holy Orders may receive this Sacrament.

Bishops

Bishops receive the fullness of the Sacrament of Holy Orders. They are the successors of the Apostles and the chief teachers of the Church. Under the authority of the Pope, a bishop usually leads a diocese. A diocese is made up of Catholic parishes and schools and may include Catholic universities and hospitals.

Priests

Priests are coworkers with their bishop. They are ordained by their bishops to celebrate the Sacraments, especially the Eucharist, and to proclaim the Word of God.

There are two kinds of priests. Diocesan priests are ordained to serve in a diocese usually as pastors or vicars of parishes. Religious priests belong to a religious order, such as the Benedictines, Franciscans, Dominicans, or Jesuits. They serve wherever the bishop of a diocese has invited and approved them to work among the people.

Deacons

Deacons are helpers of bishops and priests. They are ordained by their bishops to help priests with the work of the parish. Deacons can officiate at the Sacraments of Baptism and Matrimony. They can also read the Gospel and give the Homily at Sunday Mass.

There are two kinds of deacons. Transitional deacons are men who are preparing for the priesthood. Permanent deacons do not become priests, and they may be single or married. A deacon may not remarry if his wife dies after he has been ordained.

? How are the roles of the deacon and the priest different and alike?

The Rite of Ordination

The Rite of Ordination initiates baptized men into the Order of Bishops, the Order of Priests, and the Order of Deacons. Bishops, priests, and deacons share in the ministry of Jesus that he shared with the Apostles. The Holy Spirit guides these men and gives them the graces they need to fulfill their responsibilities and to serve the Church throughout their lives. The ordination of a priest contains these parts:

Laying on of Hands

In silence, the ordaining bishop lays his hands on the heads of the candidates to be ordained. Next, all the priests who are present do the same. This shows that a person has been chosen for a special office or is receiving a special responsibility.

Prayer of Consecration

The ordaining bishop prays the prayer of consecration. This is the essential part of the Rite of Ordination of a priest. The bishop prays, in part, "Almighty Father, grant to these servants of yours the dignity of the priesthood."

Investiture with Stole and Chasuble

Each of the newly ordained priests receives a stole and a chasuble and puts them on. The stole is the symbol of the priest's office and authority. It is worn for sacramental celebrations. The chasuble is the outside vestment the priest wears for the celebration of Mass.

Anointing of Hands

The palms of the hands of the newly ordained are anointed with Sacred Chrism as the bishop prays, "The Father anointed our Lord Jesus Christ through the power of the Holy Spirit. May Jesus preserve you to sanctify the Christian people to offer sacrifice to God."

Activity Make a list of the three qualities needed to serve as a priest.

_____

_____

_____

139

I FOLLOW JESUS

All the baptized are called to be lights in the world. One way we can be lights in the world is to serve others as Jesus did. God calls you to serve others. The things you are doing now to help others are preparing you to continue serving the Church as an adult.

SERVING THE CHURCH

Choose one talent God has blessed you with. Write it in the center of the circle. Then, around the outside of the circle, name ways you can use this talent to serve the Church.

MY FAITH CHOICE

This week, I will work with others to do the work of the Church. I will

_____

_____

Pray, "Lord God, I live the gift of faith not only in words but also in deeds. Help me live my Baptism by living my faith. Amen."

Chapter Review

Fill in the blanks in each sentence so that the sentence is correct.

1. Through Baptism, we receive the call, or _____, and the graces to continue the work of Christ.

2. The Sacrament of Holy Orders consecrates certain men to serve the whole Church as bishops, priests, and _____.

3. In the Rite of Ordination, the _____ shows that the person has been chosen for a special office or responsibility.

Love One Another

Praying the Scriptures provides us the time to listen to God's Word and discern how we are to live our faith.

Leader: Let us remember that Jesus said that whenever two or more gather in his name, he is there among them. Jesus is with us today.

Jesus taught us what it means to serve people. We are to love others as he loves us.

Reader: A reading from the Letter to the Colossians.

(Read Colossians 3:12–15.)

The word of the Lord.

All: Thanks be to God.

Leader: Let us ask the Holy Spirit to teach us ways to serve others as Jesus taught us to do. (Pause.) Now let us share a sign of peace with one another.

> **TO HELP YOU REMEMBER**

1. All the baptized are called to continue the work of Christ, to build up the Church, and to prepare the way for the coming of the Kingdom of God.

2. Holy Orders consecrates, or sets aside for a holy purpose, some men of the Church to serve the whole Church. It is one of the two Sacraments at the Service of Communion.

3. In Holy Orders, a baptized man is consecrated to serve the whole Church as a bishop, priest, or deacon.

With My Family

This Week . . .

In Chapter 15, "The Sacrament of Holy Orders," your child learned:

▶ God calls some members of the Church to serve the whole Church.

▶ The Sacrament of Holy Orders and the Sacrament of Matrimony are called Sacraments at the Service of Communion.

▶ Through Holy Orders, baptized men are ordained to serve the whole Church by continuing the unique work Jesus entrusted to the Apostles.

▶ The Theological Virtue of faith is a gift from God that helps us respond to his invitation to know and believe in him.

For more about related teachings of the Church, see the *Catechism of the Catholic Church*, 1536–1600, and the *United States Catholic Catechism for Adults*, pages 261–275.

■ Sharing God's Word

Read together 1 Corinthians 12:12–30. Emphasize that each member of the Church has an important role as a member of the Body of Christ.

■ We Live as Disciples

The Christian home and family is a school of discipleship. Choose one of the following activities to do as a family, or design a similar activity of your own:

▶ Place a small piece of posterboard on your refrigerator with the heading "We Serve the Lord." Place the name or a photo of each family member down the left side. Each day, invite each family member to add at least one way he or she served others.

▶ Faith involves a response to God's call. When you take part in Mass this week, look in the parish bulletin. Identify a service group within the parish with whom you will work to live out your baptismal calling.

■ Our Spiritual Journey

Sometimes children in Catholic schools would write at the top of their schoolwork the words: "All for the honor and glory of God." Teach your children to use these words as a brief morning prayer before starting their day. If you gather for breakfast, pray it together.

For more ideas on ways your family can live as disciples of Jesus, visit **www.BeMyDisciples.com**

Looking Ahead

In this chapter, the Holy Spirit invites you to ▶

EXPLORE how a Catholic family was a living sign of Christ's love.

DISCOVER how we celebrate Matrimony.

DECIDE how you will honor your parents and your family.

The Sacrament of Matrimony

? If you have attended a wedding, what do you remember about it?

Imagine you and your family are at a Catholic wedding. Someone comes up to the ambo and reads:

Love is patient, love is kind. It is not jealous, . . . it does not rejoice over wrongdoing but rejoices with the truth. It bears all things, believes all things, hopes all things, endures all things. 1 CORINTHIANS 13:4, 6–7

? Why do you think this reading is so popular for weddings?

Humility

Humility is the ability to acknowledge that all of our blessings come from God. This virtue enables us to see ourselves and value ourselves and all other people as children of God. It enables us to bless God for all the good in our lives.

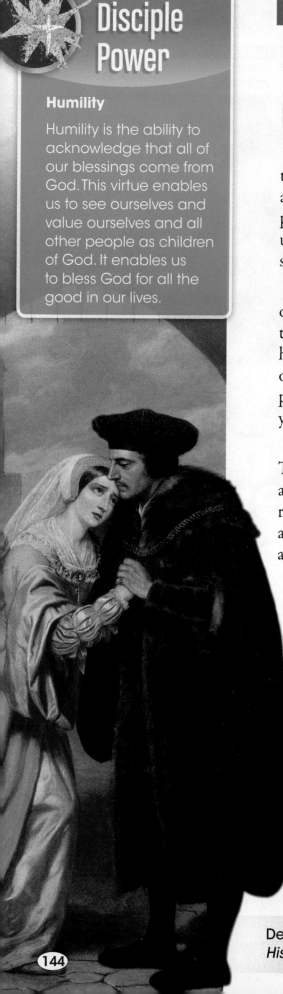

THE CHURCH FOLLOWS JESUS

In Good Times and in Bad Times

Jesus told his disciples that they would have to take up their cross as he did. Married life is made up of good times and bad times. When they marry, a man and a woman promise to remain faithful in good times and in bad times until their death. The life of Thomas More and his family show us what it means to be faithful to those promises.

Sir Thomas More and his wife, Jane, are an example of a married couple who cared deeply for each other and their family in good times and in bad times. More than five hundred years ago, Thomas More was a lawyer and a member of the Parliament in England. Thomas and Jane were the parents of four children. Jane died when the children were young, and Thomas married a widow, Alice Middleton.

The Mores were an intelligent and fun-loving family. Thomas and Alice made sure that their daughters received an education equal to that of their son. At dinner, the family read and discussed the New Testament. After dinner, a lute and harp would be brought out. Thomas and Alice played and sang while the children danced.

The Mores lived in England when King Henry VIII named himself the head of the Church in England. This caused Catholics in England to make a decision to follow either the king or the Pope. Thomas and Alice often discussed what to do. Thomas clearly knew what he would do. Thomas was an important man in England, but he was also humble. He would be the "king's good servant, but God's first."

Thomas decided not to share his views with his wife to protect her. Then the king could not punish her and the children. Thomas was eventually put in prison and put to death. Today the Church honors Thomas More as Saint Thomas More.

? What important values has your family taught you?

Detail from *Sir Thomas More's Farewell to His Daughter,* Edward Matthew Ward

A Sacred Covenant

Marriage is a sign of God's faithful love for all people. Every married person shares in God's love and has the vocation to share that love with others.

God created man and woman to be together and gave them the sacred gift of marriage. In marriage, they are to share God's love with each other and to be willing to bring children into the world.

God blessed them, saying to them, "Be fertile and multiply. . . . This is why a man [and a woman] leave their father and mother. And the man and woman become one."

BASED ON GENESIS 1:28 AND 2:24

Married couples share the gift of love with the children God may give them. They raise their children to love God and others.

Christian Marriage

Christian married couples are called to be living signs of Christ's love for the Church. The **Sacrament of Matrimony** unites a baptized man and a baptized woman in marriage and makes the couple a sign of Christ's love for the Church.

Matrimony is another name for marriage. In the Sacrament of Matrimony, the man and woman receive the grace to live their vocation to be a sign of God's love for all people and of Christ's love for the Church. The Christian married couple "become one" (Genesis 2:24). They are closer to each other than to anyone else. They are to share that love within their families and with others.

Activity Create a headline for a poster advertising the two Sacraments at the Service of Communion. Your headline should say what these two Sacraments have in common.

_____

_____

_____

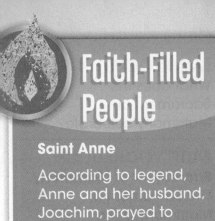
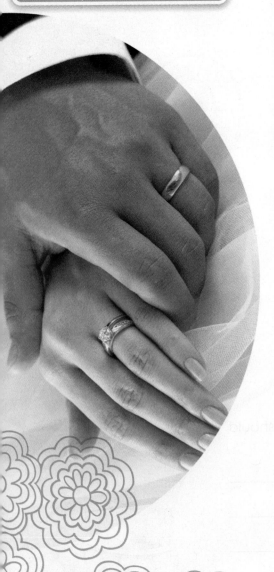

The Rite of Marriage

The celebration of the Sacrament of Matrimony usually takes place within the celebration of Mass. The ministers of this Sacrament are the couple being married. The priest or deacon is the official witness of the marriage.

The celebration of Matrimony takes place right after the Liturgy of the Word. This is what happens:

The bride and groom individually tell the priest or deacon and everyone present they are marrying freely.

They promise to accept the children God may give them and to raise their children according to God's Law.

They give their consent that they will love and honor each other and will be faithful to each other as husband and wife until they die.

There is the blessing and exchange of rings. The newly married couple usually gives each other rings to wear as a sign of their never-ending love and commitment to each other.

The priest leads everyone present in the Prayer of the Faithful, and the Nuptial Blessing. The priest asks God to bless the newly married couple.

The Rite of Marriage concludes with the praying of the Our Father and the final blessing.

The Church has the duty to support married couples and their families and to help them wherever necessary to meet their responsibilities to one another. The Church speaks out in support of families to help them remain strong.

? Families depend on each other for care and support. What are some of the ways you support your parents?

The Christian Family

A man and a woman united in the Sacrament of Matrimony are a sign of love and service. In their daily lives, in both big and little ways, a married couple serves each other with love.

The married couple forms a new family in the Church. Families pass on faith. Some families have children; some do not. Through the everyday work of family life, the married couple serves each other, their children, their friends, and those in need. By the way they care for each other and their families, married couples are an example of God's caring love for all people.

The Domestic Church

The Church calls the family the "domestic Church" and recognizes that parents are the primary educators of their children. Parents teach their children right from wrong and how to make good and wise choices in life. Parents work to provide food and shelter for their children and care for them when they are sick. They guide their children in coming to know their vocation.

Catholics Believe

Wedding Rings

When a man and a woman marry, they may exchange rings. The exchange of rings is a sign of lasting love and a promise to be true to each other in good times and in bad times for all of their lives.

Activity Some married couples have words engraved inside their wedding rings to express their commitment. Design two wedding rings. Write the words they might choose underneath the rings.

I FOLLOW JESUS

Christian married life involves many choices. A husband and wife choose to be loving, generous, faithful, and open to having children. Loving choices are not just for married couples. God calls you to make loving choices too. The good and wise choices you are now making help you support your parents and family. They also strengthen you to make good and wise choices in the future.

GOOD AND WISE CHOICES

Complete the activity below by writing your responses on the lines provided.

1. In your own words, describe some of the qualities of a faithful and responsible child.

_____

_____

_____

_____

2. Share one way you have been faithful to your family.

_____

_____

_____

_____

MY FAITH CHOICE

This week, I will respect my parents and honor my family. I will

_____

_____

_____

 Ask the Holy Spirit to help you continue to be a responsible member of your family. Pray for an increase in the virtue of humility.

Chapter Review

Circle the word or phrase that completes each sentence correctly.

1. The Sacrament of Matrimony is most related to _____.

   a. healing   **b.** water   **c.** service

2. The official witness of the Sacrament of Matrimony is the _____.

   a. priest   **b.** deacon   **c.** priest or deacon

3. The Sacrament of Matrimony is usually celebrated _____.

   a. during winter   **b.** at Mass   **c.** on a weekday

What is the most important thing you learned in this lesson? Why is it the most important?

_____

_____

A Family Blessing

Together, ask God's blessing on your families. Ask God to help your families follow Jesus' example of loving service.

Leader: Generous God, you have made us for love. Let us rejoice always in your blessing and gift of love.

   All: **Bless our families that we might glorify you in all we say and do.**

Leader: Show us how to be of service in your Church and in the world.

   All: **Bless our families that we might glorify you in all we say and do.**

Leader: Help us to see what you want us to do. Give us vision, courage, and friends who encourage us to do your work.

   All: **Bless our families that we might glorify you in all we say and do. Amen.**

With My Family

This Week . . .

In Chapter 16, "The Sacrament of Matrimony," your child learned:

▶ God calls some members of the Church to serve the whole Church through the Sacrament of Matrimony.

▶ In Matrimony, a baptized man and a baptized woman are united in a lifelong bond of faithful love and become a sign of Christ's love for the Church.

▶ The virtue of humility helps a married couple and their family live its vocation.

For more about related teachings of the Church, see the *Catechism of the Catholic Church*, 1601–1666, and the *United States Catholic Catechism for Adults*, pages 277–292.

◼ Sharing God's Word

Read Colossians 3:12–17 together. Discuss together how the qualities named in this reading are important for a strong marriage and a strong family.

◼ We Live as Disciples

The Christian home and family is a school of discipleship. Choose one of the following activities to do as a family, or design a similar activity of your own:

▶ Recall any weddings you have been to as a family. Discuss the different aspects of a Catholic wedding and invite your child to describe what he or she witnessed.

▶ Share that family life is a call, or vocation, to live our Baptism. Discuss with your child the ways that your family is continuing the work of Christ to build up the Church and to prepare for the coming of the Kingdom of God.

◼ Our Spiritual Journey

There is an adage that reads, "The family that prays together stays together." Integrate the spiritual discipline of daily prayer into the life of your marriage and into the life of your family. Use the prayer refrain on page 149 in your prayer.

For more ideas on ways your family can live as disciples of Jesus, visit

www.BeMyDisciples.com

Unit 4 **Review**

Name _____

A. Choose the Best Word

Fill in the blanks to complete each of the sentences.
Use the words from the word bank.

| man | sin | deacons |
| forgiveness | woman | sick |

1. God is always ready to forgive us when we _____.

2. _____ are helpers of bishops and priests.

3. Everyone needs _____.

4. The Oil of the _____ is blessed during Holy Week.

5. A baptized _____ and a baptized _____
unite in the Sacrament of Matrimony.

B. Show What You Know

Match the items in Column A with those in Column B.

Column A

1. Sacrament of Matrimony

2. Sacrament of Holy Orders

3. Sacrament of the Anointing
of the Sick

4. parents

5. Sacrament of Penance
and Reconciliation

Column B

_____ **a.** teach their children right from wrong
and provide them with food and
shelter

_____ **b.** unites a baptized man and a
baptized woman in a lifelong bond

_____ **c.** We receive both God's forgiveness
for the sins we commit after Baptism
and his grace not to sin.

_____ **d.** A baptized man is consecrated to
serve the whole Church as a bishop,
priest, or deacon.

_____ **e.** strengthens our faith, hope, and love
for God when we are seriously ill,
weakened by old age, or dying

C. Connect with Scripture

Reread the Scripture passage on page 117.
What connection do you see between this passage and
what you learned in this unit?

_____

_____

_____

D. Be a Disciple

1. *Review the four pages in this unit titled The Church Follows*
Jesus. What person or ministry of the Church on these
pages will inspire you to be a better disciple of Jesus?
Explain your answer.

_____

_____

_____

2. *Work with a group. Review the four Disciple Power virtues*
or gifts you have learned about in this unit. After jotting
down your own ideas, share with the group practical
ways that you will live these virtues or gifts day by day.

_____

_____

_____

Love Your Enemies

One day, Jesus was teaching a great crowd. He said,

"But to you who hear I say, love your enemies, do good to those who hate you, bless those who curse you, pray for those who mistreat you. To the person who strikes you on one cheek, offer the other one as well, and from the person who takes your cloak, do not withhold even your tunic. Give to everyone who asks of you, and from the one who takes what is yours, do not demand it back."

BASED ON LUKE 6:27–30

What I Have Learned

What is something you already know about these faith concepts?

The Beatitudes

_____

_____

_____

Covenant

_____

_____

Holiness

_____

_____

Faith Terms to Know

Put an X next to the faith terms you know. Put a ? next to faith terms you need to learn more about.

_____ conscience

_____ Cardinal Virtues

_____ Decalogue

_____ Great Commandment

_____ obedience

_____ Kingdom of God

_____ venial sin

_____ mortal sin

The Bible

What do you know about the Beatitudes?

_____

_____

_____

The Church

What does the Church teach about how to make good decisions?

_____

_____

_____

Questions I Have

What questions would you like to ask about making good choices to live a holy life?

_____

_____

_____

Looking Ahead

In this chapter, the Holy Spirit invites you to ▶

EXPLORE how Father Solanus Casey lived a life of holiness.

DISCOVER the path to holiness.

DECIDE how you will grow in holiness.

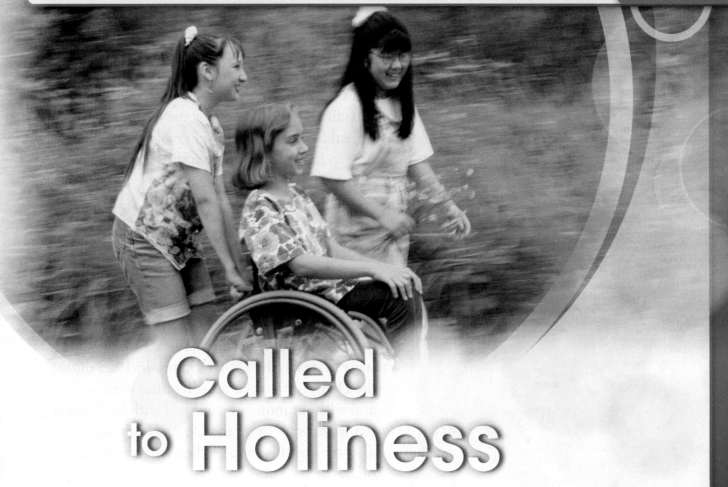

Called to Holiness

? What makes every person special?

God created us to be holy. When you think of a holy person, whom do you think of? We live holy lives when we live our Catholic faith and follow the example of Jesus.

> . . . but, as he who called you is holy, be holy yourselves in every aspect of your conduct, for it is written, "Be holy because I [am] holy."
>
> 1 PETER 1:15–16

? What are the qualities of a holy person?

Disciple Power

Goodness

Goodness is a Fruit of the Holy Spirit. We exhibit goodness when we honor God by avoiding sin and always trying to do what we know is right.

THE CHURCH FOLLOWS JESUS

Venerable Solanus Casey

God invites everyone to share his life and love. He invites everyone to live a holy life. Sometimes people who live holy lives are named Saints, or canonized, by the Church. The Church has named Bernard Casey a venerable of the Church. This is the first step in naming him a Saint of the Church.

Bernard Casey was the sixth child of a family of ten boys and six girls. They lived on a farm in Wisconsin near the Mississippi River. At the age of twenty-one, he entered St. Francis Seminary in Milwaukee. Five years later, he received the name Solanus when he entered the Franciscan Capuchin Order.

After he was ordained a priest, Father Solanus devoted his life to serving the sick and the poor in many places in the United States. In 1929 during the Depression when most families were hungry and without money, he worked with his brother Franciscans to set up the Detroit Soup Kitchen. The work of this soup kitchen still continues today.

Father Solanus Casey truly loved others as Jesus loved him. One day before he died, he said, "I looked on my whole life as giving, and I want to give until there is nothing left."

❓ Think of a person you know who is living a holy life. How is that person making a difference in the lives of other people?

Our Call to Holiness

God created every person to be holy. God created us in his image and likeness. The Scriptures tell us that we are all called to holiness. Holiness is sharing in the very life and love of God. Jesus lived and taught the way of holiness. After he taught his disciples the Beatitudes, Jesus told his disciples they were to be lights in the world (see Matthew 5:14–16). At the Last Supper, he told them how to do this. He said:

> "As the Father loves me, so I also love you. . . .
> This I command you: love one another."

JOHN 15:9, 17

Our choices, both words and actions, are to show our love for God and for one another. Each day, we ask the Holy Spirit to help us try our best to love, forgive, and care for others as Jesus showed us.

Activity God the Father sends us a gift to help us live holy lives. Use this code to discover the gift.

A	.-	H	....	O	---	V	...-
B	-...	I	..	P	.--.	W	.--
C	-.-.	J	.---	Q	--.-	X	-..-
D	-..	K	-.-	R	.-.	Y	-.--
E	.	L	.-..	S	...	Z	--..
F	..-.	M	--	T	-		
G	--.	N	-.	U	..-		

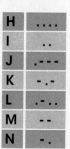
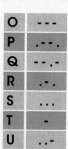
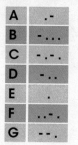

- .... .

.... --- .-.. -.--

... .--. .. .-. .. -

Perpetua and Felicity

Saint Perpetua and Saint Felicity are examples of the power of God's grace working in our lives. These North African women suffered martyrdom because of their faithfulness to Christ. They gave each other a sign of peace as they were attacked by wild animals. The Church celebrates the feast day of Saints Perpetua and Felicity on March 7.

Living by God's Grace

Our parents share the gift of life, love, and faith in Jesus with us. Through Baptism, God shares the gift of his life and love with us. We call this gift **sanctifying grace**. The word *sanctifying* means "making holy." Through this grace, all that separates us from God is taken away. Sin is forgiven. We are made holy.

God also intervenes and gives us the additional gift of his help to live holy lives. We call this help from God **actual grace**. The Holy Spirit teaches us and helps us live as followers of Jesus Christ. Without the grace of the Holy Spirit, we could never live as children of God.

We strengthen our love for God and receive his grace to live holy lives when we take part in the celebration of the Sacraments, especially the Eucharist. Reading the Bible and praying also help us say yes to God's invitation to live as his children.

How can you show that you are saying yes to God's gift of grace?

Choosing the Way of Holiness

We can choose to live Jesus' command, "Love one another," or we can choose not to live it. We can choose to make decisions not to live the way of holiness. When we freely choose not to live as God wants us to live, we sin. The decision to sin can begin with a temptation. All sin offends God and hurts us, but all sins are not the same.

Mortal sin. Serious, or grave, sins that separate us from God are called mortal sins. Three things are necessary to commit a mortal sin. They are

1. The thing that we choose to do or not to do must be very seriously wrong.

2. We must know that what we are choosing to do or not to do is seriously wrong.

3. We must freely choose to do what we know is seriously wrong.

Venial sins. Less serious sins are called venial sins. A sin is venial when one, two, or three of the conditions named above for a mortal sin are not fully present. Venial sins damage and weaken our love for God and for others. They do not break our relationship with God. Ignoring our venial sins or failing to be sorry for them can lead us to sin seriously.

Activity

1. Describe a time when you resisted a temptation and chose to do the right thing even though it was difficult.

_____

_____

_____

2. Write two ways your Catholic faith helps you keep your eyes focused on God.

_____

_____

_____

I FOLLOW JESUS

You are holy and are called to live a holy life. God will give you the grace you need if you ask him and do your best to make good choices.

GROWING IN HOLINESS

Faced with these situations, what are some good choices that would help you grow in holiness and goodness?

A friend of yours makes the team, but you do not. How might you react?

I might

_____

_____

Your parents really want you to go someplace important with the family, but you want to go somewhere with your friends. How would you feel? What would you do?

I would feel

_____

_____

I would

_____

_____

MY FAITH CHOICE

This week, I will look for ways to make choices that will help me grow in holiness. I will _____

_____

_____

 Pray to God, asking that you may live a holy life filled with goodness.

Chapter Review

Solve this crossword puzzle.

Across

3. Sins that weaken our love for God and for others

4. Grace that helps us live as children of God and followers of Jesus

5. Living as children of God

Down

1. Serious sin by which we choose to separate ourselves from God's love

2. Grace that is the gift of God's life and love that makes us holy

A Prayer of Blessing

The Church prays the psalms every day. Pray these psalm verses. Ask God to help you walk the way of holiness that Jesus taught.

Group 1: Make known to me your ways, LORD; teach me your paths.

Group 2: Guide me in your truth and teach me, for you are God my savior.

Group 1: For you, I wait all the long day, because of your goodness, LORD.

Group 2: Let honesty and virtue preserve me; I wait for you, O LORD.

PSALM 25:4–5, 21

With My Family

This Week . . .

In Chapter 17, "Called to Holiness," your child learned:

▶ Christians are called to live the way of holiness Jesus lived and taught his disciples to live.

▶ Through Baptism, we receive the gift of sanctifying grace. We are made sharers in the life and love of God the Father, the Son, and the Holy Spirit.

▶ We can accept or reject God's invitation and his help to live holy lives. When we freely choose not to live as we know God wants us to live, we sin.

▶ Your child also learned that goodness is a Fruit of the Holy Spirit that helps us honor God by always trying to do what we know is right.

For more about related teachings of the Church, see the *Catechism of the Catholic Church,* 1846–1869 and 1987–2016, and the *United States Catholic Catechism for Adults,* pages 307–338.

■ Sharing God's Word

Read together 1 Peter 1:15–16. Emphasize that God created every person to be holy. Talk about what your family can do to become more holy.

■ We Live as Disciples

The Christian home is a school of discipleship. Choose one of the following activities to do as a family, or design a similar activity of your own:

▶ Ask family members to think of a friend or relative they believe lives a holy life. Then have family members share how those people are making a difference in the lives of others. Have each family member prepare a card thanking the person for the gift he or she has been to your family.

▶ Together research the lives of your family's patron Saints in a book or on a Catholic Web site. Talk about why that person was named a Saint, a model of holiness.

■ Our Spiritual Journey

A rich prayer life is an important step in growing in holiness. Take time as a family to determine how prayer can become an important part of your daily life. In this chapter, your child prayed a prayer based on Psalm 25. Read and pray together this prayer on page 161.

For more ideas on ways your family can live as disciples of Jesus, visit **www.BeMyDisciples.com**

Looking Ahead

In this chapter, the Holy Spirit invites you to: ▶

EXPLORE how Saint John Bosco made good decisions.

DISCOVER habits that can help us make good decisions.

DECIDE how you will make good moral decisions.

CHAPTER
18

Making Moral Decisions

? What are some decisions you make every day?

Every day, you make choices and decisions. Your choices tell people a lot about you. Use the following psalm verse as a prayer every time you are being called to make an important decision.

> Make known to me your ways, LORD;
> teach me your paths.
>
> PSALM 25:4

? How do you know if your decision is a good one?

Disciple Power

Prudence

Prudence is the virtue that helps a person know what is good and choose to do it. It is an important virtue in making Christian decisions.

Saint John Bosco

Saints are people who make Christian decisions and choose what is good and right. In the 1800s, a Saint named Father John Bosco lived in Italy. God called John to work with children who had no one to guide them. Because they were poor, hundreds of children had left their families to work in the cities. John helped the children find shelter and work. He provided them with food and an education. He played games with them, sang songs with them, and even juggled to make them laugh.

John also taught the children about Jesus and about how to live a Christian life. Because he was a priest, John always said Mass for the children. John knew that by loving the children and teaching them the Scriptures, he was helping them learn to make good and prudent choices. Many of these children grew up to be holy people.

? Who are some people in your life who have shown you how to make good choices and be a disciple of Jesus? Tell a partner about them.

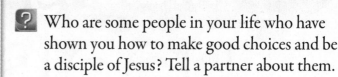

Choosing Good

FAITH FOCUS
Why is it important to make good moral decisions?

God created us to know him, to love him, and to serve him. **Moral decisions** are the good choices we make to live as children of God and followers of Christ. They bring us closer to living the life that God created us to live. They build up our relationship with God, the Church, and others. Good decisions strengthen our character and lead us toward the happiness God created us to have. Our intellect, free will, and feelings can help us make good moral decisions.

Intellect. Our intellect gives us the ability to learn more and more about God, ourselves, others, and the world in which we live.

Free will. Our free will is the power God gives us to make our own decisions and to love him and others. We can choose to do what we know is good or evil.

Feelings. Our feelings, or emotions, are neither good nor bad. They can help us do good or they can weaken us to do evil.

Sadly, we live in a world in which Original Sin has weakened our intellect and will. We do not always use our feelings to help us choose what we know is good. We struggle to overcome temptation. Temptation is everything that moves us to make decisions that lead us away from living as children of God.

The Holy Spirit always helps and guides us to make good decisions and to overcome temptation. We just need to remember to ask for help.

FAITH VOCABULARY

moral decisions
Moral decisions are the good choices we make to live as children of God and followers of Jesus Christ.

conscience
Conscience is the gift of God that is part of every person and that guides us to know and judge what is right and wrong.

Activity On a separate piece of paper or card, write and decorate a phrase that can help you and others remember to make moral decisions. Keep your card where you will see it often.

Saint Catherine of Siena

Catherine of Siena worked with the leaders of the Church and local government to help them overcome the temptation to settle their problems by fighting. Because of her work, Saint Catherine of Siena is honored as a Doctor, or great teacher, of the Church and a peacemaker. The Church celebrates her feast day on April 29.

The Gift of Conscience

Every person is born with a gift that helps us make moral decisions. This gift is our **conscience**. Our conscience guides us to know and judge what is right and what is wrong. Just as we develop our gifts to play a sport, do math, use computers, play a musical instrument, or dance or sing, we also need to develop our ability to make moral decisions. Here are some ways we can develop or train our conscience:

▶ Pray to the Holy Spirit.

▶ Take part in the celebration of the Sacraments, especially the Eucharist and Reconciliation.

▶ Read, study, and pray the Bible, especially the Gospels.

▶ Study what the Church teaches about how we should live.

▶ Learn from the lives of others, such as the Saints, who have lived holy lives.

▶ Ask the advice of our parents and other adults who teach us about our faith.

Our ability to use and follow our conscience can also become weakened. We can develop a bad conscience. It is very important that we work hard at forming a good conscience. This is something we have the responsibility to do all of our lives.

Activity You have read about six ways you can train your conscience. Choose one of these ways. Write how you will use it to train your conscience.

_____

_____

_____

_____

_____

The Four Cardinal Virtues

The more we train our voice to sing or practice our serve in tennis, the more improvement we see. We develop good habits, or ways of doing things, that seem natural. The same is true in following a well-trained conscience and making moral decisions. The more we cooperate with the grace of the Holy Spirit and work at making moral decisions, the better we become at it. We develop Moral Virtues.

The Moral Virtues are spiritual powers, or habits, that give us the strength to do what is right and live holy lives. The four Moral Virtues are also called Cardinal Virtues. The word *cardinal* comes from a word meaning "to hinge on." The four Cardinal Virtues are

Prudence. Prudence helps us evaluate situations and judge whether they will lead us to do good or evil.

Justice. Justice directs us to give to God what rightfully belongs to him and to give to our neighbors what rightfully belongs to them.

Fortitude. Fortitude keeps us steady in doing what is good, especially when difficulties arise.

Temperance. Temperance helps us use and enjoy things in a way that is not harmful to us or others.

Our moral life and moral decision making hinge on the moral virtues. They help us live as children of God and followers of Christ.

Activity Read these two situations. Name a moral virtue that will help each person make a good decision and put it into practice.

1. Robert enjoys playing electronic games. He has been playing a game for forty-five minutes. His mom says, "Robert, it's seven o'clock. How's the homework coming?"

_____

2. Elena is with a group of her friends at the mall. Her friends decide to go into a movie that she knows her mother does not want her to see. They encourage her to go with them anyway.

_____

I FOLLOW JESUS

Each day you try to grow as a Christian and make decisions to live the life that God asks you to live. Your conscience and the guidance of the Holy Spirit will assist you.

DECISIONS, DECISIONS!

You are the host of a student talk show, "Decisions! Decisions!" Today the topic is "Helpful Decisions Made by Fifth Graders." Create a dialogue you might have with a student about a good decision he or she made and the good consequences that come from that decision.

MY FAITH CHOICE

This week, I will try to be more aware of how I go about making good decisions. Before I make an important decision, I will

_____

_____

Ask the Holy Spirit to help you live a prudent life, guiding you always to make good decisions.

Chapter Review

Fill in the circle next to each correct answer.

1. A _____ is a habit or spiritual power that helps us do what is right and avoid what is wrong.

    ○ temptation　　○ conscience　　○ virtue

2. Our _____ is our ability to know God, ourselves, and other people more clearly.

    ○ intellect　　○ free will　　○ soul

3. _____ is the gift of God that is part of every person and helps us know and judge what is right and wrong.

    ○ Virtue　　○ Free will　　○ Conscience

4. _____ is the Cardinal Virtue that keeps us steady when problems arise in living holy lives.

    ○ Justice　　○ Fortitude　　○ Kindness

TO HELP YOU REMEMBER

1. Moral decisions help us grow as children of God and live as followers of Jesus Christ.

2. Conscience is our ability to know and judge what is right and what is wrong.

3. The Cardinal Virtues of prudence, justice, fortitude, and temperance are good habits that help us live holy lives.

An Examination of Conscience

An examination of conscience is like a mini-retreat. Set aside time each day to reflect on your actions. Use this examination of conscience:

1. Sit in a comfortable place. Remember that God is with you.

2. Spend some time thinking about the day.

3. Answer these questions:

    a. How have I shown or not shown love and respect for God?

    b. How have I shown or not shown love and respect for myself?

    c. How have I shown or not shown love and respect for other people?

    d. How have I used or misused the gifts of God's creation?

4. Spend some time talking to God. Ask him to help you make better decisions.

5. Promise that you will try to do your best.

6. Close by praying the Act of Contrition.

With My Family

This Week . . .

In Chapter 18, "Making Moral Decisions," your child learned:

▶ Making moral decisions is an important part of the Christian life. Such decisions guide us in living as children of God and followers of Christ.

▶ Each of us has been given a conscience, an intellect, a free will, and feelings, or emotions. All these natural gifts give us the ability to make decisions that guide us in living holy lives.

▶ The four virtues of prudence, justice, fortitude, and temperance are called the Cardinal Virtues. These virtues strengthen our desire and ability to choose what is good, to overcome the temptation to do evil, and to avoid doing what is not good.

▶ Your child also focused on the Cardinal Virtue of prudence and how this virtue helps us make good decisions.

For more about related teachings of the Church, see the *Catechism of the Catholic Church*, 1699–1709, 1716–1724, 1730–1742, 1762–1770, 1776–1794, and 1803–1811, and the *United States Catholic Catechism for Adults*, pages 307–321.

■ Sharing God's Word

Read together Wisdom 8:7. Emphasize that the four Cardinal Virtues play a pivotal role in helping us make good decisions to live holy lives.

■ We Live as Disciples

The Christian home and family is a school of discipleship. Choose one of the following activities to do as a family, or design a similar activity of your own:

▶ Invite family members to share the things that have helped them develop a good conscience. Encourage each other to make decisions to live holy lives.

▶ Identify ways your family can help one another make decisions to live holy lives. Choose one thing you will do this week to help each other make prudent decisions.

■ Our Spiritual Journey

An examination of conscience helps us reflect on our moral decisions. Talk about why it is important to think about our moral decisions before, during, and after we make them. Encourage the children to review their actions before going to bed each night using the form on page 169.

For more ideas on ways your family can live as disciples of Jesus, visit **www.BeMyDisciples.com**

Looking Ahead

In this chapter, the Holy Spirit invites you to ▶

EXPLORE God's Covenant with his people.

DISCOVER God's faithfulness to the Covenant.

DECIDE how you will respond to God's Covenant with you.

CHAPTER
19

Living the Covenant

❓ Why is it hard sometimes to keep our promises?

God always keeps his promises. Even though we feel God is not with us at times, the truth is that we are so connected with God that he is always present to us. Listen to how the writer of Psalm 117:2 shares his faith in God's presence.

> The LORD's love for us is strong;
>   the LORD is faithful forever.
> Hallelujah!
>
> PSALM 117:2

❓ How do you feel when you read that God is always faithful, even when we turn away from him?

Disciple Power

Obedience

Obedience is to freely choose to follow God's ways because of our love for God and our trust in his faithfulness to the Covenant. We know that God only desires what is best for us.

Solemn Agreements

God has made solemn agreements, or covenants, with certain people like Noah, Abraham, and Moses. These agreements were mostly verbal, or spoken. They were not written legal agreements.

After an agreement was reached, it was sealed, or made final, with symbolic rituals, a sacrifice, a special blessing, or even a ritual meal. For example, after the Great Flood, God made a Covenant with Noah. He told Noah that he would bless him and his descendents and that the world would not be destroyed by water ever again. It was sealed by a rainbow, so that every time a rainbow is seen, we are reminded of that Covenant made long ago. In other places in the Bible, agreements between God and people were sealed with the sacrifice of an animal, usually a lamb.

Jesus is the new and everlasting Covenant. In him, God promises Salvation for everyone. In Baptism, we are made sharers of that promise. At that moment, we enter into a Covenant with God. It is sealed by water being poured on our head. We are then dressed in a white garment. A lighted candle is given to our parents to symbolize that we are children of light and belong to God. We are Christians.

God will always be faithful to the Covenant he made with us. It is up to us to be faithful to the Covenant we made with God.

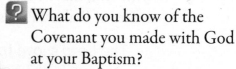 What do you know of the Covenant you made with God at your Baptism?

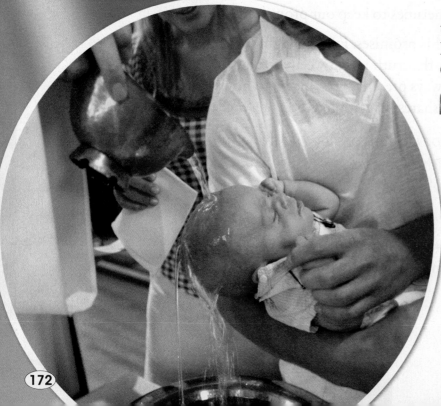

A Covenant People

God began the everlasting **Covenant** with all people when he promised Noah that he would never again destroy the Earth by flood. This expression of the Covenant was a loving and sacred relationship between God and his people. Noah, and later Abraham, honored the Covenant they and God made by being faithful to him.

Jacob was the son of Isaac, who was the son of Abraham and Sarah. He would have twelve sons whose children would become the Twelve Tribes, or large family groups, of Israel. This reflected the Covenant and original promise God made to Abraham, namely, the promise that he would have as many descendants as stars in the sky (see Genesis 15:5-6).

At Mass, we proclaim that Abraham is our father in faith. All the baptized have been made sharers in the Covenant that binds God and Abraham. Saint Paul reminds us of this Covenant connection with Abraham. He teaches,

If you belong to Christ, then you are Abraham's descendant, heirs according to the promise.

GALATIANS 3:29

FAITH FOCUS
Why is it important to remember God's Covenant with us?

FAITH VOCABULARY
Covenant
A covenant is a sacred agreement or relationship, sometimes sealed by a ritual or ceremony.

Activity Look up and read Genesis 15:1–16, the story of the Covenant that God and Abraham made. In this space, write three promises God made to Abraham.

_____

_____

_____

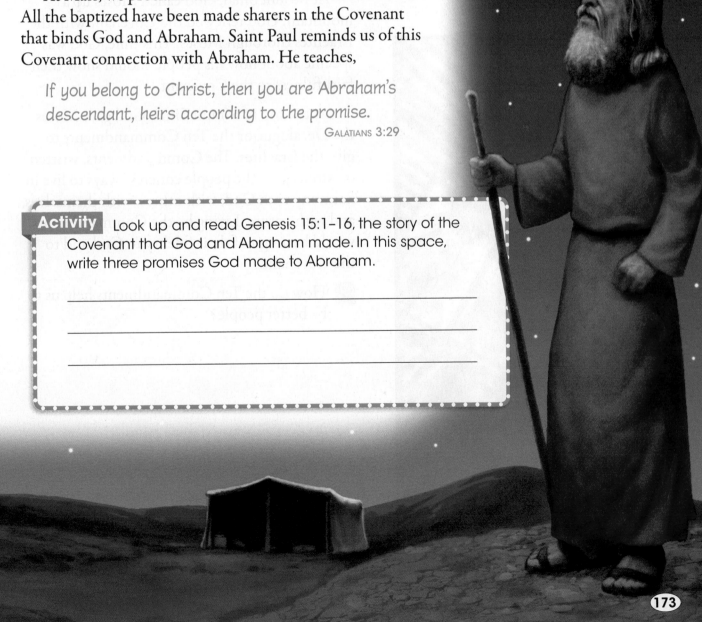

Abraham

Christians honor Abraham as our "Father in Faith." His name was Abram, and God changed it to Abraham after God made the Covenant with him. Solely on God's promise to them, Abraham and Sarah and their family packed up all their belongings and did as God asked.

The Covenant with Moses

God has never stopped loving his creation. God always offers people the chance to come back and live in harmony with him. However, the descendants of Isaac and Jacob, the Israelites, broke their side of the Covenant.

God nevertheless remained faithful to them and to the Covenant. He never turned away from his people. God is more dependable than the sun rising in the morning. God is always faithful.

God sent Moses to bring the Israelites, or Hebrews as they were also known, out of slavery in Egypt. During the Israelites' Exodus from Egypt and their journey through the desert, God invited them to enter a special Covenant with him.

At Mount Sinai, God called Moses up a mountain. God renewed the Covenant with the Israelites thorough Moses. This time, God was specific about how his people should show their faithfulness to the Covenant.

At the top of Mount Sinai, God gave Moses the Decalogue or the Ten Commandments to give the Israelites. The Commandments, written on stone, gave the people concrete ways to live in harmony with God, with others, with themselves, and with nature. Living by the Commandments would be a sign of their fidelity to God and to the Covenant.

❓ How do the Ten Commandments help us to be better people?

The New Covenant

As central to the Covenant as the Ten Commandments are, they are not the final statement of our responsibilities for living the Covenant. In the fullness of time, God the Father sent his Son, Jesus Christ, the Word of God and the Savior of the world, to live among us. Jesus is the new and everlasting Covenant. Joined to him in Baptism, we have been made sharers in the new Covenant.

Jesus came to reconcile all people with God, with one another, and with all of creation. As part of his mission, Jesus taught:

"Do not think that I have come to abolish the law or the prophets. I have come not to abolish but to fulfill."

MATTHEW 5:17

Jesus, the Word of God, clearly reveals what we must do to be faithful to God and to share in the promise of Salvation.

"Whoever obeys and teaches these commandments will be called the greatest in the kingdom of heaven."

MATTHEW 5:19

This new Covenant was no longer to be simply engraved on stone. It is written in our hearts as God himself revealed through the prophet Jeremiah.

I will place my law within them, and write it upon their hearts; I will be their God, and they shall be my people.

JEREMIAH 31:33

Activity God says that his Commandments are written on our hearts. That means they are part of who we are and what we know is true. Think of a rule that is written on your heart.

Write the rule in this space.

_____

_____

_____

_____

_____

I FOLLOW JESUS

God has, is, and always will be faithful to the Covenant.
God invites us and gives us the grace to do the same.

MY COMMITMENT TO THE COVENANT

Create a symbol that shows your faithfulness to God. Then write how you
will try to be faithful to God just as he is faithful to you.

_____

_____

_____

_____

_____

_____

_____

_____

_____

_____

_____

_____

MY FAITH CHOICE

This week, I will remain true to my Covenant with God. I will

_____

_____

_____

Pray, "My heart is steadfast, God; my heart is steadfast. I will sing
and chant praise."

PSALM 108:2

Chapter Review

Find and circle the covenant words hidden in the word search. Write a brief paragraph about the Covenant using these words.

```
J   A   C   O   B   G   C
A   B   R   A   H   A   M
C   L   J   X   N   D   O
O   O   N   E   W   I   S
B   N   O   C   S   Y   E
H   E   A   R   T   U   S
N   C   H   T   D   X   S
```

_____

_____

_____

_____

▶ TO HELP YOU REMEMBER

1. We are Covenant people. Our Baptism binds us in an everlasting Covenant with God.

2. God gave Moses the Ten Commandments on Mount Sinai to guide us in living the Covenant.

3. Jesus, the Son of God, is the new and everlasting Covenant who came to fulfill the law and the prophets.

Prayer of Commitment

Prayer is a sign that we live in Covenant with God. Pray this prayer silently in your heart.

Father in Heaven, when the Spirit came down upon Jesus at his baptism in the Jordan River, you revealed him to be your own beloved Son.

Keep me (Say your name), your child, born of water and the Holy Spirit, faithful to our Covenant.

May I, who share in our Covenant as your adopted child through Baptism, follow in Christ's path of service to people.

May I live as your child, following the example of Jesus. Amen.

With My Family

This Week . . .

In Chapter 19, "Living the Covenant," your child learned:

▶ Our Baptism binds us in an everlasting Covenant with God. God never breaks his part of the Covenant.

▶ The Ten Commandments are a guide to help us live in harmony.

▶ Jesus Christ is the fulfillment of the old Covenant.

▶ The virtue of obedience is to freely choose to follow God's ways because of our love for God and our trust in his faithfulness to the Covenant.

For more about related teachings of the Church, see the *Catechism of the Catholic Church*, 26–231, and the *United States Catholic Catechism for Adults*, pages 11–76.

■ Sharing God's Word

Read Psalm 108:1–5. Focus on how the psalmist gives thanks to God for God's faithfulness and love. Reflect on how you can be like the psalmist.

■ We Live as Disciples

The Christian home and family is a school of discipleship. Choose one of the following activities to do as a family, or design a similar activity of your own:

▶ Make a short list of family rules that will help you live as faithful Christians in harmony with God and one another. Post the list in a place where everyone can see it and be reminded of the family rules.

▶ Make a list of how each of the family members live out their baptismal Covenant with God daily. Share it with each other.

■ Our Spiritual Journey

God invites and gives us the grace to be faithful and obedient to his ways. We live the Covenant with God. He walks with us side by side, step by step. We always have the gift of his presence—even when we turn away from him. Pray the covenant prayer on page 177 aloud as a family this week.

For more ideas on ways your family can live as disciples of Jesus, visit **www.BeMyDisciples.com**

Looking Ahead

In this chapter, the Holy Spirit invites you to ▶

EXPLORE how Christians are signs of God's love.

DISCOVER what it means to be truly blessed by God.

DECIDE how you will live the Beatitudes.

CHAPTER
20

The Beatitudes

? Where do you think true happiness comes from?

Everyone wants to be happy. Everyone spends their whole life seeking happiness. Jesus taught us the true meaning of happiness. If we live a life of holiness, even when it is difficult, Jesus told us that we would discover happiness.

"Rejoice and be glad, for your reward will be great in heaven."
MATTHEW 5:12

? What are some of the ways you know that Jesus wants you to live?

Disciple Power

Justice

Justice is the Cardinal Virtue that helps us give to God what rightfully belongs to him and to give to our neighbors what rightfully belongs to them.

Habitat for Humanity

Jesus encouraged us to help others and told us that by doing so we would find happiness. Habitat for Humanity International is a Christian housing organization. It brings together Catholic and other Christian volunteers to work together for justice and righteousness. They build simple, decent, and affordable housing in partnership with those who need it.

Many Catholics participate in Habitat for Humanity. Its volunteers have built more than 150,000 homes all over the world. This includes more than 50,000 in the United States. These homes are for people who cannot afford to buy a home of their own. The people themselves often participate.

Habitat for Humanity volunteers build homes for people of all races, religions, and ethnic groups. Their work is a sign of God's love for all people and helps all people place their trust in him. You can imagine the happiness that families feel when they move into a home built by Habitat for Humanity.

Activity How does your parish help to build a better world? Write some of the things your parish does on the lines below.

_____

_____

_____

_____

_____

_____

Former President Jimmy Carter and Mrs. Carter assist in a Habitat for Humanity building project.

The Way of Happiness

During his life on Earth, Jesus taught his disciples many things. He gave his disciples concrete guidelines on how he wanted them to live. Matthew has gathered many of the teachings of Jesus in chapters 5, 6, and 7 of his Gospel. This part of Matthew's Gospel is called the **Sermon on the Mount**.

The Sermon on the Mount begins with the **Beatitudes**. The Beatitudes are the sayings or teachings of Jesus that describe both the qualities and the actions of people blessed by God. The words *blessed* and *kingdom* are the key to understanding Jesus' teachings in the Beatitudes.

Blessed. The Jewish people described people who trusted and hoped in God above everyone and everything else as "blessed."

Kingdom. The Jewish people living in Jesus' time were under the rule of the Romans. They wanted to be free of that rule and prayed that God would establish the kingdom he had promised to Abraham, Moses, and David. Jesus' listeners and disciples hoped that Jesus would bring about that kingdom.

How do you think Jesus' understanding of the Kingdom of God differed from what many people thought it would be?

FAITH FOCUS
How do the Beatitudes help us make decisions to live as Christians?

FAITH VOCABULARY

Sermon on the Mount
The Sermon on the Mount includes the teachings of Jesus that are grouped together in chapters 5, 6, and 7 in the Gospel of Matthew.

Beatitudes
Beatitudes are the sayings or teachings of Jesus that are found in the Sermon on the Mount. They describe both the qualities and the actions of people blessed by God.

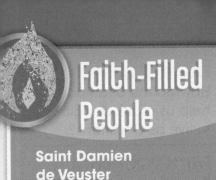

The Beatitudes

Jesus traveled throughout Galilee and Judea preaching the Good News of the coming of the Kingdom of God. One day, a crowd followed Jesus up a mountainside in Galilee. Seeing the crowd, he began to teach them. He said:

"Blessed are the poor in spirit,
　　for theirs is the kingdom of heaven.

Blessed are they who mourn,
　　for they will be comforted.

Blessed are the meek,
　　for they will inherit the land.

Blessed are they who hunger and thirst for righteousness,
　　for they will be satisfied.

Blessed are the merciful,
　　for they will be shown mercy.

Blessed are the clean of heart,
　　for they will see God.

Blessed are the peacemakers,
　　for they will be called children of God.

Blessed are they who are persecuted for the sake of righteousness,
　　for theirs is the kingdom of heaven."

MATTHEW 5:3–12

Jesus concluded by telling his listeners that living the Beatitudes would not be easy. People would make fun of them and even persecute them. He told them to have the courage to live the Beatitudes. If they did, they would discover happiness.

❓ Who is a person you know or have learned about who lives the Beatitudes?

Saint Damien de Veuster, St. Joseph's, Louvain, Beligum

The New Covenant

The Kingdom of God is not a kingdom of power on Earth, but of happiness with God. By understanding the meaning of the Beatitudes, we can better understand what it means to be blessed by God.

The poor in spirit. People who are poor in spirit place all their trust in God.

Those who mourn. People who mourn have suffered a loss in their lives. They are strong because they know God is always with them.

The meek. People who are meek are considerate. They treat others kindly and respectfully.

Those who hunger and thirst for righteousness. These people work so that everyone is treated fairly and justly.

The merciful. Merciful people are generous and kind to others.

The clean of heart. The clean of heart place God above everyone and everything else in their lives.

The peacemakers. Peacemakers work to solve problems without harming anyone and to build the kind of world God wants.

Those persecuted for righteousness. These people do what God wants even when it is difficult.

The Beatitudes are guides for living as Jesus taught us to live. The rewards promised to the blessed will be received in the Kingdom of God.

Activity The headline "Workers Meet to Settle Salary Demands" might describe "Blessed are the peacemakers." Create a headline for one other Beatitude in action.

_____

_____

_____

I FOLLOW JESUS

When you live the Beatitudes, you are a sign to others of what it means to be blessed by God. You have your eyes on living in the Kingdom of Heaven.

LIVING THE BEATITUDES

Think about each of these actions as a way of living the Beatitudes. Then name the Beatitude that each puts into action and write one way you could live that Beatitude.

Action	Beatitude	How I Lived It
You are kind to someone others are picking on.		
You listen to someone you disagree with. Together you solve your problem.		

MY FAITH CHOICE

I believe that the Holy Spirit calls me to live the Beatitudes. This week, I will

_____

_____

 Ask Jesus to help you live the Beatitudes, acting with justice in all your daily life.

Chapter Review

Match the parts of the Beatitudes.

____ **1.** "Blessed are the meek

____ **2.** "Blessed are the peacemakers

____ **3.** "Blessed are the poor in spirit

____ **4.** "Blessed are the clean of heart

____ **5.** "Blessed are they who mourn

a. for theirs is the kingdom of heaven."

b. for they will see God."

c. for they will be comforted."

d. for they will inherit the land."

e. for they will be called children of God."

TO HELP YOU REMEMBER

1. The Beatitudes show ways Jesus wants his disciples to live.

2. The Beatitudes are sayings of Jesus that describe the qualities and actions of people blessed by God.

3. The Beatitudes guide us to prepare the way for the coming of the Kingdom of God, which will come about at the end of time.

Live the Beatitudes

Ask God to help us live for the Kingdom of God. Ask God to help you live the Beatitudes.

Leader: Loving Father, send us the Holy Spirit. Teach us to be poor in spirit

All: **that we will receive the gift of the Kingdom.**

Leader: Teach us to mourn

All: **that we will receive the gift of your comfort.**

Leader: Teach us to be meek

All: **that we will inherit the earth.**

Leader: Teach us to hunger and thirst for righteousness

All: **that we will be satisfied.**

Leader: Teach us to be merciful

All: **that we will be shown mercy.**

Leader: Teach us to be clean of heart

All: **that we will see you.**

Leader: Teach us to be peacemakers

All: **that we will be called children of God.**

Leader: Teach us to have courage when we are treated harmfully because of our love for you

All: **that we will receive the gift of the Kingdom.**

BASED ON MATTHEW 5:3–10

With My Family

This Week . . .

In Chapter 20, "The Beatitudes," your child learned:

▶ The Beatitudes are found in the Sermon on the Mount in Matthew's Gospel.

▶ The Beatitudes name qualities and rewards of those blessed by God.

▶ The disciples of Jesus are called to live in such a way that we witness to the coming of the Kingdom of Heaven.

▶ We are to be living signs of the blessedness, or happiness, God wishes for all.

▶ Your child also learned how the Cardinal Virtue of justice can help us live the Beatitudes.

For more about related teachings of the Church, see the *Catechism of the Catholic Church*, 1716–1724, and the *United States Catholic Catechism for Adults*, pages 307–321.

■ Sharing God's Word

Read together Matthew 5:3–12. Emphasize that Jesus taught the Beatitudes to identify people who were truly blessed by God. Talk about what your family can do to live the Beatitudes in your daily lives.

■ We Live as Disciples

The Christian home and family is a school of discipleship. Choose one of the following activities to do as a family, or design a similar activity of your own:

▶ We live the Beatitudes when we are peacemakers. Name concrete ways that you can live as peacemakers at home, at school, at work, and in your community.

▶ Write each of the Beatitudes on an index card and put the cards in a container near the entrance of your home. Each day this week, have each family member choose a card, read it, place it back in the container, and try to put that Beatitude into practice that day.

■ Our Spiritual Journey

In this chapter, your child prayed a prayer of petition, asking God for the grace to live the Beatitudes. Read and pray together this prayer on page 185.

For more ideas on ways your family can live as disciples of Jesus, visit **www.BeMyDisciples.com**

Unit 5 **Review**

Name _____

A. Choose the Best Word

Fill in the blanks to complete each of the sentences.
Use the words from the word bank.

image	Merciful	Mount Sinai
likeness	conscience	Peacemakers

1. _____ work to solve problems without harming anyone and to build the kind of world God wants.

2. Our _____ guides us to know and judge what is right and what is wrong.

3. At _____, God gave the Israelites the Ten Commandments as a guide.

4. _____ people are generous and kind to others.

5. God created us in his _____ and _____.

B. Show What You Know

Match the items in Column A with those in Column B.

Column A

1. Sermon on the Mount

2. free will

3. actual grace

4. obedience

5. prudence

Column B

_____ **a.** helps us evaluate situations and judge whether they will lead us to do good or evil

_____ **b.** the power God gives us to make our own decisions

_____ **c.** the teachings of Jesus that are grouped together in chapters 5, 6, and 7 of the Gospel of Matthew

_____ **d.** strengthens us to respect people in authority

_____ **e.** the gift of God's presence with us to help us live as children of God and followers of Jesus Christ

C. Connect with Scripture

*Reread the Scripture passage on page 153.
What connection do you see between this passage and
what you learned in this unit?*

_____

_____

_____

D. Be a Disciple

1. *Review the four pages in this unit titled The Church Follows
Jesus. What person or ministry of the Church on these
pages will inspire you to be a better disciple of Jesus?
Explain your answer.*

_____

_____

_____

2. *Work with a group. Review the four Disciple Power virtues
or gifts you have learned about in this unit. After jotting
down your own ideas, share with the group practical
ways that you will live these virtues or gifts day by day.*

_____

_____

_____

We Live

Part Two

The Great Commandment

A man tried to test Jesus. "Teacher, which commandment in the law is the greatest?" He said to him, "You shall love the Lord, your God, with all your heart, with all your soul, and with all your mind. This is the greatest and the first commandment. The second is like it: You shall love your neighbor as yourself. The whole law and the prophets depend on these two commandments."

MATTHEW 22:36–40

What I Have Learned

What is something you already know about these faith concepts?

Old Covenant

_____

_____

_____

New Covenant

_____

_____

Ten Commandments

_____

_____

Faith Terms to Know

Put an X next to the faith terms you know. Put a ? next to faith terms you need to learn more about.

_____ manna

_____ Lord's Day

_____ Great Commandment

_____ Good Samaritan

_____ steward

_____ truth

_____ Lord's Prayer

_____ prayer

The Bible

What do you know about the Golden Rule?

_____

_____

_____

The Church

When does the Church pray the Our Father?

_____

_____

_____

Questions I Have

What questions would you like to ask about how to follow the Ten Commandments?

_____

_____

_____

Looking Ahead

In this chapter, the Holy Spirit invites you to ▶

EXPLORE how Saint Dominic Savio honored God.

DISCOVER the ways we must honor God.

DECIDE how to honor God in our lives.

CHAPTER
21

Love of God

? Why are rules important?

Rules help us respect one another and live together as a community. The Ten Commandments outline our responsibilities to love and respect God, others, and ourselves. Listen to what the writer of Psalm 119 says about obeying God's Law:

> Lord, teach me the way of your laws; . . .
> Give me insight to observe your teaching,
>   to keep it with all my heart.   Psalm 119:33–34

? Why is it important for us to obey God's Commandments?

Meekness

Meekness is the virtue that helps us to maintain our confidence in God when difficulties come into our lives rather than being overcome by the difficult condition itself.

THE CHURCH FOLLOWS JESUS

The Child Saint

The Saints of the Church learned and lived God's Law. They valued God's Laws, or Commandments, and kept them.

Often when we think of the Saints, we think of adults. Most Saints were ordinary people who did ordinary things in an extraordinary way. There are even child Saints in the Church.

Dominic Savio (1842–1857) is an example of a young boy who is a Saint. He was an ordinary boy, one of ten children, and high-spirited. He knew how important rules were, and he knew when he was breaking rules. For example, Dominic got into trouble with his teachers because he would often break out laughing in class.

When Dominic was getting ready to make his First Communion, he made four rules to live by. The first was that he would go to Confession and Holy Communion as often as possible. The second was to celebrate Sundays and holy days in a special way. The third was that Jesus and Mary would be his friends. The fourth was that he would try not to sin.

In 1857, at the age of fifteen, Dominic caught the lung disease tuberculosis, which eventually caused his death. Dominic's meekness allowed him to keep faith in God when he was dying. As his father was praying with him, Dominic's face lit up with an intense joy. He said to his father: "I am seeing most wonderful things!" Dominic saw what Jesus promised. He is now with God in Heaven. Dominic Savio was canonized, or named a Saint of the Church, in 1954.

What rules help you live your Catholic faith?

Living the Covenant

The story of God's Revelation of the Ten Commandments is part of the story of the Covenant. The Covenant is the solemn agreement that God entered into with the Israelites. He promised that he would be their God, and the Israelites promised they would worship him alone as God.

After Moses led the Israelites out of slavery in Egypt, they journeyed for forty years in the desert. During this time, God provided them with **manna** from Heaven to eat. Nevertheless, the Israelites grew angry with God, with Moses, and with one another. They forgot the Covenant they had entered into with God.

Sacred Scripture tells us that God saw all that was happening and called Moses up to the mountain. There he gave Moses the **Ten Commandments** to guide his people in living the Covenant. After Moses came down from the mountain, he explained to the Israelites:

"These then are the commandments, . . . which the LORD, your God, has ordered that you be taught to observe."
DEUTERONOMY 6:1

The Ten Commandments also guide the followers of Christ in living the New Covenant that God has made with all people. Jesus is the new and everlasting Covenant. He came to fulfill, not to do away with, the Commandments that were revealed to Moses.

FAITH FOCUS
How do the First, Second, and Third Commandments tell us to respond to God's love?

FAITH VOCABULARY

manna
Manna is the food miraculously sent to the Israelites during their forty years in the desert.

Ten Commandments
The Ten Commandments are the laws of the Covenant revealed to Moses and the Israelites on Mount Sinai.

Activity Imagine that you are among the people when Moses came down from the mountain. How would you have reacted to Moses' message from God? Act out the scene with your class.

Moses

Acting on God's behalf, Moses led the Israelites out of slavery from Egypt. He went up on Mount Sinai and carried down the Ten Commandments. He prepared the Israelites to enter the land of Canaan.

The First Three Commandments

The First, Second, and Third Commandments describe our privilege and responsibility to worship God. They also show us how we are to show our love for God.

The First Commandment

I am the Lord your God: you shall not have strange gods before me.   BASED ON EXODUS 20:2–3

Through the First Commandment, God calls us to believe and hope in him, and love him above all else. We are not to let things, such as money or being popular, become more important to us than God.

The Second Commandment

You shall not take the name of the Lord, your God, in vain.   BASED ON EXODUS 20:7

The Second Commandment teaches us that we are to use God's name truthfully and with respect. We use God's name in vain when we take an oath to tell the truth and then lie. When we do this, we call upon God as a witness to a lie as if it were the truth. We also use God's name in vain when we use the name God or Jesus in anger or in any inappropriate way. This is called profanity.

How can others see that you please God first in your life?

Former President Ronald Reagan as he took the Oath of Office.

The Third Commandment

Remember to keep holy the Lord's Day.

BASED ON EXODUS 20:8

In the story of creation, we read that

God blessed the seventh day and made it holy, because on it he rested from all the work he had done in creation.

GENESIS 2:3

For the Israelites and the Jewish people today, the seventh day of the week is a holy day, the Sabbath.

For Christians, Sunday is the Lord's Day. It is the day on which Jesus was raised from the dead. Taking part in Mass on the Lord's Day, either on Saturday evening or Sunday, is a serious obligation for Catholics. Those who do not have a serious reason for not participating in Mass, such as an illness, and deliberately choose not to fulfill their obligation commit a serious sin.

The Lord's Day is a time to worship God the Creator. It is a time to rest from our work and make sure all the work we do is God's work. It is a time to nourish our faith and our life.

Catholics Believe

Saturday Evening Mass

The Church begins the celebration of Sunday and holy days of obligation by celebrating Mass on Saturday evening or the evening before the holy day. This custom of the Church is based on the ancient Jewish custom of defining a day as sundown to sundown.

Activity

What are ways your family keeps Sunday, the Lord's Day, holy? Fill in the spaces below.

_____

_____

_____

_____

_____

_____

_____

_____

_____

I FOLLOW JESUS

You are growing in your love for God each day. The virtue of meekness allows you to do many things to show others that God is at the center of your life.

THE CENTER OF MY LIFE

In each part of the circle, write or draw one thing you can do to help you make God the center of your life.

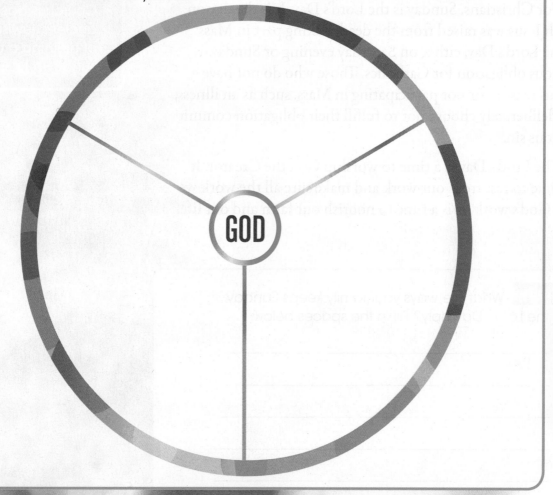

GOD

MY FAITH CHOICE

This week, I will keep Sunday as a holy and special day dedicated to the Lord. I will

_____

 Pray, "Father, blessed is your Son, Jesus, whom you sent to show us how we can love you. Fill our hearts with the Holy Spirit, so we may follow your laws. Amen."

Chapter Review

Match the terms in Column A with their descriptions in Column B.

Column A

___ **1.** First Commandment

___ **2.** Second Commandment

___ **3.** Third Commandment

Column B

a. Keep the Lord's Day as a holy day.

b. Use God's name truthfully and respectfully.

c. Worship only God and love him above all things.

▶ **TO HELP YOU REMEMBER**

1. God revealed the Ten Commandments to guide us in making moral decisions.

2. The First, Second, and Third Commandments describe our privilege and responsibility to worship God.

3. The Lord's Day is a holy day and a time to rest from our work. Sunday is the Lord's Day for Christians.

You Are God

The *Te Deum* ("You Are God") is an ancient hymn of the Church. Written in the 300s, it is a great hymn of praising God.

All: **Holy God, we praise your name.**

Group 1: You are God: we praise you;
You are the Lord: we acclaim you;

Group 2: You are the eternal Father:
All creation worships you.

All: **Holy God, we praise your name.**

Group 1: The glorious company of Apostles praises you.
The noble fellowship of prophets praises you.
The white-robed army of martyrs praises you.

Group 2: Throughout the world, the holy Church acclaims you:
Father, of majesty unbounded, your true and only Son,
worthy of all worship, and the Holy Spirit,
Advocate and Guide.

All: **Holy God, we praise your name.**

Based on the *Te Deum*

With My Family

This Week . . .

In Chapter 21, "Love of God," your child learned:

▶ The First, Second, and Third Commandments describe our privilege and responsibility to worship, respect, and reverence God as God.

▶ The First Commandment calls us to believe in, hope in, and love God above all else.

▶ The Second Commandment teaches us to respect God by only calling on his name truthfully.

▶ The Third Commandment obliges us to worship God together at Mass and to nourish our relationship with both him and our family.

▶ The virtue of meekness helps us keep confidence in God in spite of difficulties.

For more about related teachings of the Church, see the *Catechism of the Catholic Church*, 2083–2132, 2142–2159, and 2168–2188, and the *United States Catholic Catechism for Adults*, pages 339–371.

▇ Sharing God's Word

There are two Scripture passages for the Ten Commandments: Exodus 20:2–17, and Deuteronomy 5:6–21. Read the two Scripture accounts of the Ten Commandments with your family.

▇ We Live as Disciples

The Christian home and family is a school of discipleship. Choose one of the following activities to do as a family, or design a similar activity of your own:

▶ The First, Second, and Third Commandments teach us to show our love and respect for God. Talk about how you show your love and respect for God during Mass and how you show your love and respect for God at home. Set a good example by always using God's name with reverence.

▶ The Third Commandment teaches us to keep holy the Lord's Day, Sunday. Talk about how your family celebrates Sunday as a holy day. Choose one thing you can do to make your Sunday a day for the Lord.

▇ Our Spiritual Journey

The *Te Deum* is an ancient hymn of praise dating from the fourth century. It is a more solemn version of the *Gloria* we sing at Mass. The praises follow the outline of the Apostles' Creed. Pray the opening words of praise from this prayer as a family each day this week.

For more ideas on ways your family can live as disciples of Jesus, visit **www.BeMyDisciples.com**

Looking Ahead

In this chapter, the Holy Spirit invites you to ▶

EXPLORE who is your neighbor.

DISCOVER the call to love your neighbor as yourself.

DECIDE how to respond to God's call to love others.

CHAPTER 22

Love of Neighbor

? What are some of the ways we show respect for one another?

Throughout the Bible, God speaks to us and reminds us that we are to live the Covenant. Jesus reminded the people of his time that the Great Commandment summarizes how we are to live the Covenant. We are to keep God's Word in our hearts.

> In my heart I treasure your promise,
> that I may not sin against you.
>
> PSALM 119:11

? Who has helped to make God's ways known to you?

Disciple Power

Temperance

Temperance gives balance to the way we act and speak in a good way. This Cardinal Virtue also enables a person to express his or her feelings appropriately.

Responding to God's Love

Every day, you experience people whose words and actions show respect for themselves and for others. You also experience people whose words and actions do not. And you know the difference! You know well the good that comes about when someone truly lives God's ways as the psalmist prayed.

Rose of Lima (1586–1617) was one of those people who lived the way of the Lord. Her love for God was so deep that it overflowed into a very practical love for people. Her day was filled with prayer, hard work, and helping sick and poor people in her community.

Rose brought them to her little shed where she fed and cared for them. She sold her fine needlework and grew beautiful flowers that she sold at the market. With the money she made, she supported her family and works of charity. Rose showed people not only how much she loved them but also how much God loved them.

Rose became a lay member of the Dominican Order. Rose was named a Saint of the Church. The more we learn about the life of Saint Rose of Lima, the more we will come to know and follow God's ways, and the better we will live the Covenant we made with God at Baptism.

? How does Rose's life help you to show love and respect for your family and for other people?

St. Rose of Lima, St. Francis Cathedral, Santa Fe, NM

Respecting Ourselves and Others

FAITH FOCUS
What do the Ten Commandments teach us about loving our neighbor as we love ourselves?

FAITH VOCABULARY
chastity
The virtue of chastity is the respecting and honoring of our sexuality. Chastity guides us to share our love with others in appropriate ways.

Jesus taught that there is one Great Commandment, which has two parts. We are to love God above all, and we are to love our neighbors as we love ourselves.

In the parable of the Good Samaritan, Jesus teaches who our neighbor is. Our neighbor is every living person. God calls us to love everyone. All are neighbors in God's eyes. The Ten Commandments help us live this part of the Great Commandment.

The Fourth Commandment

Honor your father and your mother.

EXODUS 20:12

The Fourth Commandment teaches that we are to love, honor, and respect the members of our family, especially our parents. The family is the first and most important group in society. It is our responsibility to strengthen our family relationships.

Activity

Discuss family rules that help family members show respect for one another. Choose one of the rules and write about it here. Tell why it is a good rule.

_____

_____

_____

_____

_____

_____

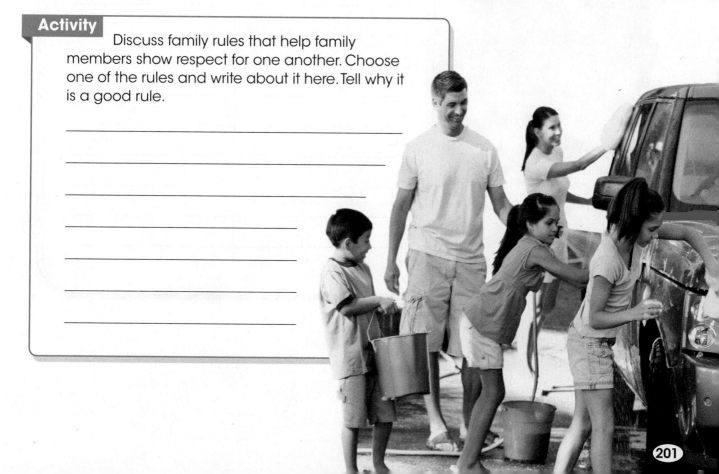

The Good Samaritan

Jesus tells a story of a man who was beaten and robbed. Three persons passed by him. The first two did not help, but the third, a Samaritan, stopped and helped. Jesus then asked, "Who was the neighbor to the robbed man?" The answer is "the one who showed him mercy." Jesus then tells us to go and do the same. He tells us to do what the Good Samaritan did.

The Fifth Commandment

You shall not kill.   BASED ON EXODUS 20:13

All life is sacred. The life of every person is sacred, regardless of age, race, gender, health, physical ability, or mental ability. The Fifth Commandment teaches that we are to respect and treat all human life as sacred. We are to take care of our own lives and health and to respect and protect the lives and health of others.

The Fifth Commandment also requires us to honor and respect the spiritual life of ourselves and others. We are not to scandalize others. This means we are not to deliberately do or say anything that leads people away from their love for God.

Activity   What kind of video game would a person who is following the Fifth Commandment choose and avoid? List your ideas here. Share and discuss your list with your class.

Choose	Avoid

The Sixth and Ninth Commandments

You shall not commit adultery. You shall not covet your neighbor's wife. BASED ON EXODUS 20:14, 17

God has given each person the gift of being either a boy or a girl who will grow to be a man or a woman. This gift is called our sexuality.

The Sixth and Ninth Commandments teach that we are to respect our own sexuality and the sexuality of others. We are to express and share our friendship and love for others in appropriate ways. **Chastity** is one of the virtues that helps us do this. The Sixth and Ninth Commandments also teach that the love and life of a husband and wife are sacred, or holy. A husband and wife are to love and honor each other their whole lives long.

The Ninth Commandment teaches that other people are to help married people grow in love. They are not to do or say things that tempt married people to be unfaithful or break up a marriage or a family.

? How does the virtue of chastity help us in our relationship with others?

I FOLLOW JESUS

The Holy Spirit teaches and helps you live the Ten Commandments each day. You pray. You respect and honor your parents and teachers. You treat your classmates and friends with respect in all ways.

LOVING AND RESPECTING OTHERS

Write a story, draw a picture, or outline a skit that shows ways you and other fifth graders can live the Fifth Commandment.

MY FAITH CHOICE

Each day, I will have many opportunities to show my love for others as Jesus taught. This week, I will

_____

_____.

 Pray, "O God, you know how firmly I believe in you and dedicate myself to you. I love you above all things. Help me to love my neighbor as myself. Amen."

Chapter Review

Write the number of the Commandment that names these moral principles.

____ **1.** Respect the gift of sexuality.

____ **2.** Reverence and respect all life.

____ **3.** Honor and respect parents and those in authority.

____ **4.** Be faithful in marriage.

____ **5.** Build happy and holy families.

A Peace Prayer

Pray this prayer of Saint Francis and learn it by heart.

Lord, make me an instrument of your peace.

Where there is hatred, let me sow love;

where there is injury, pardon;

where there is doubt, faith;

where there is despair, hope;

where there is darkness, light;

and where there is sadness, joy.

O Divine Master, grant that I may not so much seek

to be consoled as to console;

to be understood as to understand;

to be loved as to love.

For it is in giving that we receive;

it is in pardoning that we are pardoned;

and it is in dying that we are born to eternal life.

Amen.

PRAYER OF SAINT FRANCIS OF ASSISI

1. The Fourth Commandment teaches us to obey and respect our parents and those in authority.

2. The Fifth Commandment teaches us to respect all human life as sacred.

3. The Sixth and Ninth Commandments teach us to be chaste and to express our love and friendship for others in appropriate ways.

With My Family

This Week . . .

In Chapter 22, "Love of Neighbor," your child learned:

▶ The Fourth Commandment teaches us to honor our parents by respecting and obeying them.

▶ The Fifth Commandment teaches us to respect the life of every person as sacred regardless of age, race, gender, health, physical ability, or mental ability.

▶ The Sixth and Ninth Commandments teach us that we are to share our love for others in a faithful and chaste manner.

▶ Temperance gives balance in the way we act and speak. It helps us to use our gifts in good ways.

For more about related teachings of the Church, see the *Catechism of the Catholic Church*, 2196–2400 and 2514–2533, and the *United States Catholic Catechism for Adults*, pages 373–416, 439–446.

Sharing God's Word

Read together Matthew 5:17–20. Emphasize that Jesus fulfilled the Commandments.

We Live as Disciples

The Christian home and family is a school of discipleship. Choose one of the following activities to do as a family, or design a similar activity of your own:

▶ Watch TV together and keep track of the Commandments that are kept and broken as you watch each show.

▶ The Fourth Commandment teaches us to honor our mother and father and for parents to love and respect their children. How does your family honor one another?

Our Spiritual Journey

There is an adage that reads, "The family that prays together stays together." Integrate the spiritual discipline of daily prayer into the life of your marriage and into the life of your family. Create special times throughout the week in which your family can pray together, even if only briefly. Help your children to learn the Prayer of Saint Francis by praying it together daily.

For more ideas on ways your family can live as disciples of Jesus, visit **www.BeMyDisciples.com**

Looking Ahead

In this chapter, the Holy Spirit invites you to ▶

EXPLORE the importance of acting with justice.

DISCOVER the fruits of living justly.

DECIDE ways to prepare the way for God's Kingdom.

CHAPTER

23

Living a Just and Truthful Life

? Have you ever noticed someone being treated unfairly? How did you respond?

The Scriptures are filled with stories and passages telling us about God's desire for a world where people are always treated fairly.

Let justice descend, O heavens, like dew from above,
   like gentle rain let the skies drop it down.
Let the earth open and salvation bud forth;
   let justice also spring up!
   I, the LORD, have created this.

ISAIAH 45:8

? Who is the One who brings God's justice most fully?

Disciple Power

Integrity

This virtue enables a person to be the person God created him or her to be. A person of integrity says and does what he or she knows and believes is the right thing to do and say.

Blessed Miguel Pro

There are many people of faith who have met many challenges and faced many dangers in order to continue the work of the Church and celebrate God's love with others. Blessed Miguel Pro is one of those people who gave his very life for his faith.

Miguel Pro was born in Mexico in 1891. His father was an engineer who worked in the mines. His mother was a homemaker. Miguel's family was devoutly Catholic. When he grew up, Miguel entered the Jesuit order to become a priest. During this time, the government of Mexico was persecuting the Catholic Church. The Catholic faith had been outlawed.

Father Pro secretly celebrated the Sacraments and helped the poor. He avoided the police and used disguises so that he would not be arrested. Sometimes he would dress like a beggar and pretend to beg for alms outside someone's home. But once inside, he would celebrate Mass secretly or perform a Baptism. He even visited prisons by pretending to be a policeman! Once he was past the guards, Father Pro would hear the prisoners' confessions and give them Holy Communion.

After two years, Father Pro was arrested. He was charged with trying to kill the future president of Mexico. He was completely innocent, but the government wanted to get rid of him. In 1927, he was executed. Before he died, he held out his arms in the form of a cross and forgave his executioners. His last words were "Viva Cristo Rey!" In English, this means "Long live Christ the King!"

Father Miguel Pro was beatified in 1998. His feast day is November 23.

? How did Father Miguel Pro demonstrate his integrity?

Love Your Neighbor

The Seventh, Eighth, and Tenth Commandments teach us to live the second part of the Great Commandment. They teach us to treat all people with **justice**, to care for others, to respect other people's goods and their reputations.

The Seventh Commandment

You shall not steal.

EXODUS 20:15

The Seventh Commandment tells us that friends of Jesus are people of justice and mercy. We are to give God and others what is their due. Taking things that do not belong to us is an act against both God and neighbor. When we cheat or steal, or misuse creation, we are not living as children of God and friends of Jesus.

We are to make reparation if we damage things that belong to others. We are to return or replace what we have taken or damaged. When we do this, we are acting justly.

Activity Imagine that a classmate admits in a text message to you that she stole something and has now broken it, so she can't return it. Text her back and give her advice on what to do now.

FAITH FOCUS
What is the importance of living the Seventh, Eighth, and Tenth Commandments?

FAITH VOCABULARY

▶ **justice**
The Cardinal Virtue of justice is the giving to God and all people what is rightfully due to them.

▶ **honesty**
Honesty is the refusal to lie, steal, or deceive in any way.

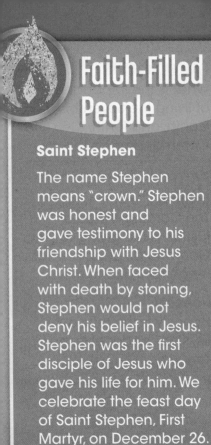

The name Stephen means "crown." Stephen was honest and gave testimony to his friendship with Jesus Christ. When faced with death by stoning, Stephen would not deny his belief in Jesus. Stephen was the first disciple of Jesus who gave his life for him. We celebrate the feast day of Saint Stephen, First Martyr, on December 26.

The Eighth Commandment

You shall not bear false witness against your neighbor.
BASED ON EXODUS 20:16

The Eighth Commandment teaches that we are to practice **honesty**. We are not only to be truthful in what we say but also in what we do. Saint Paul teaches:

[We are to] speak the truth, each one to his neighbor, for we are members one of another.
EPHESIANS 4:25

"To speak the truth" means more than not lying. We are also to respect the reputation, or good name, of others. We are not to gossip, or tell lies about and make up stories, about people either. When we gossip, we are not acting as a friend of Christ.

Lying and gossiping create a division between us and our neighbor. They also create a division between us and God. When we have created division, we must repair the relationship with our neighbor and with God. Depending on what was said or done, an example might be apologizing to the person. If we seriously harm the good name or reputation of someone, we are to confess that sin in the Sacrament of Penance and Reconciliation.

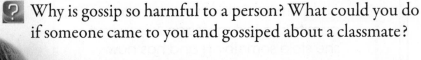 Why is gossip so harmful to a person? What could you do if someone came to you and gossiped about a classmate?

The Tenth Commandment

You shall not covet your neighbor's goods.

BASED ON EXODUS 20:17

All the good things that we have are gifts from God. The Tenth Commandment helps us value and respect all those gifts. We learn about sharing not only our material blessings, such as money, but other blessings, such as our talents.

This Commandment helps us appreciate that God is the origin and source of all things. Just as God shared with us the gift of creation, we are commanded to share with others. We are called to be good stewards of God's creation. We are to share our time, talents, and treasures freely and generously, especially with people in need.

Being a good steward extends beyond sharing with people. We are to take care of creation. We are to work to protect and preserve it. We are to use it responsibly. We are always to keep in mind that no part of creation belongs just to us. Creation is God's, and he has given it to all people.

We are to use natural resources to make the world a better place for all and not just to make our lives better. Being a good steward is the work of a disciple and friend of Christ.

Catholics Believe

Social Justice

This deals with the essential needs of people that flow from their dignity. These needs include food, clothing, shelter, health care, education, and an income that supports the family.

Activity Think of one thing a friend has that you would like to have too. Then tell why you want it and why you can live without it.

What I want: _____

Why I want it: _____

Why I don't need it: _____

I FOLLOW JESUS

The Bible tells us that, when Jesus comes again in glory, there will be a new creation, the Kingdom of God. The Seventh, Eighth, and Tenth Commandments name ways that we can prepare the way for the coming of the kingdom.

FAITHFUL TO GOD'S WORD

The Seventh, Eighth, and Tenth Commandments are listed below. For each Commandment, tell one practical thing you could do better to be faithful to it.

Seventh Commandment — "You shall not steal."

_____

_____

Eighth Commandment — "You shall not bear false witness against your neighbor."

_____

_____

Tenth Commandment — "You shall not covet your neighbor's goods."

_____

_____

MY FAITH CHOICE

This week, I will be a person of integrity. I will be true to myself by

_____

_____

Pray, "Lord God, your spirit of wisdom fills the Earth and teaches me your ways. Help me to always give witness to Jesus, who is the way, the truth, and the life. Amen."

Chapter Review

Match the terms in Column A with the statements in Column B.

Column A

_____ 8ᵗʰ Commandment

_____ disciple

_____ 10ᵗʰ Commandment

_____ stewardship

_____ 7ᵗʰ Commandment

Column B

A. The responsibility to use creation justly, fairly, and share it generously.

B. It is important to be generous with my time, talents, and treasures.

C. A follower of Jesus Christ

D. No matter what, always tell the truth.

E. If it is not mine, I must not take it.

Praying Psalm 19

Honey never loses its sweetness. Even after thousands of years, honey found in jars buried in Egyptian tombs still tastes sweet! Psalm 19 says that God's Law is even sweeter than honey.

Leader: The law of the Lord is perfect, refreshing the soul.

All: We will choose life.

Leader: The law of the Lord is trustworthy, giving wisdom to those who follow it.

All: We will be faithful.

Leader: The law of the Lord is right, rejoicing the heart.

All: We will be loving.

Leader: The laws of the lord are true, enduring forever.

All: They are more precious than gold, sweeter than honey.

Glory be to the Father . . .

BASED ON PSALM 19:8–12

With My Family

This Week . . .

In Chapter 23, "Living a Just and Truthful Life," your child learned:

▶ Stealing is wrong. It is an act against both God and neighbor.

▶ Telling the truth is expected of all Christians.

▶ God calls us all to be good stewards by sharing our time, talents, and treasures.

▶ Integrity is a virtue that enables a person to be the person God created him or her to be.

For more about related teachings of the Church, see the *Catechism of the Catholic Church*, 2401–2513 and 2534–2557, and the *United States Catholic Catechism for Adults*, pages 417–438, 447–457.

▪ Sharing God's Word

Read John 15:1–17 together. Emphasize in your own words that our friendship with Jesus is at the center of our relationship with him.

▪ We Live as Disciples

The Christian home and family is a school of discipleship. Choose one of the following activities to do as a family, or design a similar activity of your own:

▶ The Eighth Commandment teaches us about the importance of telling the truth. Discuss, "How does telling the truth help us to grow in our faith?"

▶ The Tenth Commandment teaches us that we are to be good stewards of creation. Name ways that your family is living this Commandment. Point out that truthfulness is an important way of being true to ourselves.

▪ Our Spiritual Journey

The goal of the Church's work of sharing the faith of the Church with others is to invite others to grow in intimacy and knowledge of Jesus Christ. Two ways we can do this are by keeping God's Law and through prayer. Pray the prayer on page 213 with your family. Psalm 19 praises God and honors his Laws.

For more ideas on ways your family can live as disciples of Jesus, visit **www.BeMyDisciples.com**

Looking Ahead

In this chapter, the Holy Spirit invites you to ▶

EXPLORE the importance of prayer.

DISCOVER the power of prayer.

DECIDE how to pray.

CHAPTER
24

Lord, Teach Us to Pray

? What is your favorite way to pray?

We can pray alone or with others. We can use the psalms to pray alone or to pray with others. Listen to how the psalmist speaks to God:

> But I pray to you, LORD,
>   for the time of your favor.
> God, in your great kindness answer me
>   with your constant help.
>
> PSALM 69:14

? How would you describe the prayer of the psalmist? When have you prayed in this way?

Monks of Gethsemani

Disciple Power

Piety

Piety is a Gift of the Holy Spirit that leads to a devotion to God. It is an expression of a person's deep reverence for God. It flows from one's recognition of the value a person places on his or her relationship with God. Piety also is an expression of one's deep respect for one's parents and family.

Christians are people of prayer. We pray in many different ways; we pray in many different languages. There are religious communities of men and religious communities of women in the Church who dedicate their lives to praying. These religious are called contemplatives. They live in convents, monasteries, or abbeys. They organize their day so that everything they do centers around prayer.

The Trappist monks of the Abbey of Gethsemani in Trappist, Kentucky, are contemplatives. They set aside times for praying all during the day and night. They gather seven times a day to pray the Liturgy of the Hours. The Liturgy of the Hours is the official public daily prayer of the Church. In addition, each monk spends time every day prayerfully reading the Scriptures, the writings of the Saints, and other spiritual writings.

The monks of the Abbey of Gethsemani earn their living by making cheese, fruitcake, and fudge. They also care for guests who come there to make a retreat. Everything the monks do, in one way or another, leads to prayer and is a form of prayer. Everything they do gives glory to God. It is an act of devotion to God and an expression of the gift of piety.

? When does your parish gather to pray?
How might your family center its life around prayer?

The Lord's Prayer

In Matthew's account of the Gospel, we read that Jesus went up a mountain to pray. Mountains had a special meaning to the Jewish people who had become disciples of Jesus. A disciple is a person who learns from and follows the teachings of another person. A mountain was a special place of God's presence. It was on Mount Sinai that God spoke to Moses and entered into the Covenant with Moses and the Israelites.

In Matthew's Gospel, Jesus teaches his disciples about prayer while they are together on a mountainside. It was at this time that Jesus taught his disciples to pray the **Our Father**. This emphasizes how important prayer, especially praying the Our Father, is for all Christians.

Many believe that the Our Father in Matthew's Gospel was a prayer the early Church had often prayed. Praying the Our Father had become part of what the Church does when we gather for prayer.

FAITH FOCUS
Why do we pray the Our Father?

FAITH VOCABULARY
Lord's Prayer
The early Christians called the Our Father the Lord's Prayer because it was given to them by Jesus. The Church teaches us that the Lord's Prayer is a summary of the whole Gospel.

Activity Share with a partner why prayer is an essential part of being a disciple of Jesus.

Hillside near the Sea of Galilee

The Our Father

Imagine you are sitting with the disciples on the mountainside and listening to Jesus. You are learning much about what it means to live as one of his disciples.

Jesus says:

"This is how you are to pray:
Our Father in heaven,
hallowed be your name,
your kingdom come,
your will be done,
on earth as in heaven.
Give us today our daily bread;
and forgive us our debts,
as we forgive our debtors;
and do not subject us to the final test,
but deliver us from the evil one." MATTHEW 6:9–13

The Our Father is also called the **Lord's Prayer**. It is the prayer that Jesus, our Lord, taught us.

If you were to divide this prayer into two parts, where would the first part end? Why?

218

A Summary of the Gospel

The Lord's Prayer has been called a summary of the Gospel. Praying the Our Father teaches us to pray and to live as disciples of Jesus.

Our Father. We do not pray "my Father" but "our Father." We belong to God as his adopted children. God is our *Abba*.

Who art in heaven. God, our Father, is glorious and majestic. He is above and beyond everything and everyone else in this world.

Hallowed be thy name. *Hallowed* means "very holy" and "very honored." We want everyone to know and love God, the Creator and Redeemer of the universe.

Thy kingdom come. We live in hope and wait with trust for the day when God's kingdom of justice, peace, love, and wisdom will completely take hold of our world.

Thy will be done. God's will is that all will be saved in Jesus. We pray that we will follow God's will and live as Jesus taught us to live.

Give us this day our daily bread. Each day and every moment of our lives, we depend on God to give us life. We place our trust in him.

Forgive us our trespasses as we forgive those who trespass against us. We ask God to forgive us. We promise to forgive all people who hurt us.

Lead us not into temptation, but deliver us from evil. We ask God's grace to overcome whatever and whoever would separate us from him.

Activity At Mass, we conclude the Our Father by praying, "for the kingdom, the power, and the glory are yours, now and forever." List the most important ways you give glory to God.

_____

_____

_____

I FOLLOW JESUS

Each time you pray the Our Father, the Holy Spirit helps you grow as a child of God. You learn both how to pray and how to live the Gospel.

GOD IS OUR FATHER

Write or draw something you could do to help others understand that God is the Father of all people.

MY FAITH CHOICE

This week, I will show that I am proud to call God, "Our Father." I will

_____

_____

_____

 Pray, "Holy Father, you have arranged the changing of the times and seasons; you formed us in your own image. May we for ever praise you in your mighty works. Amen." (Based on Preface V of the Sundays in Ordinary Time, *Roman Missal*)

Chapter Review

Imagine that you were on the mountain listening as Jesus taught the disciples the Our Father. Create a headline and write a brief news report describing what happened. See how many of these words and phrases you can include in your report.

mountain	worship	Lord's Prayer
trust	love	God the Father
Jesus	forgive	justice

_____

_____

_____

_____

_____

The Lord's Prayer

The Our Father, or Lord's Prayer, is the prayer of all Christians. Pray it every day.

Leader: Jesus prayed, "Father, I pray that they all may be one, as we are one" (based on John 17:20–22). Together, let us join hands and pray as Jesus taught us:

All: **Our Father . . .**

Leader: Let us share a sign of peace to show that we are all children of God, our Father.

With My Family

This Week . . .

In Chapter 24, "Lord, Teach Us to Pray," your child learned:

▶ In Matthew's Gospel, Jesus teaches the Our Father, or Lord's Prayer, to the disciples on a mountainside.

▶ The Lord's Prayer is a summary of the Gospel.

▶ When we pray the Our Father, the Holy Spirit teaches us both how to pray and how to live the Gospel.

▶ Your child also learned that piety, a Gift of the Holy Spirit, leads to devotion to God.

For more about related teachings of the Church, see the *Catechism of the Catholic Church*, 2558–2865, and the *United States Catholic Catechism for Adults*, pages 481–495.

■ Sharing God's Word

Read Matthew 6:5–14 together. Emphasize that the Our Father is also called the Lord's Prayer and that praying the Lord's Prayer helps us to live the Gospel.

■ We Live as Disciples

The Christian home and family is a school of discipleship. Choose one of the following activities to do as a family, or design a similar activity of your own.

▶ Jesus reminds us that God is our Father. Every member of your family is a child of God. Name the things your family is doing to live as God's children.

▶ Choose a petition of the Lord's Prayer to focus on as a family this week, for example, "give us this day our daily bread." Pray for those in your community and in the world who are hungry. Explore a concrete way that you can help as a family so your children know that it is important to you.

■ Our Spiritual Journey

From the earliest days of the Church, Christians have prayed the Lord's Prayer as their daily prayer. If you do not pray the Liturgy of the Hours, pray the Lord's Prayer to begin each day, pray it again in the mid-morning, at noon, in the mid-afternoon, in the evening, and at bedtime.

For more ideas on ways that your family can live as disciples of Jesus, visit **www.BeMyDisciples.com**

Unit 6 **Review**

Name _____

A. Choose the Best Word

Fill in the blanks to complete each of the sentences.
Use the words from the word bank.

Sabbath	gossiping	Ten Commandments
lying	Great Commandment	Lord's Prayer

1. The _____ is to love God
   above all else and to love people as we love ourselves.

2. Keep holy the _____.

3. The _____ are the laws God
   gave us to help us live happy and holy lives.

4. The _____ is another name for the Our Father.

5. Acts of _____ and _____ create division
   between us and our neighbor.

B. Show What You Know

Match the items in Column A with those in Column B.

Column A

1. Fifth Commandment

2. the Our Father

3. Second Commandment

4. temperance

5. Eighth Commandment

Column B

____ **a.** teaches us that are we to use God's
name truthfully and with respect

____ **b.** to speak the truth means more than
not lying

____ **c.** teaches that we are to respect and
treat all life as sacred

____ **d.** the prayer that Jesus, our Lord,
taught us

____ **e.** This Cardinal Virtue enables a
person to express his or her feelings
appropriately.

C. Connect with Scripture

Reread the Scripture passage on page 189.
What connection do you see between this passage and
what you learned in this unit?

_____

_____

_____

D. Be a Disciple

1. *Review the four pages in this unit titled The Church Follows*
   Jesus. What person or ministry of the Church on these
   pages will inspire you to be a better disciple of Jesus?
   Explain your answer.

_____

_____

_____

2. *Work with a group. Review the four Disciple Power virtues,*
   or gifts, you have learned about in this unit. After jotting
   down your own ideas, share with the group practical
   ways that you will live these virtues day by day.

_____

_____

_____

WE CELEBRATE THE CHURCH YEAR

The Year of Grace

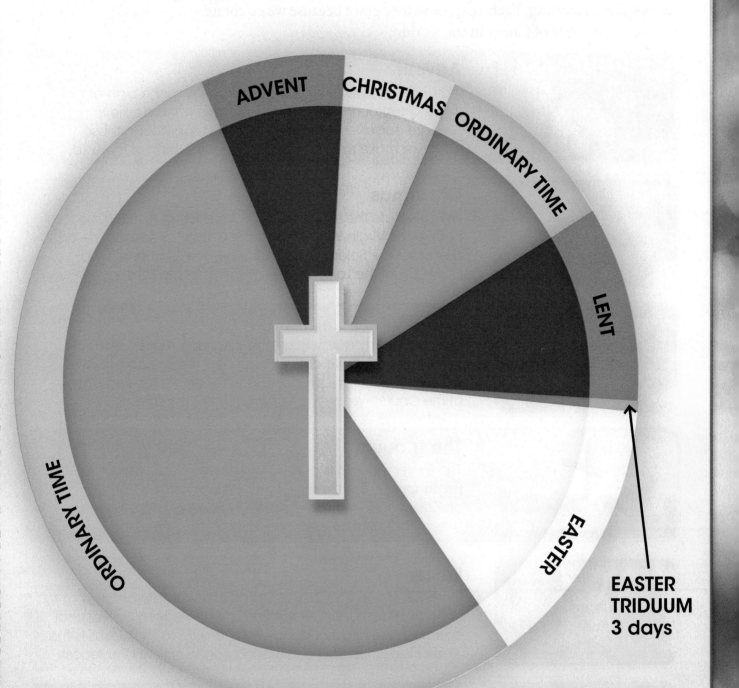

ADVENT

CHRISTMAS

ORDINARY TIME

LENT

EASTER

ORDINARY TIME

EASTER TRIDUUM 3 days

The Liturgical Year

While many things you see and hear at Mass are always the same, other things change. The readings change, as do the colors of banners and vestments. All of the changes help us know what part of the Church year we are celebrating. Each year is a year of grace because we celebrate the saving presence of Christ in the world.

Advent

We begin the liturgical year by anticipating the birth of Jesus Christ during the season of Advent. It is a time to prepare ourselves through prayer and sacrifice. In these ways, we make room in our hearts for the birth of the Lord.

Christmas

We celebrate the Incarnation of Jesus Christ through his birth to the Virgin Mary. During the Christmas season, we also celebrate the Solemnity of Mary, the Holy Mother of God, Epiphany of the Lord, and the Baptism of the Lord.

Lent

During the forty days of Lent, we pray and make personal sacrifices so that we can turn our hearts more completely toward God. We are preparing for the greatest celebration of the Church year—the Resurrection of the Lord.

The Triduum

The Easter Triduum is at the center of our year of worship. Beginning on the evening of Holy Thursday and ending on Easter Sunday evening, the Triduum is our three-day solemn celebration of the Paschal Mystery.

Easter

On each of the fifty days of Easter, we celebrate our new life in the Risen Christ. At the Easter Vigil, we light the Paschal candle in the midst of darkness to remind us that Jesus is the light of the world. Our celebration continues until Pentecost.

Ordinary Time

The rest of the Church year is called Ordinary Time. We celebrate many events in the life and ministry of Jesus. We also celebrate other great feasts and solemnities honoring Jesus, Mary, and the Saints.

Faith Focus
What is the Communion of Saints?

The Word of the Lord
Choose one of the readings for the Solemnity of All Saints. Ask your family to read it with you. Talk about the reading with them.

First Reading
Revelation 7:2–4, 9–14

Second Reading
1 John 3:1–3

Gospel
Matthew 5:1–12a

All Saints

The Church celebrates the Solemnity of All Saints on November 1. On this day, we honor all the disciples of Christ who have died and now share eternal happiness with God in Heaven. Some people have been officially recognized, or canonized, by the Church as Saints. These holy men and women are models of discipleship. Some are known for their lives of heroic virtue. Other Saints are known for the great sacrifices they made for their faith. Mary, the Mother of Jesus, is the greatest of all the Saints.

The Saints come from every time, every culture, every race, and from every nation on Earth. They were young and old, poor and wealthy. Some were great scholars while others never learned to read. Some Saints were from royal families; others were peasants. Many of these Saints have special feast days on the Church calendar to honor their unique contributions to the Church. There are also many Saints in Heaven who are known only to God. The Church teaches that anyone in Heaven is a saint. On the Solemnity of All Saints we honor all the Saints in Heaven, those we know and those we do not know.

On the Solemnity of All Saints, we rejoice in the Communion of Saints. The Communion of Saints includes all the faithful followers of Jesus, both living and dead—those in Heaven, those in Purgatory, and those living on Earth. When we pray in the Apostles' Creed that we believe in the Communion of Saints, we profess our belief that we are united as a people of faith.

Mary, Saint
Kateri Tekakwita,
Saint Martin de Porres,
Saint Rose of Lima

227

A Tapestry of Saints

In the three sections below, draw or write about three Saints whom you admire. You might include relatives who have died whom you and your family believe now live with God in Heaven. Beneath the images, tell about your favorite canonized Saint.

My Favorite Saint

_____

_____

_____

MY FAITH CHOICE

This week, I will imitate the discipleship of the Saints. I will

_____

_____

_____.

Pray, "Thank you God, for the holy men, women, and children who teach us how to live holy lives. Amen."

The Word of the Lord
These are the Gospel readings for the First Sunday of Advent. Choose this year's reading. Read and discuss it with your family.

Year A
Matthew 24:37–44

Year B
Mark 13:33–37

Year C
Luke 21:25–28, 34–36

What You See
The Advent wreath is made of evergreens with four candles. The candles are lighted successively each week of Advent to symbolize the coming of Christ, the Light of the world.

Advent

New things happen all the time. In the spring, we see new life everywhere. In school, we learn new things every day. Watching television, we learn things about the world we never knew before.

Advent begins a new year for Catholics. It is a new year and a new time to renew our love for God and for one another. It is a time to accept the Holy Spirit's invitation to make room in our hearts for Jesus.

John the Baptist announced, "Prepare the way of the Lord" (Luke 3:4). During the four weeks of Advent, we do just that. We listen to the Scripture readings each Sunday during Mass and are reminded to prepare for the coming of the Lord in our lives. The Lord came not only on that first Christmas but in every moment of every day. He will come again in glory at the end of time.

During Advent, we prepare our hearts every day to welcome Jesus. Then we will be ready to celebrate the birth of Jesus with great joy at Christmas.

Awaiting the Lord's Coming

Look up these stories in your Bible. Each is about a person whose words and example help prepare us for the Lord's coming. In the spaces, write the name of the person in each story.

Read Mark 1:1–8. Who first used the words:
"Behold, I am sending my messenger ahead of you;
he will prepare your way"?   Mark 1:2

_____

Read Luke 1:46–56. Who said yes to God and sang these words:
"My soul proclaims the greatness of the Lord"?   Luke 1:46

_____

Read Matthew 1:18–25. Who believed Isaiah's words:
"Behold, the virgin shall be with child and bear a son,
and they shall name him Emmanuel"?   Matthew 1:23

_____

Read Matthew 3:1–7. Who announced Jesus' coming and preached repentance by saying:
"Prepare the way of the Lord"?   Matthew 3:3

_____

MY FAITH CHOICE

This week, I will prepare the way of the Lord. I will

_____

_____

_____ .

Pray, "Father in Heaven, help me to welcome Jesus, the Light of the world, into my heart. Amen."

The Word of the Lord
These are the readings for the Solemnity of the Immaculate Conception. Choose one and read it. Talk about the reading with your family.

First Reading:
Genesis 3:9–15, 20

Second Reading:
Ephesians 1:3–6, 11–12

Gospel:
Luke 1:26–38

The Immaculate Conception

During the four weeks of Advent, the Church celebrates a time of anticipation and preparation to welcome Jesus into our hearts at Christmas.

Each year during Advent, the Church celebrates the unique gift God gave to Mary. Long before Jesus was born, God prepared Mary to be the Mother of his only Son.

On December 8, the Church celebrates the Solemnity of the Immaculate Conception of the Blessed Virgin Mary. Mary was conceived without Original Sin and was filled with grace from the first moment of her life. We call this belief the Immaculate Conception.

Mary, Model of Holiness

Mary never lost the gift of her original holiness. She remained sinless during her entire life. She always chose to obey God's will. She lived as a faithful child of God. Because of this, Mary is the model of a true disciple and the perfect example of Christian holiness.

Mary is our greatest Saint. She now lives in Heaven. We can pray to her, and she prays for us. Her prayers help strengthen us to do God's will and to avoid sin.

Mary prays that we will live as true disciples of her Son as she did. She prays that we will live with her and all the Saints in Heaven. We raise our voices to pray, "Holy Mother of God, make us worthy of the promises of Christ" (based on the Litany of the Blessed Virgin Mary).

Mary and Jesus, mosaic artwork from Thailand

Saying "Yes!" to God

Think of the times when it has been hard for you to obey God's will. In the space, write or draw about some of the times you said yes to God.

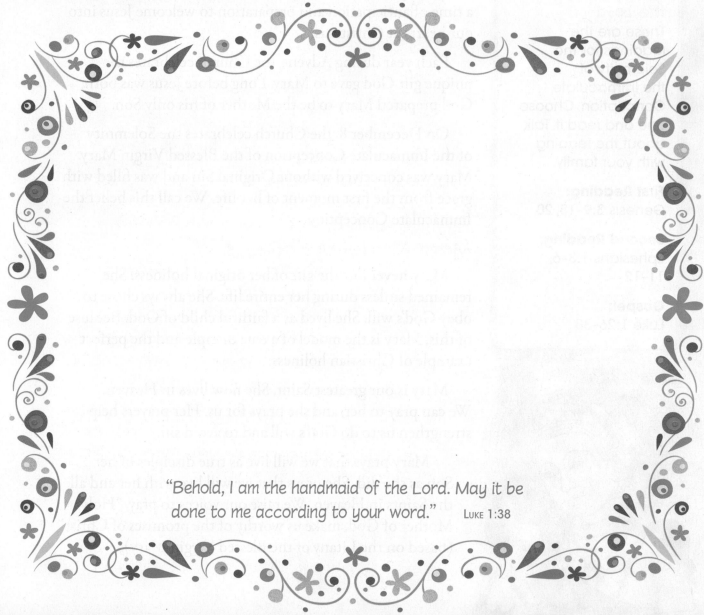

"Behold, I am the handmaid of the Lord. May it be done to me according to your word." LUKE 1:38

MY FAITH CHOICE

This week, I will follow Mary's example of discipleship. I will

_____

_____

_____.

Pray, "Mary, Mother Immaculate, help us to avoid sin and to live holy lives. Amen."

Faith Focus
Why does the Church honor Our Lady of Guadalupe?

The Word of the Lord
Choose one of the readings for the Feast of Our Lady of Guadalupe. Read and discuss the reading with your family.

Isaiah 7:10–14
Galatians 2:4–7
Luke 1:39–48

Our Lady of Guadalupe

We honor Mary's love as our mother in a special way each year on December 12 when we celebrate the Feast of Our Lady of Guadalupe. This feast recalls the appearance of the Blessed Virgin Mary in A.D. 1531 to a native Mexican peasant, Juan Diego.

One day, Juan saw a vision of Mary dressed as an Aztec Indian princess. Mary gave him a message for his bishop. The "Lady," as Juan called her, wanted a church built on the hill where she appeared. She promised to help anyone who visited the church and prayed to her.

Juan delivered the message, but the bishop did not believe him. Mary gave Juan a sign for the bishop. She pointed to a plot of blooming roses, a surprising sight in winter. Juan gathered the roses in his cloak and hurried to the bishop's house.

When he opened his cloak, he saw that Mary had given the bishop an even more wondrous sign. Inside the cloak, a beautiful image of Mary, looking just as Juan described, had replaced the roses. The bishop immediately ordered a shrine to be built.

The Basilica of Our Lady of Guadalupe is visited by millions of people each year. On her feast day, we pray, "[May] we who rejoice in Our Lady of Guadalupe live united and at peace in this world until the day of the Lord dawns in glory" (Prayer after Communion, *Roman Missal*).

Our Lady of Guadalupe is a reminder that God cares for all people, especially the poor and suffering. Mary is the mother of all God's children, in all places and all times.

Making a Pilgrimage

A pilgrimage is a prayer journey to a shrine or other holy place. Prayerfully make a virtual pilgrimage to the Basilica of Our Lady of Guadalupe. "Walk" through the maze below to the shrine at the center. As you travel, copy the letters you find on the lines below.

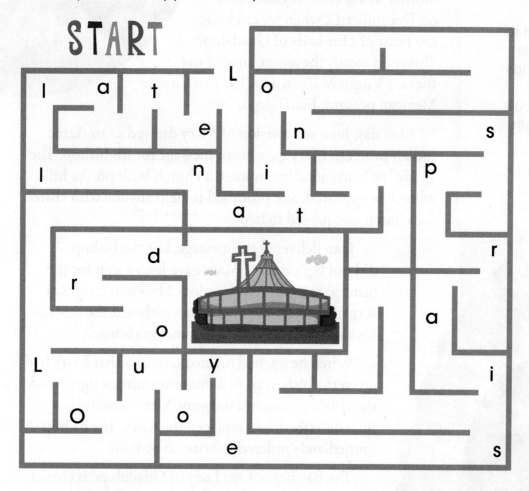

START

"
_____

_____ , _____ "

BASED ON THE RESPONSORIAL PSALM, FEAST OF OUR LADY OF GUADALUPE

MY FAITH CHOICE

This week, I will show respect for people in my school and my family. I will

_____

_____

_____

Pray, "Our Lady of Guadalupe, help me to care for people in need. Amen."

Christmas

Imagine a world filled with peace and harmony. Think of a world in which no one is homeless and all children eat well every day. What would that world be like?

The Son of God became one of us and lived among us to show us how to build such a world. It is a task we will need to work at until Jesus comes again at the end of time.

During the Christmas season, we remember and celebrate that "a savior has been born for you who is Messiah and Lord" (Luke 2:11). Joining with the angels, we sing:

"Glory to God in the highest
and on earth peace to those on whom his
favor rests." LUKE 2:14

We proclaim that Jesus is the Prince of Peace, who makes all things new. Announcing the kingdom of peace, Isaiah says:

The calf and the young lion shall browse
together,
with a little child to guide them.

ISAIAH 11:6

When Jesus was born, God's plan for all people to live in peace was born again too. All creatures, even those who now treat each other as enemies, are called to live together in peace. Jesus is the Prince of Peace. With him, we work to build a world of peace. We prepare for the coming of the Kingdom of God.

Making All Things New

Here is a prayer you and your family may use to bless a Christmas tree. Use it now to bless your classroom tree or wreath.

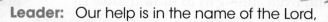

Leader: Our help is in the name of the Lord,

All: **who made Heaven and Earth.**

Reader 1: Sing to the Lord, bless his name.

All: **Sing to the Lord a new song.**

Reader 2: Bring gifts and enter his courts; bow down to the Lord, splendid in holiness.

All: **Sing to the Lord a new song.**

Reader 3: Let the heavens be glad and the earth rejoice; . . . / Then let all the trees of the forest rejoice / before the LORD who comes, who comes to govern the earth, / To govern the world with justice / and the peoples with faithfulness.   PSALM 96:11–13

Leader: Let us pray:
Bless these boughs and all the trees of the forest. May their green life remind us of eternal life. May their decorations remind us to celebrate your coming among us as light and joy. We ask this in the name of Jesus, your Son, born of the Virgin Mary for us.

All: **Amen.**

This week, I will work to build peace in the world. I will

_____

_____

_____

Pray, "Jesus, Prince of Peace, help us prepare for the Kingdom of God. Amen."

The Word of the Lord
Choose one of the readings for the Solemnity of Mary, the Holy Mother of God. Read and discuss it with your family.

First Reading
Numbers 6:22–27

Second Reading
Galatians 4:4–7

Gospel
Luke 2:16–21

Mary, the Holy Mother of God

Throughout her history, the Church has honored the Blessed Virgin Mary under many different titles. Each of these title professes in some way the faith and teachings of the Catholic Church about Mary. Some of her titles include "Mother of Jesus," "Mother of Peace," and "Queen of Heaven."

On January 1 each year, the Church celebrates the belief that Mary is truly the Mother of God. We believe this because Jesus is true God and true man. Because Mary is the Mother of Jesus, the Church teaches that she is the Mother of God.

We call Mary *Theotokos*. The word *theotokos* is a Greek word that means "God-bearer." By saying yes to being the Mother of Jesus, Mary agreed to cooperate in God's plan of Salvation for all people. She brought Jesus into this world through the power of the Holy Spirit.

Mary, our Blessed Mother, is the first disciple of her Son. As disciples of Jesus Christ, we are also called to bring God to others. We do this by the example of our lives. When we are kind and merciful, we bring God to others. When we help the poor or teach others about Jesus, we bring God to others.

The Solemnity of Mary, the Holy Mother of God, is a holy day of obligation. When we participate in Mass on this day and receive Holy Communion, we receive the grace to live as disciples of Jesus. We begin the year with God's blessings. When we say yes to God's grace and glorify him by our lives, we truly honor Mary, the Mother of God. This is what she prays that we will always do.

Saying "Yes" to God

In the space below, create a reminder to honor Mary as the Mother of God. You may draw, write original words of your own, or add a Scripture quotation about Mary.

MY FAITH CHOICE

This week, I will bring God to others by

_____

_____

_____ .

Pray, "Mother of God, help me to grow in discipleship by following your example. Amen."

The Word of the Lord
This is the Gospel reading for the Solemnity of the Epiphany of the Lord. Find it in the Bible and read and discuss it with your family.

Years A, B, and C
Matthew 2:1–12

Epiphany

When Jesus was born in Bethlehem, three wise men known as Magi traveled from the East searching for a newborn king. They were led to Jerusalem by the light of a great star rising in the sky. They said to King Herod, "Where is the newborn king of the Jews? We saw his star at its rising and have come to do him homage" (Matthew 2:2).

The wise men believed the star was a sign that a new ruler had been born. They wanted to honor the child with their presence and their gifts.

The wise men followed the star until it stopped over the place in Bethlehem where Jesus had been born. Here they found the Christ Child with his mother, Mary. "They prostrated themselves and did him homage. Then they opened their treasures and offered him gifts of gold, frankincense, and myrrh" (Matthew 2:11).

In time, believers came to know that Jesus was a different kind of ruler. He came to bring the rule of peace, love, and justice into the world. He came to save all people from sin and death. He brought the light of Salvation into the world.

Like the Magi who traveled to Bethlehem to adore the newborn king, we also come to adore Christ at every Mass. We receive him in the Eucharist when we share the Body and Blood of Christ.

At Mass we pray, "A holy day has dawned upon us: Come, you nations, and adore the Lord, for a great light has come down upon the earth" (Entrance Antiphon, Weekdays of Christmas Time [Monday], *Roman Missal*).

Let Your Light Shine

There are many places in our families, our communities, and in the world where people are suffering. How might the light of Christ shine in these dark places of the world? Write your examples on the star's rays below. Share your thoughts with your class and with your family.

See, darkness covers the earth,
and thick clouds cover the peoples;
But upon you the LORD shines,
and over you appears his glory.

ISAIAH 60: 2

MY FAITH CHOICE

This week, I will bring Jesus' light into the world. I will

_____
_____
_____.

 Pray, "Jesus, let your light shine in me! Amen."

What can we do
as a sign of turning
away from sin and
back to God?

The Word of the Lord

This is the Gospel
reading for Ash
Wednesday. Read
and discuss it with
your family.

Gospel
Matthew 6:1–6,
16–18

Ash Wednesday

The season of Lent developed in the early Church as the
final period of preparation for people who wanted to join the
Church. They had spent time learning what it means to be
followers of Jesus. They had practiced the traditions of prayer,
fasting, and almsgiving as all of Jesus' followers did. Finally,
after two or three years of preparation, they were welcomed
into the Church at the Easter Vigil.

Today, the entire season of Lent is still a special time of
preparation for people who want to join the Church. The whole
Church shares in the preparation of the elect, so called because
they have elected to begin the final period of preparation for
Baptism. Fasting, prayer, and almsgiving, or doing good, are
important for all Catholics. Those who are already baptized are
called to be examples and living witnesses of what it means to be
a baptized follower of Jesus.

Likewise, the elect have a role with the members of the
Church. Their desire to become united with Christ and his
Church should awaken in every Catholic a deeper desire to live
our faith every day.

The period of preparation for Easter begins on Ash
Wednesday. The ashes that are traced on our foreheads remind
us that Jesus calls us to turn away from sin and to devote
the next six weeks to praying, fasting, and doing works of
charity. These are called the disciplines of Lent. They help us
to turn our hearts toward the sacrifice of Jesus so that we can
experience the joy of Easter. This change of heart is called
conversion.

As the ashes are blessed for Ash Wednesday all over the
world, we hear: "O God, who are moved with acts of
humility and respond with forgiveness to works of
penance, lend your merciful ear to our prayers"
(Blessing and Distribution of Ashes, Ash
Wednesday, *Roman Missal*).

Ash Wednesday Challenge

On Ash Wednesday, after the priest blesses the ashes, he places them on the foreheads of those who come forward and repeats a verse based on the words of Jesus in Mark 1:15.

Unscramble the words below to reveal that verse. When you discover the words of the verse, write them on the lines. In the space below the words, design a poster for your parish calling all its members to observe Lent. You may incorporate the words you wrote.

hTe goidKnm fo oOGd si ta nhda. ptneRe, nad iebvele ni eth solegp.

_____

_____

242

Faith Focus
Why do we call Lent the Church's springtime?

The Word of the Lord
These are the Gospel readings for the First Sunday of Lent. Choose this year's reading. Read and discuss it with your family.

Year A
Matthew 4:1–11

Year B
Mark 1:12–15

Year C
Luke 4:1–13

What You See
During Lent, the color of the vestments is purple or violet. Purple is a symbol of sorrow and penance. We remember Jesus' Passion and prepare to celebrate his Resurrection.

Lent

Spring is a season of rebirth and renewal. During springtime, flowers begin to grow. Leaves begin to sprout and cover the bare branches of winter. Ice and snow begin to melt. Flowing down mountainsides, streams fill the forests with sounds of new life. Nature begins its long return from death to new life.

Lent is the Church's sacred springtime. It is a season of spiritual rebirth and renewal. It is the time when people make final preparations to receive new life in Christ through Baptism. It is a time when the baptized renew their new life in Christ.

During Lent, we walk with Jesus and stand with him as we reflect on his Passion and Death. Lent is also a time when we look forward to the Resurrection at Easter.

During Lent, we strengthen our decision to be faithful to the Great Commandment, which calls us to love God and love our neighbor as ourselves. We make decisions that increase our efforts to

- give alms, or share our time, talents, and other gifts with which God has blessed us
- fast, or eat less, and share in the sufferings of Jesus;
- pray, or talk things over with God more often

Learning About Lent

Throughout Lent, we make private decisions to fulfill our baptismal promise. We also join with other members of the Church to work and pray together.

Find a classmate who can help you complete these statements about Lent. Write your answers in the spaces provided and have your classmate put his or her initials on the lines. You may need to research some of the answers to these questions at home.

The color used to celebrate Lent is

_____. Initials: _____

A Lenten devotion is

_____. Initials: _____

Lent lasts this many days:

_____. Initials: _____

Lent begins on

_____. Initials: _____

Lent ends on

_____. Initials: _____

Lent is a season of

_____. Initials: _____

MY FAITH CHOICE

The season of Lent is a time of sacrifice, rebirth, and renewal. To increase my Lenten efforts, I will

_____

_____.

 Pray every day, "Lord, help me to live the new life I received at Baptism. Amen."

Faith Focus
Why do we say
that Holy Week is a
celebration of being
forgiven and growing
in forgiveness?

The Word of the Lord

These are the Gospel readings for Palm Sunday of the Passion of the Lord. Choose this year's reading. Read and discuss it with your family.

Year A
Matthew 26:14–27:66
or Matthew 27:11–54

Year B
Mark 14:1–15:47
or Mark 15:1–39

Year C
Luke 22:14–23:56
or Luke 23:1–49

What You See

Palm branches are blessed, carried in procession, and held high as we listen to the reading of "The Passion of our Lord Jesus Christ."

Palm Sunday of the Passion of the Lord

Forgiving others and being forgiven by others are two very important actions. A forgiving word or look, a hug or a smile for someone who has been hurt helps people grow closer. An apology to someone you have hurt can make a friendship stronger. Forgiveness, reconciliation, and new life are essential to the life of a disciple of Jesus.

Holy Week places us at the center of the story of God's plan of forgiveness. On Palm Sunday of the Passion of the Lord, we listen as Jesus was cheered when he rode into Jerusalem on a donkey. Only a few days later, the cheering of the crowds would turn into jeering. Jesus would be crucified so we could be forgiven.

Throughout his life on Earth, Jesus taught that we are to have forgiving hearts. We are to forgive as God forgives—not once, not twice, but over and over again. We are to be merciful and forgiving—"not seven times but seventy-seven times"—as many times as necessary. (Matthew 18:22).

Celebrating Forgiveness

Holy Week is a good time to reflect on how we are living as forgiving people. We need to ask the Holy Spirit to strengthen and guide us to act as a forgiving people. As disciples of Jesus we continue his work of forgiveness throughout our lives. Pray this service of forgiveness together.

Leader: My friends, we gather to seek forgiveness and to forgive one another as God has forgiven us. Let us listen to God's promise of forgiveness.

Reader: *Read Ezekiel 36:25–28*

Leader: Give thanks to the Lord for his goodness.

All: God's mercy lasts forever.

Leader: The Lord lifts the burdens of our sin.

All: God's mercy lasts forever.

Leader: The Lord grants us the strength and courage to forgive and to seek forgiveness.

All: God's mercy lasts forever.

Leader: As a sign of thanks for God's forgiveness and our decision to try to live as forgiving people, let us pray the Our Father together.

All: Our Father . . .

Leader: Father, we bless you for your forgiving love. Look kindly on us. Lead us to peace with you and with one another. Amen.

Let us now offer a sign of peace to one another.

All: Amen.
(Everyone shares a sign of peace.)

MY FAITH CHOICE

I will imitate Jesus' example of mercy and forgiveness. This week, I will

_____

_____

_____ .

Pray that we will forgive others as God forgives us.

Faith Focus
How does taking part in the liturgy on Holy Thursday help us strengthen our love for God and for one another?

The Word of the Lord
These are the Scripture readings for the Evening Mass of the Lord's Supper on Holy Thursday. Choose one reading. Read and discuss it with your family.

First Reading
Exodus 12:1–8, 11–14

Second Reading
1 Corinthians 11:23–26

Gospel
John 13:1–15

Triduum: Holy Thursday

There is a saying that goes, "You can't judge a book by its cover." In other words, you cannot know what the book is really about until you read it. The same might be said about people. We really cannot know someone simply by looking at him or her. We need to listen to them and see them in action.

The last three days of Holy Week are called the Triduum, a word that means "a period of three days." The Church's celebration of the Triduum includes the celebration of the Evening Mass of the Lord's Supper on Holy Thursday, the celebration of the Lord's Passion on Good Friday, Easter Vigil on Holy Saturday night, and the liturgy on Easter Sunday. The Triduum ends with the celebration of Evening Prayer on Easter Sunday evening.

On Holy Thursday, after we listen to the story of the Last Supper proclaimed to us, the priest wraps a cloth around his waist. Kneeling before twelve members of the assembly, he washes and dries their feet. This reminds us that we are to do what Jesus did. Each day, we are to "wash one another's feet." We are to look for opportunities to be kind and generous. We are to treat everyone fairly and respectfully. We are to serve one another as Jesus did.

After washing the disciples' feet, Jesus returned to the table and shared the Last Supper with them. He took bread and said, "This is my body." Then he took the cup of wine and said, "This is the cup of my blood." We remember Jesus' greatest act of love for us. We share in the memorial of the sacrifice of his life for our Salvation.

The words and actions of our lives, as those of Jesus' life did, are to show our love for God and for one another. We are to live as Christians in addition to calling ourselves Christians.

No Greater Love

Jesus tells us to love one another unselfishly. Act out and discuss this short play. Do you think there are many people today who would act like the two brothers? Why or why not?

Narrator: *Once upon a time, two brothers farmed together. They divided everything evenly. But one day this changed.*

Unmarried Brother: My brother is married and has children. He should have more than half of the wheat crop.

Married Brother: My brother is not married. He will have no one to take care of him in his old age. He should have more than half of the wheat crop.

Narrator: *So on the night of the new moon, the brother who was not married secretly carried sacks of wheat into his married brother's storage. The married brother did the same for his unmarried brother! This went on night after night.*

Unmarried Brother: Hmmmm. I have the same amount of wheat.

Married Brother: Hmmmm. I have the same amount of wheat.

Narrator: *One dark night the brothers ran into each other. They dropped their sacks of wheat. They paused. They understood. They hugged each other. They laughed for joy.*

The place where they met is a holy place. For where love is, there is God.

BASED ON A HASSIDIC TALE

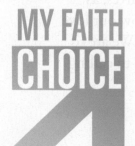

MY FAITH CHOICE

This week, I will be kind, generous, and fair. I will

_____

_____

_____ .

Pray, "Dear Jesus, plant the seeds of love in my heart that I may show my love for others as you do. Amen."

The Word of the Lord
These are the Scripture readings for Good Friday. Choose one reading. Read and discuss it with your family.

First Reading
Isaiah 52:13–53:12

Second Reading
Hebrews 4:14–16, 5:7–9

Gospel
John 18:1–19:42

Triduum: Good Friday

We are surrounded by symbols. A symbol is an object or action that has a special meaning for us. For example, the flag of our nation is a symbol of the values on which our nation is built. It represents the people who have built and continue to build our nation, especially those who have given their lives for us.

The cross, or crucifix, is the central symbol of Christianity. On Good Friday, Catholics around the world gather and pray:

> We adore your Cross, O Lord, we praise and glorify your holy Resurrection, for behold, because of the wood of a tree joy has come to the whole world (Adoration of the Holy Cross, Good Friday, *Roman Missal*).

Dressed in red vestments, the ministers silently enter the church. When they reach the altar steps, they lie facedown for a moment of reflection. Rising, they go to their places and join us in listening to the retelling of the story of God's promise of Salvation and its fulfillment in Jesus Christ.

After the Liturgy of the Word concludes, the deacon or priest enters the church and walks through the assembly. Holding the crucifix up high, he sings aloud three times, "Behold the wood of the Cross, on which hung the salvation of the world." Each time we respond, "Come, let us adore."

Everyone in the assembly then approaches the Cross and reverences it as the choir sings an appropriate song.

The cross stands for the life-giving sacrifice of Jesus. It reminds us of the love of Jesus for his Father and for all people. It stands for the life that we who have been baptized into the Death-Resurrection of Christ are called to live.

Making the Right Choice

Make a list of a few of the many choices you have made or might be asked to make each day because of your love for God and others. Rate each choice as 1, easy; 2, not so easy; or 3, really difficult. Circle your most difficult choice. With a partner, act out a situation in which you have the courage to make the correct choice.

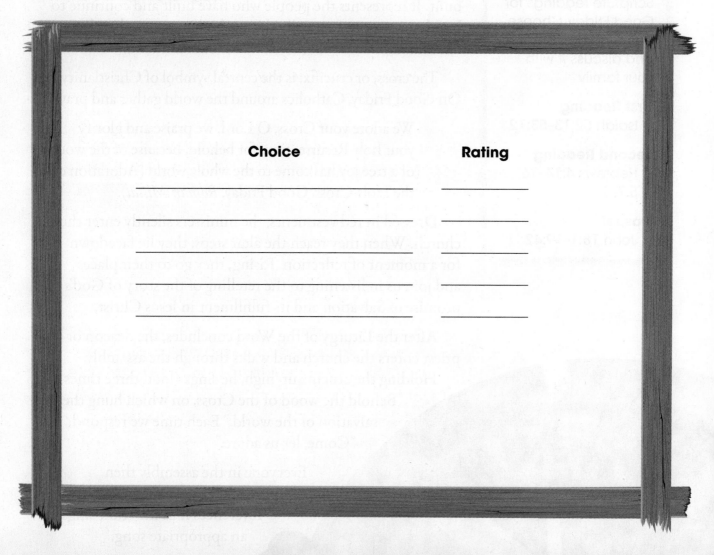

Choice	Rating
_____	_____
_____	_____
_____	_____
_____	_____

MY FAITH CHOICE

This week, I will remember that the cross is a symbol of Jesus' love. I will

_____

_____

_____

Pray, "Lord, help me to do your will. Amen."

There is something special about a farm when crops begin to grow and fill a field. The air is filled with new scents as the smell of winter dirt is transformed into the fresh aroma of new, green life. What signs of spring and new life fill the places where you live and play?

Signs of the new life we have in Christ fill our churches during Easter. At the Easter Vigil Mass, the newly lighted Easter candle stands tall and shines in the darkness. Standing and holding lighted candles that flood the church with light, the worshiping assembly listens as the Church proclaims the Exsultet:

Exult, let them exult, the hosts of heaven,
exult, let Angel ministers of God exult,
let the trumpet of salvation
sound aloud our mighty King's triumph!

Everyone rejoices. Easter is the Church's season of new life. On Easter Sunday, the Church around the world breaks into joyful song and sings, "This is the day the Lord has made; let us be glad and rejoice in it" (Easter Proclamation).

We fill our homes and lives with signs of joy and new life. Flowers and candles decorate our homes. Special foods, such as Easter breads and colored eggs, remind us that this is a life-giving feast. Throughout the day and for fifty days afterward, our celebration of Easter continues. We sing aloud and in the quiet of our hearts, "Alleluia! Alleluia! Alleluia!"

Alleluia! Christ Is Risen!

Design an Easter banner in this space. Then, using your
design, work with your family to make the banner and hang
it in your home.

MY FAITH CHOICE

Easter is a time to celebrate the gift of new life. I will celebrate by

_____

_____

_____

Pray, "This is the day the Lord has made. Let us rejoice and be glad.
Alleluia!"

Faith Focus
Why is the Ascension of the Lord a time of joy?

The Word of the Lord
Each year, this is the Second Reading for the Ascension of the Lord. Ask your family to read it with you. Talk about the reading with them.

Second Reading
Ephesians 1:17–23

Ascension of the Lord

Forty days after Easter, the Church celebrates the Ascension of the Lord. On this day, we celebrate Jesus Christ's entry into Heaven. We recall this glorious day, the culmination of the Paschal Mystery, when we pray the Nicene Creed:

He ascended into heaven
   and is seated at the right hand
   of the Father.

He will come again in glory to judge
   the living and the dead. . . .

During the forty days after his Resurrection on Easter Sunday, Jesus appeared to his disciples on many occasions. He shared meals with them and continued to teach them. He promised to send the Holy Spirit to be with them always. Jesus gave the Apostles the mission to "make disciples of all nations, baptizing them in the name of the Father, and of the Son, and of the holy Spirit, teaching them to observe all that I have commanded you" (Matthew 28:19–20a).

Saint Luke describes what happened next:

Then he led them [out] as far as Bethany, raised his hands, and blessed them. As he blessed them he parted from them and was taken up to heaven. They did him homage and then returned to Jerusalem with great joy."
                                                                    Luke 24:50–52

On the Solemnity of the Ascension of the Lord, we follow the example of the Apostles. We celebrate the Eucharist. We praise God for his Son, Jesus, who lives and reigns with God in Heaven. We are filled with joy for the Savior who sacrificed his life on the Cross, rose from the dead, and returned to his Father in Heaven to prepare a place for us so that we may one day be with him forever in the Kingdom of God.

Jesus Our Joy

On the banner below, draw a symbol that will remind you of the Ascension of the Lord. Pray the words on the banner with your class before you begin to draw. After you draw your symbol, decorate the banner.

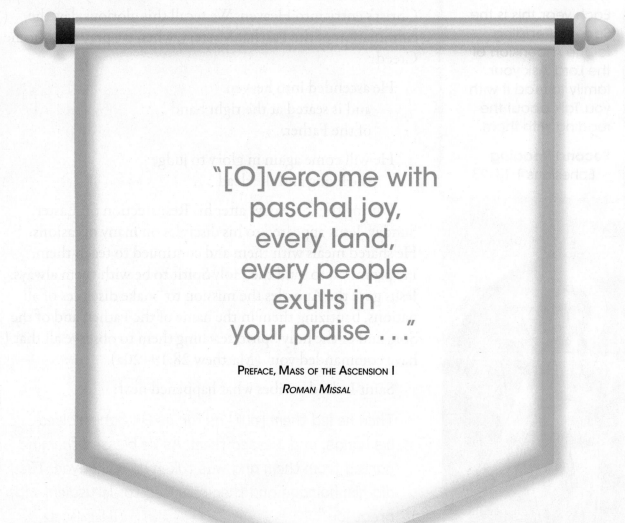

"[O]vercome with
paschal joy,
every land,
every people
exults in
your praise . . ."

PREFACE, MASS OF THE ASCENSION I
ROMAN MISSAL

MY FAITH CHOICE

This week, I will celebrate the Ascension of the Lord by bringing joy to someone. I will

_____

_____

_____.

Pray, reflecting on the words of Jesus: "I am with you always, until the end of the age" (Matthew 28:20b).

Faith Focus
How does celebrating Pentecost each year remind us of our Baptism?

The Word of the Lord
These are the Gospel readings for Pentecost. Choose this year's reading. Read and discuss it with your family.

Year A
John 20:19–23

Year B
John 20:19–23 or John 15:26–27, 16:12–15

Year C
John 20:19–23 or John 14:15–16, 23–26

Pentecost

When we play a game, we feel team spirit. That spirit gives us the courage and enthusiasm to do our best. When do you feel a spirit that moves you to be courageous or generous or kind?

After the Risen Lord ascended to his Father in Heaven, his disciples gathered in a house in Jerusalem. There, on the Jewish feast of Pentecost, a great wind filled the room. Flames, like tongues of fire, settled above them. This was a sign that the Holy Spirit had come to the disciples as Jesus promised. The Holy Spirit filled the disciples with joy and courage.

When Peter preached about Jesus to people who had come to Jerusalem from many countries, each person understood Peter in his or her own language. Many listened, and the Holy Spirit moved them to be baptized.

Each year, the Church celebrates Pentecost. On Pentecost, we stand and sing:

Come, Holy Spirit, fill the hearts of the faithful and kindle in them the fire of your love.

GOSPEL ANTIPHON, PENTECOST

Christians are temples of the Holy Spirit. The Holy Spirit is so close to us that he lives within us. Each Pentecost, we remember that we have received the gift of the Holy Spirit at Baptism. We ask the Holy Spirit to fill us with his gifts to live our Baptism.

Fruits of the Holy Spirit

Saint Paul named nine signs, or fruits, of living a life guided by the Holy Spirit. Read Galatians 5:22–23 to discover these signs. List them in the space below.

_____	_____
_____	_____
_____	_____
_____	_____
_____	

MY FAITH CHOICE

This week, I will remember that I am a temple of the Holy Spirit. I will

_____

_____

_____.

Pray, "Come, Holy Spirit, kindle in me the fire of your love. Amen."

Catholic Prayers and Practices

Sign of the Cross

In the name of the Father,
and of the Son,
and of the Holy Spirit. Amen.

Signum Crucis

In nómine Patris,
et Fílii,
et Spíritus Sancti. Amen.

Our Father

Our Father, who art in heaven,
hallowed be thy name;
thy kingdom come,
thy will be done
on earth as it is in heaven.
Give us this day our daily bread,
and forgive us our trespasses,
as we forgive those who trespass
   against us;
and lead us not into temptation,
but deliver us from evil.
Amen.

Pater Noster

Pater noster, qui es in cælis:
sanctificétur nomen tuum;
advéniat regnum tuum;
fiat volúntas tua,
sicut in cælo, et in terra.
Panem nostrum cotidiánum
   da nobis hódie;
et dimítte nobis débita nostra,
sicut et nos dimíttimus debitóribus
   nostris;
et ne nos indúcas in tentatiónem;
sed líbera nos a malo. Amen.

Glory Be (Doxology)

Glory be to the Father
and to the Son
and to the Holy Spirit,
as it was in the beginning
is now, and ever shall be
world without end. Amen.

Gloria Patri

Glória Patri
et Fílio
et Spirítui Sancto.
Sicut erat in princípio,
et nunc et semper
et in sæcula sæculórum. Amen.

The Hail Mary

Hail, Mary, full of grace,
the Lord is with thee.
Blessed art thou among women
and blessed is the fruit
   of thy womb, Jesus.
Holy Mary, Mother of God,
pray for us sinners,
now and at the hour of our death.
Amen.

Ave, Maria

Ave, María, grátia plena,
Dóminus tecum.
Benedícta tu in muliéribus,
et benedíctus fructus ventris tui, Iesus.
Sancta María, Mater Dei,
ora pro nobis peccatóribus,
nunc et in hora mortis nostræ.
Amen.

Apostles' Creed

(from the *Roman Missal*)

I believe in God,
the Father almighty,
Creator of heaven and earth,
and in Jesus Christ, his only Son,
  our Lord,

(At the words that follow, up to and including the Virgin Mary, all bow.)

who was conceived by the Holy Spirit,
born of the Virgin Mary,
suffered under Pontius Pilate,
was crucified, died and was buried;
he descended into hell;
on the third day he rose again
  from the dead;
he ascended into heaven,
and is seated at the right hand of God
  the Father almighty;
from there he will come to judge
  the living and the dead.

I believe in the Holy Spirit,
the holy catholic Church,
the communion of saints,
the forgiveness of sins,
the resurrection of the body,
and life everlasting. Amen.

Nicene Creed

(from the *Roman Missal*)

I believe in one God,
the Father almighty,
maker of heaven and earth,
of all things visible and invisible.

I believe in one Lord Jesus Christ,
the Only Begotten Son of God,
born of the Father before all ages.

God from God, Light from Light,
true God from true God,
begotten, not made, consubstantial
  with the Father;
through him all things were made.
For us men and for our salvation
he came down from heaven,

(At the words that follow up to and including and became man, *all bow.)*

and by the Holy Spirit was incarnate
  of the Virgin Mary,
and became man.

For our sake he was crucified under
  Pontius Pilate,
he suffered death and was buried,
and rose again on the third day
in accordance with the Scriptures.
He ascended into heaven
and is seated at the right hand of the Father.
He will come again in glory
to judge the living and the dead
and his kingdom will have no end.

I believe in the Holy Spirit, the Lord,
  the giver of life,
who proceeds from the Father and the
  Son,
who with the Father and the Son is
  adored and glorified,
who has spoken through the prophets.

I believe in one, holy, catholic and
  apostolic Church.
I confess one Baptism for the forgiveness
  of sins
and I look forward to the
resurrection of the dead
and the life of the world to come. Amen.

Morning Prayer

Dear God,
as I begin this day,
keep me in your love and care.
Help me to live as your child today.
Bless me, my family, and my friends
    in all we do.
Keep us all close to you. Amen.

Grace Before Meals

Bless us, O Lord,
    and these thy gifts,
which we are about to receive
    from thy bounty,
    through Christ our Lord.
Amen.

Grace After Meals

We give thee thanks,
    for all thy benefits, almighty God,
who lives and reigns forever.
Amen.

Evening Prayer

Dear God,
I thank you for today.
Keep me safe throughout the night.
Thank you for all the good I did today.
I am sorry for what I have chosen
    to do wrong.
Bless my family and friends. Amen.

A Vocation Prayer

God, I know you will call me
for special work in my life.
Help me follow Jesus each day
and be ready to answer your call. Amen.

Prayer to the Holy Spirit

Come, Holy Spirit, fill the hearts
    of your faithful.
And kindle in them the
    fire of your love.
Send forth your Spirit and
    they shall be created.
And you will renew the
    face of the earth. Amen.

Act of Contrition

My God,
I am sorry for my sins
    with all my heart.
In choosing to do wrong
and failing to do good,
I have sinned against you,
whom I should love above all things.
I firmly intend, with your help,
to do penance,
to sin no more,
and to avoid whatever leads me to sin.
Our Savior Jesus Christ
suffered and died for us.
In his name, my God, have mercy. Amen.

The Beatitudes

"Blessed are the poor in spirit,
    for theirs is the kingdom of heaven.
Blessed are they who mourn,
    for they will be comforted.
Blessed are the meek,
    for they will inherit the land.
Blessed are they who hunger
        and thirst for righteousness,
    for they will be satisfied.
Blessed are the merciful,
    for they will be shown mercy.
Blessed are the clean of heart,
    for they will see God.
Blessed are the peacemakers,
    for they will be called children of God.
Blessed are they who are persecuted for
        the sake of righteousness,
    for theirs is the kingdom of heaven."

MATTHEW 5:3–10

The Angelus

Leader: The Angel of the Lord declared unto Mary,

Response: And she conceived of the Holy Spirit.

All: Hail, Mary . . .

Leader: Behold the handmaid of the Lord,

Response: Be it done unto me according to your Word.

All: Hail, Mary . . .

Leader: And the Word was made flesh,

Response: And dwelt among us.

All: Hail, Mary . . .

Leader: Pray for us, O Holy Mother of God,

Response: That we may be made worthy of the promises of Christ.

Leader: Let us pray.

All: Pour forth, we beseech you, O Lord, your grace into our hearts; that we, to whom the Incarnation of Christ your Son was made known by the message of an Angel, may by his Passion and Cross be brought to the glory of his Resurrection. Through the same Christ our Lord. Amen.

The Ten Commandments

1. I am the LORD your God: you shall not have strange gods before me.
2. You shall not take the name of the LORD your God in vain.
3. Remember to keep holy the LORD's Day.
4. Honor your father and your mother.
5. You shall not kill.
6. You shall not commit adultery.
7. You shall not steal.
8. You shall not lie.
9. You shall not covet your neighbor's wife.
10. You shall not covet your neighbor's goods.

BASED ON EXODUS 20:2–3, 7–17

Precepts of the Church

1. Participate in Mass on Sundays and holy days of obligation, and rest from unnecessary work.
2. Confess sins at least once a year.
3. Receive Holy Communion at least during the Easter season.
4. Observe the prescribed days of fasting and abstinence.
5. Provide for the material needs of the Church, according to one's abilities.

The Great Commandment

"You shall love the Lord, your God, with all your heart, with all your soul, and with all your mind. . . . You shall love your neighbor as yourself."

MATTHEW 22:37, 39

The Law of Love

"This is my commandment: love one another as I love you."

JOHN 15:12

Corporal Works of Mercy

Feed people who are hungry.
Give drink to people who are thirsty.
Clothe people who need clothes.
Visit people who are in prison.
Shelter people who are homeless.
Visit people who are sick.
Bury people who have died.

Spiritual Works of Mercy

Help people who sin.
Teach people who are ignorant.
Give advice to people who have doubts.
Comfort people who suffer.
Be patient with other people.
Forgive people who hurt you.
Pray for people who are alive and for those who have died.

Rosary

Catholics pray the Rosary to honor Mary and remember the important events in the lives of Jesus and Mary. There are twenty mysteries of the Rosary. Follow the steps from 1 to 5.

4 Repeat step No. 3 for each of the next four mysteries.

5 Pray the Hail, Holy Queen prayer. Make the Sign of the Cross.

3 Think of the first mystery. Pray an Our Father, ten Hail Marys, and the Glory Be.

2 Pray an Our Father, three Hail Marys, and the Glory Be.

1 Make the Sign of the Cross and pray the Apostle Creed.

Joyful Mysteries

1 The Annunciation
2 The Visitation
3 The Nativity
4 The Presentation in the Temple
5 The Finding of the Child Jesus After Three Days in the Temple

Luminous Mysteries

1 The Baptism at the Jordan
2 The Miracle at Cana
3 The Proclamation of the Kingdom and the Call to Continuing Conversion
4 The Transfiguration
5 The Institution of the Eucharist

Sorrowful Mysteries

1 The Agony in the Garden
2 The Scourging at the Pillar
3 The Crowning with Thorns
4 The Carrying of the Cross
5 The Crucifixion and Death

Glorious Mysteries

1 The Resurrection
2 The Ascension
3 The Descent of the Holy Spirit at Pentecost
4 The Assumption of Mary
5 The Crowning of the Blessed Virgin as Queen of Heaven and Earth

Hail, Holy Queen

Hail, holy Queen, Mother of mercy:
Hail, our life, our sweetness,
    and our hope.
To you do we cry, poor banished
    children of Eve.
To you do we send up our sighs,
mourning and weeping
    in this valley of tears.
Turn then, most gracious advocate,
your eyes of mercy toward us;
and after this our exile
show unto us the blessed fruit
    of your womb, Jesus.
O clement, O loving, O sweet
    Virgin Mary.

Stations of the Cross

1. Jesus is condemned to death.

2. Jesus accepts his cross.

3. Jesus falls the first time.

4. Jesus meets his mother.

5. Simon helps Jesus carry the cross.

6. Veronica wipes the face of Jesus

7. Jesus falls the second time.

8. Jesus meets the women.

9. Jesus falls the third time.

10. Jesus is stripped of his clothes.

11. Jesus is nailed to the cross.

12. Jesus dies on the cross.

13. Jesus is taken down from the cross.

14. Jesus is buried in the tomb.

(Some parishes conclude the Stations by reflecting on the Resurrection of Jesus.)

The Seven Sacraments

Jesus gave the Church the Seven Sacraments. The Sacraments are the main liturgical signs of the Church. They make the Paschal Mystery of Jesus, who is always the main celebrant of each Sacrament, present to us. They make us sharers in the saving work of Christ and in the life of the Holy Trinity.

Sacraments of Christian Initiation

Baptism

Through Baptism, we are joined to Christ and become members of the Body of Christ, the Church. We are reborn as adopted children of God and receive the gift of the Holy Spirit. Original Sin and all personal sins are forgiven.

Confirmation

Confirmation completes Baptism. In this Sacrament, the gift of the Holy Spirit strengthens us to live our Baptism.

Eucharist

Sharing in the Eucharist joins us most fully to Christ and to the Church. We share in the one sacrifice of Christ. The bread and wine become the Body and Blood of Christ through the power of the Holy Spirit and the words of the priest. We receive the Body and Blood of Christ.

Sacraments of Healing

Penance and Reconciliation

Through the ministry of the priest, we receive forgiveness of sins committed after our Baptism. We need to confess all mortal sins.

Anointing of the Sick

Anointing of the Sick strengthens our faith and trust in God when we are seriously ill, dying, or weak because of old age.

Sacraments at the Service of Communion

Holy Orders

Through Holy Orders, a baptized man is consecrated to serve the whole Church as a bishop, priest, or deacon in the name of Christ. Bishops, who are the successors of the Apostles, receive this Sacrament most fully. They are consecrated to teach the Gospel, to lead the Church in the worship of God, and to guide the Church to live holy lives. Bishops are helped in their work by priests, their coworkers, and by deacons.

Matrimony

Matrimony unites a baptized man and a baptized woman in a lifelong bond of faithful love to honor each other always and to accept the gift of children from God. In this Sacrament, the married couple is consecrated to be a sign of God's love for the Church.

We Celebrate the Mass

The Introductory Rites

We remember that we are the community of the Church.
We prepare to listen to the Word of God and to celebrate the Eucharist.

The Entrance

We stand as the priest, deacon, and other ministers enter the assembly. We sing a gathering song. The priest and deacon kiss the altar. The priest then goes to the chair where he presides over the celebration.

Sign of the Cross and Greeting

The priest leads us in praying the Sign of the Cross. The priest greets us, and we say,
"And with your spirit."

The Penitential Act

We admit our wrongdoings.
We bless God for his mercy.

The Gloria

We praise God for all the good that he has done for us.

The Collect

The priest leads us in praying the Collect.
We respond, **"Amen."**

The Liturgy of the Word
God speaks to us today. We listen and respond to God's Word.

The First Reading from Scripture
We sit and listen as the reader reads from the Old Testament or from the Acts of the Apostles. The reader concludes, "The word of the Lord." We respond,

> **"Thanks be to God."**

The Responsorial Psalm
The song leader leads us in singing a psalm.

The Second Reading from Scripture
The reader reads from the New Testament, but not from the four Gospels. The reader concludes, "The word of the Lord." We respond,

> **"Thanks be to God."**

The Acclamation
We stand to honor Christ, present with us in the Gospel. The song leader leads us in singing **"Alleluia, Alleluia, Alleluia"** or another chant during Lent.

The Gospel

The deacon or priest proclaims,
"A reading from the holy Gospel according to (name of Gospel writer)." We respond,
> **"Glory to you, O Lord."**

He proclaims the Gospel. At the end he says,
"The Gospel of the Lord."
We respond,
> **"Praise to you, Lord Jesus Christ."**

The Homily

We sit. The priest or deacon preaches the Homily. He helps the people gathered to understand the Word of God spoken to us in the readings.

The Profession of Faith

We stand and profess our faith.
We pray the Nicene Creed together.

The Prayer of the Faithful

The priest leads us in praying for our Church and her leaders, for our country and its leaders, for ourselves and others, for those who are sick and those who have died. We can respond to each prayer in several ways. One way that we respond is
> **"Lord, hear our prayer."**

The Liturgy of the Eucharist
We join with Jesus and the Holy Spirit to give thanks and praise to God the Father.

The Preparation of the Gifts
We sit as the altar is prepared and the collection is taken up. We share our blessings with the community of the Church and especially with those in need. The song leader may lead us in singing a song. The gifts of bread and wine are brought to the altar.

The priest lifts up the bread and blesses God for all our gifts. He prays, "Blessed are you, Lord God of all creation. . . ." We respond,
 "Blessed be God for ever."

The priest lifts up the cup of wine and prays, "Blessed are you, Lord God of all creation. . . ." We respond,
 "Blessed be God for ever."

The priest invites us,
 "Pray, brothers and sisters, that my sacrifice and yours may be acceptable to God, the almighty Father."

We stand and respond,
 "May the Lord accept the sacrifice at your hands for the praise and glory of his name, for our good, and the good of all his holy Church."

The Prayer over the Offerings
The priest leads us in praying the Prayer over the Offerings.
We respond, **"Amen."**

Preface

The priest invites us to join in praying the Church's great prayer of praise and thanksgiving to God the Father.

Priest: "The Lord be with you."

Assembly: "And with your spirit."

Priest: "Lift up your hearts."

Assembly: "We lift them up to the Lord."

Priest: "Let us give thanks to the Lord our God."

Assembly: "It is right and just."

After the priest sings or prays aloud the preface, we join in acclaiming,

**"Holy, Holy, Holy Lord God of hosts.
Heaven and earth are full of your glory.
Hosanna in the highest.
Blessed is he who comes in the name of the Lord.
Hosanna in the highest."**

The Eucharistic Prayer

The priest leads the assembly in praying the Eucharistic Prayer. We call on the Holy Spirit to make our gifts of bread and wine holy so that they become the Body and Blood of Jesus. We recall what happened at the Last Supper. The bread and wine become the Body and Blood of the Lord. Jesus is truly and really present under the appearances of bread and wine.

The priest sings or says aloud, "The mystery of faith." We respond using this or another acclamation used by the Church,

"We proclaim your Death, O Lord, and profess your Resurrection until you come again."

The priest then prays for the Church. He prays for the living and the dead.

Doxology

The priest concludes the praying of the Eucharistic Prayer. He sings or prays aloud,

"Through him, and with him,
    and in him,
O God, almighty Father,
in the unity of the Holy Spirit,
all glory and honor is yours,
for ever and ever."

We respond by singing **"Amen."**

The Communion Rite

The Lord's Prayer
We pray the Lord's Prayer together.

The Sign of Peace
The priest invites us to share a sign of peace, saying, "The peace of the Lord be with you always." We respond,

"And with your spirit."

We share a sign of peace.

The Fraction, or the Breaking of the Bread
The priest breaks the host, the consecrated bread. We sing or pray aloud,

"Lamb of God, you take away
the sins of the world,
    have mercy on us.
Lamb of God, you take away
the sins of the world,
    have mercy on us.
Lamb of God, you take away
the sins of the world,
    grant us peace."

Communion
The priest raises the host and says aloud,
    "Behold the Lamb of God,
    behold him who takes away the sins
      of the world.
    Blessed are those called to the supper
      of the Lamb."

We join with him and say,
    "Lord, I am not worthy that
    you should enter under my roof,
    but only say the word
    and my soul shall be healed."

The priest receives Communion. Next, the deacon, the extraordinary ministers of Holy Communion, and the members of the assembly receive Communion.

The priest, deacon, or extraordinary minister of Holy Communion holds up the host. We bow, and the priest, deacon, or extraordinary minister of Holy Communion says, "The Body of Christ." We respond, **"Amen."** We then receive the consecrated host in our hands or on our tongues.

If we are to receive the Blood of Christ, the priest, deacon, or extraordinary minister of Holy Communion holds up the cup containing the consecrated wine. We bow, and the priest, deacon, or extraordinary minister of Holy Communion says, "The Blood of Christ." We respond, **"Amen."** We take the cup in our hands and drink from it.

The Prayer After Communion
We stand as the priest invites us to pray, saying, "Let us pray." He prays the Prayer After Communion. We respond,
"Amen."

The Concluding Rites
We are sent forth to do good works, praising and blessing the Lord.

Greeting
We stand. The priest greets us as we prepare to leave. He says, "The Lord be with you."
We respond,
"And with your spirit."

Final Blessing
The priest or deacon may invite us,
"Bow down for the blessing."
The priest blesses us, saying,
"May almighty God bless you,
the Father, and the Son,
and the Holy Spirit."
We respond, **"Amen."**

Dismissal of the People
The priest or deacon sends us forth, using these or similar words,
"Go in peace, glorifying the Lord
by your life."
We respond,
"Thanks be to God."
We sing a hymn. The priest and the deacon kiss the altar. The priest, deacon, and other ministers bow to the altar and leave in procession.

The Sacrament of Penance and Reconciliation

Individual Rite

Greeting
"When the penitent comes to confess [his or her] sins, the priest welcomes [him or her] warmly and greets [the penitent] with kindness" (*Rite of Penance* 41).

Scripture Reading
"[T]hrough the word of God Christians receive light to recognize their sins and are called to conversion and to confidence in God's mercy" (*Rite of Penance* 17).

Confession of Sins and Acceptance of Penance
"[The priest] urges [the penitent] to be sorry for [his or her] faults, reminding [him or her] that through the sacrament of penance the Christian dies and rises with Christ and is renewed in the paschal mystery" (*Rite of Penance* 44).

Act of Contrition
"The most important act of the penitent is contrition. . . . The genuineness of penance depends on [a] heartfelt contrition" (*Rite of Penance* 6a).

Absolution
"The form of absolution indicates that the reconciliation of the penitent comes from the mercy of the Father" (*Rite of Penance* 19).

Closing Prayer
"After receiving pardon for sin, the penitent praises the mercy of God and gives him thanks. . . . Then the priest bids the penitent to go in peace" (*Rite of Penance* 20).

Communal Rite

Greeting
"When the faithful have assembled, they may sing a psalm, antiphon, or other appropriate song while the priest is entering the church" (*Rite of Penance* 48).

Scripture Reading
"[T]hrough his word God calls his people to repentance and leads them to a true conversion of heart" (*Rite of Penance* 24).

Homily
"The homily. . . . should lead the penitents to examine their consciences and renew their lives" (*Rite of Penance* 52).

Examination of Conscience
"A period of time may be spent in making an examination of conscience and in arousing true sorrow for sins" (*Rite of Penance* 53).

Litany of Contrition, and the Lord's Prayer
"The deacon or another minister invites all to kneel or bow, and to join in saying a general formula for confession" (*Rite of Penance* 54).

Individual Confession and Absolution
"[T]he penitents go to the priests designated for individual confession, and confess their sins. Each one receives and accepts a fitting act of satisfaction and is absolved" (*Rite of Penance* 55).

Closing Prayer
"After the song of praise or the litany [for God's mercy], the priest concludes the common prayer" (*Rite of Penance* 57).

Key Teachings of the Catholic Church

The Mystery of God

Divine Revelation

Who am I?

Every human person has been created by God to live in friendship with him both here on Earth and forever in Heaven.

How do we know this about ourselves?

We know this because every human person desires to know and love God and wants God to know and love them. We also know this because God told us this about ourselves and about him.

How did God tell us?

First of all, God tells us this through creation, which is the work of God; creation reflects the goodness and beauty of the Creator and tells us about God the Creator. Secondly, God came to us and told us, or revealed this about himself. He revealed this most fully by sending his Son, Jesus Christ, who became one of us and lived among us.

What is faith?

Faith is a supernatural gift from God that enables us to know God and all that he has revealed, and to respond to God with our whole heart and mind.

What is a mystery of faith?

The word *mystery* describes the fact that we can never fully comprehend or fully grasp God and his loving plan for us. We only know who God is and his plan for us through Divine Revelation.

What is Divine Revelation?

Divine Revelation is God's free gift of making himself known to us and giving himself to us by gradually communicating in deeds and words his own mystery and his divine plan for humanity. God reveals himself so that we can live in communion with him and with one another forever.

What is Sacred Tradition?

The word *tradition* comes from a Latin word meaning "to pass on." Sacred Tradition is the passing on of Divine Revelation by the Church through the power and guidance of the Holy Spirit.

What is the deposit of faith?

The deposit of faith is the source of faith that we draw from in order to pass on God's Revelation. The deposit of faith is the unity of Sacred Scripture and Sacred Tradition handed on by the Church from the time of the Apostles.

What is the Magisterium?

The Magisterium is the teaching authority of the Church. Guided by the Holy Spirit, the Church has the responsibility to authentically and accurately interpret the Word of God, both in Sacred Scripture and in Sacred Tradition. She does this to assure that her understanding of Revelation is faithful to the teaching of the Apostles.

What is a dogma of faith?

A dogma of faith is a truth taught by the Church as revealed by God and to which we are called to give our assent of mind and heart in faith.

Sacred Scripture

What is Sacred Scripture?

The words *sacred scripture* come from two Latin words meaning "holy writings." Sacred Scripture is the collection of all the writings God has inspired authors to write in his name.

What is the Bible?

The word *bible* comes from a Greek word meaning "book." The Bible is the collection of the forty-six books of the Old Testament and the twenty-seven books of the New Testament named by the Church as all the writings God has inspired human authors to write in his name.

What is the canon of Scripture?

The word *canon* comes from a Greek word meaning "measuring rod," or standard by which something is judged. The canon of Scripture is the list of books that the Church has identified and teaches to be the inspired Word of God.

What is biblical inspiration?

Biblical inspiration is a term that describes the Holy Spirit guiding the human authors of Sacred Scripture so that they faithfully and accurately communicate the Word of God.

What is the Old Testament?

The Old Testament is the first main part of the Bible. It is the forty-six books inspired by the Holy Spirit, written before the birth of Jesus and centered on the Covenant between God and his people, Israel, and the promise of the Messiah or Savior. The Old Testament is divided into the Torah/Pentateuch, historical books, wisdom literature, and writings of the prophets.

What is the Torah?

The Torah is the Law of God that was revealed to Moses. The written Torah is found in the first five books of the Old Testament, which are called the "Torah" or the "Pentateuch."

What is the Pentateuch?

The word *pentateuch* means "five containers." The Pentateuch is the first five books of the Old Testament, namely Genesis, Exodus, Leviticus, Numbers, and Deuteronomy.

What is the Covenant?

The Covenant is the solemn agreement of fidelity that God and his people freely entered into. It was renewed and fulfilled in Jesus Christ, the new and everlasting Covenant.

What are the historical books of the Old Testament?

The historical books tell about the fidelity and infidelity of God's people to the Covenant and about the consequences of those choices.

What are the Wisdom writings of the Old Testament?

The Wisdom writings are the seven books of the Old Testament that contain inspired practical advice and common-sense guidelines for living the Covenant and the Law of God. They are the Book of Job, Book of Psalms, Book of Ecclesiastes, Book of Wisdom, Book of Proverbs, Book of Sirach (Ecclesiasticus), and Song of Songs.

What are the writings of the prophets in the Old Testament?

The word *prophet* comes from a Greek word meaning "those who speak before others." The biblical prophets were those people God had chosen to speak in his name. The writings of the prophets are the eighteen books of the Old Testament that contain the message of the prophets to God's people. They remind God's people of his unending fidelity to them and of their responsibility to be faithful to the Covenant.

What is the New Testament?

The New Testament is the second main part of the Bible. It is the twenty-seven books inspired by the Holy Spirit and written in apostolic times that focus on Jesus Christ and his saving work among us. The main parts are the four Gospels, the Acts of the Apostles, the twenty-one letters, and the Book of Revelation.

What are the Gospels?

The word *gospel* comes from a Greek word meaning "good news." The Gospel is the Good News of God's loving plan of Salvation, revealed in the Passion, Death, Resurrection, and Ascension of Jesus Christ. The Gospels are the four written accounts of Matthew, Mark, Luke, and John. The four Gospels occupy a central place in Sacred Scripture because Jesus Christ is their center.

What is an epistle?

The word *epistle* comes from a Greek word meaning "message or letter." An epistle is a formal type of letter. Some of the letters in the New Testament are epistles.

What are the Pauline Epistles and letters?

The Pauline Epistles and letters are the fourteen letters in the New Testament traditionally attributed to Saint Paul the Apostle.

What are the Catholic Letters?

The Catholic Letters are the seven New Testament letters that bear the names of the Apostles John, Peter, Jude, and James, and which were written to the universal Church rather than to a particular Church community.

The Holy Trinity

Who is the Mystery of the Holy Trinity?

The Holy Trinity is the mystery of One God in Three Divine Persons—God the Father, God the Son, God the Holy Spirit. It is the central mystery of the Christian faith.

Who is God the Father?

God the Father is the First Person of the Holy Trinity.

Who is God the Son?

God the Son is Jesus Christ, the Second Person of the Holy Trinity. He is the only begotten Son of the Father who took on flesh and became one of us without giving up his divinity.

Who is God the Holy Spirit?

God the Holy Spirit is the Third Person of the Holy Trinity, who proceeds from the Father and Son. He is the Advocate, or Paraclete, sent to us by the Father in the name of his Son, Jesus.

What are the divine missions, or the works of God?

The entire work of God is common to all Three Divine Persons of the Trinity. The work of creation is the work of the Trinity, though attributed to the Father. Likewise, the work of Salvation is attributed to the Son and the work of sanctification is attributed to the Holy Spirit.

Divine Work of Creation

What is the divine work of creation?

Creation is the work of God bringing into existence everything and everyone, seen and unseen, out of love and without any help.

Who are angels?

Angels are spiritual creatures who do not have bodies as humans do. Angels give glory to God without ceasing and sometimes serve God by bringing his message to people.

Who is the human person?

The human person is uniquely created in the image and likeness of God. Human dignity is fulfilled in the vocation to a life of happiness with God.

What is the soul?

The soul is the spiritual part of a person. It is immortal; it never dies. The soul is the innermost being, that which bears the imprint of the image of God.

What is the intellect?

The intellect is an essential power of the soul. It is the power to know God, yourself, and others; it is the power to understand the order of things established by God.

What is free will?

Free will is an essential quality of the soul. It is the God-given ability and power to recognize him as part of our lives and to choose to center our lives around him as well as to choose between good and evil. By free will, the human person is capable of directing oneself toward the truth, beauty and good, namely, life in communion with God.

What is Original Sin?

Original Sin is the sin of Adam and Eve by which they choose evil over obedience to God. By doing so, they lost the state of original holiness for themselves and for all their descendants. As a result of Original Sin, death, sin, and suffering entered into the world.

Jesus Christ, the Incarnate Son of God

What is the Annunciation?

The Annunciation is the announcement by the angel Gabriel to Mary that God chose her to be the mother of Jesus, the Son of God, by the power of the Holy Spirit.

What is the Incarnation?

The word *incarnation* comes from a Latin word meaning "take on flesh." The term *Incarnation* is the event in which the Son of God, the Second Person of the Holy Trinity, truly became human while remaining truly God. Jesus Christ is true God and true man.

What does it mean that Jesus is Lord?

The word *lord* means "master, ruler, a person of authority" and is used in the Old Testament to name God. The designation, or title, "Jesus, the Lord" expresses that Jesus is truly God.

What is the Paschal Mystery?

The Paschal Mystery is the saving events of the Passion, Death, Resurrection, and glorious Ascension of Jesus Christ; the passing over of Jesus from death into a new and glorious life; the name we give to God's plan of Salvation in Jesus Christ.

What is Salvation?

The word *salvation* comes from a Latin word meaning "to save." Salvation is the saving, or deliverance, of humanity from the power of sin and death through Jesus Christ. All Salvation comes from Christ through the Church.

What is the Resurrection?

The Resurrection is the historical event of Jesus being raised from the dead to a new glorified life after his Death on the Cross and burial in the tomb.

What is the Ascension?

The Ascension is the return of the Risen Christ in glory to his Father, to the world of the divine.

What is the Second Coming of Christ?

The Second Coming of Christ is the return of Christ in glory at the end of time to judge the living and the dead; the fulfillment of God's plan in Christ.

What does it mean that Jesus is the Messiah?

The word *messiah* is a Hebrew term meaning "anointed one." Jesus Christ is the Anointed One, the Messiah, who God promised to send to save people. Jesus is the Savior of the world.

The Mystery of the Church

What is the Church?

The word *church* means "convocation," those called together. The Church is the sacrament of Salvation—the sign and instrument of our reconciliation and communion with God the Holy Trinity and with one another. The Church is the Body of Christ, the people God the Father has called together in Jesus Christ through the power of the Holy Spirit.

What is the central work of the Church?

The central work of the Church is to proclaim the Gospel of Jesus Christ and to invite all people to come to know and believe in him and to live in communion with him. We call this work of the Church "evangelization," a word that comes from a Greek word that means "to tell good news."

What is the Body of Christ?

The Body of Christ is an image for the Church used by Saint Paul the Apostle that teaches that all the members of the Church are one in Christ, who is the Head of the Church, and that all members have a unique and vital work in the Church.

Who are the People of God?

The People of God are those the Father has chosen and gathered in Christ, the Incarnate Son of God, the Church. All people are invited to belong to the People of God and to live as one family of God.

What is the Temple of the Holy Spirit?

The Temple of the Holy Spirit is a New Testament image used to describe the indwelling of the Holy Spirit in the Church and within the hearts of the faithful.

What is the Communion of Saints?

The Communion of Saints is the communion of holy things and holy people that make up the Church. It is the communion, or unity, of all the faithful, those living on Earth, those being purified after death, and those enjoying life everlasting and eternal happiness with God, the angels, Mary and all the Saints.

What are the Marks of the Church?

The Marks of the Church are the four attributes and essential characteristics of the Church and her mission, namely, one, holy, catholic, and apostolic.

Who are the Apostles?

The word *apostle* comes from a Greek word meaning "to send away." The Apostles were those twelve men chosen and sent by Jesus to preach the Gospel and to make disciples of all people.

Who are the "Twelve"?

The "Twelve" is the term that identifies the Apostles chosen by Jesus before his Death and Resurrection. "The names of the twelve apostles are these: first, Simon called Peter, and his brother Andrew; James, the son of Zebedee, and his brother John; Philip and Bartholomew, Thomas and Matthew the tax collector; James the son of Alphaeus, and Thaddaeus; Simon the Cananean, and Judas Iscariot who betrayed him" (Matthew 10:2–4). The Apostle Matthias was chosen after Jesus' Ascension.

What is Pentecost?

Pentecost is the coming of the Holy Spirit upon the Church as promised by Jesus; it marks the beginning of the work of the Church.

Who are the ordained ministers of the Church?

The ordained ministers of the Church are those baptized men who are consecrated in the Sacrament of Holy Orders to serve the whole Church. Bishops, priests, and deacons are the ordained ministers of the Church and make up the clergy.

How do the Pope and other bishops guide the Church in her work?

Christ, the Head of the Church, governs the Church through the Pope and the college of bishops in communion with him. The Pope is the bishop of Rome and the successor of Saint Peter the Apostle. The Pope, the Vicar of Christ, is the visible foundation of the unity of the whole Church. The other bishops are the successors of the other Apostles and are the visible foundation of their own particular Churches. The Holy Spirit guides the Pope and the college of bishops working together with the Pope, to teach the faith and moral doctrine without error. This grace of the Holy Spirit is called *infallibility*.

What is the consecrated life?

The consecrated life is a state of life for those baptized who promise or vow to live the Gospel by means of professing the evangelical counsels of poverty, chastity, and obedience, in a way of life approved by the Church. The consecrated life is also known as the "religious life."

Who are the laity?

The laity (or laypeople) are all the baptized who have not received the Sacrament of Holy Orders nor have promised or vowed to live the consecrated life. They are called to be witnesses to Christ at the very heart of the human community.

The Blessed Virgin Mary

What is Mary's role in God's loving plan for humanity?

Mary has a unique role in God's plan of Salvation for humanity. For this reason she is full of grace from the first moment of her conception, or existence. God chose Mary to be the Mother of the Incarnate Son of God, Jesus Christ, who is truly God and truly man. Mary is the Mother of God, the Mother of Christ, and the Mother of the Church. She is the greatest Saint of the Church.

What is the Immaculate Conception?

The Immaculate Conception is the unique grace given to Mary that totally preserved her from the stain of all sin from the very first moment of her existence, or conception, in her mother's womb and throughout her life.

What is the perpetual virginity of Mary?

The *perpetual virginity of Mary* is a term that describes the fact that Mary remained always a virgin. She was virgin before the conception of Jesus, during his birth, and remained a virgin after the birth of Jesus her whole life.

What is the Assumption of Mary?

At the end of her life on earth, the Blessed Virgin Mary was taken body and soul into heaven, where she shares in the glory of her Son's Resurrection. Mary, the Mother of the Church, hears our prayers and intercedes for us with her Son. She is an image of the heavenly glory in which we all hope to share when Christ, her Son, comes again in glory.

Life Everlasting

What is eternal life?

Eternal life is life after death. At death, the soul is separated from the body. In the Apostles' Creed we profess faith in "the life everlasting." In the Nicene Creed we profess faith in "the life of the world to come."

What is the particular judgment?

The particular judgment is the assignment given to our souls at the moment of our death to our final destiny based on what we have done in our lives.

What is the Last Judgment?

The Last Judgment is the judgment at which every human being will appear in their own bodies and give an account of their deeds. At the Last Judgment, Christ will show his identity with the least of his brothers and sisters.

What is the beatific vision?

The beatific vision is seeing God "face-to-face" in heavenly glory.

What is Heaven?

Heaven is eternal life and communion with the Holy Trinity. It is the supreme state of happiness—living with God forever for which he created us.

What is the Kingdom of God?

The Kingdom of God, or Kingdom of Heaven, is the image used by Jesus to describe all people and creation living in communion with God. The Kingdom of God will be fully realized when Christ comes again in glory at the end of time.

What is Purgatory?

Purgatory is the opportunity after death to purify and strengthen our love for God before we enter Heaven.

What is hell?

Hell is the immediate and everlasting separation from God.

Celebration of the Christian Life and Mystery

Liturgy and Worship

What is worship?

Worship is the adoration and honor given to God. The Church worships God publicly in the celebration of the liturgy. The liturgy is the Church's worship of God. It is the work of the whole Church. In the liturgy the mystery of Salvation in Christ is made present by the power of the Holy Spirit.

What is the liturgical year?

The liturgical year is the cycle of seasons and great feasts that make up the Church's year of worship. The main seasons and times of the Church year are Advent, Christmas, Lent, Easter Triduum, Easter, and Ordinary Time.

The Sacraments

What are the Sacraments?

The Sacraments are seven signs of God's love and the main liturgical actions of the Church through which the faithful are made sharers in the Paschal Mystery of Christ. They are effective signs of grace, instituted by Christ and entrusted to the Church, by which divine life is shared with us.

What are the Sacraments of Initiation?

The Sacraments of Christian Initiation are Baptism, Confirmation, and the Eucharist. These three Sacraments are the foundation of every Christian life. "Baptism is the beginning of new life in Christ; Confirmation is its strengthening; the Eucharist nourishes the faithful for their transformation into Christ."

What is the Sacrament of Baptism?

Through Baptism, we are reborn into new life in Christ. We are joined to Jesus Christ, become members of the Church, and are reborn as God's children. We receive the gift of the Holy Spirit; and Original Sin and our personal sins are forgiven. Baptism marks us indelibly and forever as belonging to Christ. Because of this, Baptism can be received only once.

What is the Sacrament of Confirmation?

Confirmation strengthens the graces of Baptism and celebrates the special gift of the Holy Spirit. Confirmation also imprints a spiritual or indelible character on the soul and can be received only once.

What is the Sacrament of the Eucharist?

The Eucharist is the source and summit of the Christian life. In the Eucharist the faithful join with Christ to give thanksgiving, honor, and glory to the Father through the power of the Holy Spirit. Through the power of the Holy Spirit and the words of the priest, the bread and wine become the Body and Blood of Christ.

What is the obligation of the faithful to participate in the Eucharist?

The faithful have the obligation to participate in the Eucharist on Sundays and holy days of obligation. Sunday is the Lord's Day. Sunday, the day of the Lord's Resurrection, is "the foundation and kernel of the whole liturgical year." Regular participation in the Eucharist and receiving Holy Communion is vital to the Christian life. In the Eucharist we receive the Body and Blood of Christ.

What is the Blessed Sacrament?

The Blessed Sacrament is another name for the Eucharist. The term is often used to identify the Eucharist reserved in the tabernacle.

What is the Mass?

The Mass is the main celebration of the Church at which we gather to listen to the Word of God (Liturgy of the Word) and through which we are made sharers in the saving Death and Resurrection of Christ and give praise and glory to the Father (Liturgy of the Eucharist).

What are the Sacraments of Healing?

Penance and Anointing of the Sick are the two Sacraments of Healing. Through the power of the Holy Spirit, Christ's work of Salvation and healing of the members of the Church is continued.

What is the Sacrament of Penance and Reconciliation?

The Sacrament of Penance is one of the two Sacraments of Healing through which we receive God's forgiveness for the sins we have committed after Baptism.

What is confession?

Confession is the telling of sins to a priest in the Sacrament of Penance. This act of the penitent is an essential element of the Sacrament of Penance. Confession is also another name for the Sacrament of Penance.

What is the seal of confession?

The seal of confession is the obligation of the priest to never reveal to anyone what a penitent has confessed to him.

What is contrition?

Contrition is sorrow for sins that includes the desire and commitment to make reparation for the harm caused by one's sin and the purpose of amendment not to sin again. Contrition is an essential element of the Sacrament of Penance.

What is a penance?

A penance is a prayer or act of kindness that shows we are truly sorry for our sins and that helps us repair the damage caused by our sin. Accepting and doing our penance is an essential part of the Sacrament of Penance.

What is absolution?

Absolution is the forgiveness of sins by God through the ministry of the priest.

What is the Sacrament of Anointing of the Sick?

The Sacrament of Anointing of the Sick is one of the two Sacraments of Healing. The grace of this Sacrament strengthens our faith and trust in God when we are seriously ill, weakened by old age, or dying. The faithful may receive this Sacrament each time they are seriously ill or when an illness gets worse.

What is Viaticum?

Viaticum is the Eucharist, or Holy Communion, received as food and strength for a dying person's journey from life on Earth through death to eternal life.

What are the Sacraments at the Service of Communion?

Holy Orders and Matrimony are the two Sacraments at the Service of Communion. These Sacraments bestow a particular work, or mission, on certain members of the Church to serve in building up the People of God.

What is the Sacrament of Holy Orders?

The Sacrament of Holy Orders is one of the two Sacraments at the Service of Communion. It is the Sacrament in which baptized men are consecrated as bishops, priests, or deacons to serve the whole Church in the name and person of Christ.

Who is a bishop?

A bishop is a priest who receives the fullness of the Sacrament of Holy Orders. He is a successor of the Apostles and shepherds a particular Church entrusted to him by means of teaching, leading divine worship, and governing the Church as Jesus did.

Who is a priest?

A priest is a baptized man who has received the Sacrament of Holy Orders. Priests are coworkers with their bishops, who have the ministry of "authentically teaching the faith, celebrating divine worship, above all the Eucharist, and guiding their Churches as true pastors."

Who is a deacon?

A deacon is ordained to assist bishops and priests. He is not ordained to the priesthood but to a ministry of service to the Church.

What is the Sacrament of Matrimony?

The Sacrament of Matrimony is one of the two Sacraments at the Service of Communion. In the Sacrament of Matrimony, a baptized man and a baptized woman dedicate their lives to the Church and to one another in a lifelong bond of faithful life-giving love. In this Sacrament they receive the grace to be a living sign of Christ's love for the Church.

What are the sacramentals of the Church?

Sacramentals are sacred signs instituted by the Church. They include blessings, prayers, and certain objects that prepare us to participate in the sacraments and make us aware of and help us respond to God's loving presence in our lives.

Life in the Spirit

The Moral Life

Why was the human person created?

The human person was created to give honor and glory to God and to live a life of beatitude with God here on Earth and forever in Heaven.

What is the Christian moral life?

The baptized have new life in Christ in the Holy Spirit. They respond to the "desire for happiness that God has placed in every human heart" by cooperating with the grace of the Holy Spirit and living the Gospel. "The moral life is a spiritual worship that finds its nourishment in the liturgy and celebration of the sacraments."

What is the way to happiness revealed by Jesus Christ?

Jesus taught that the Great Commandment of loving God above all else and our neighbor as ourselves is the path to happiness. It is the summary and heart of the Commandments and all of God's law.

What are the Ten Commandments?

The Ten Commandments are the laws of the Covenant that God revealed to Moses and the Israelites on Mount Sinai. The Ten Commandments are also known as the Decalogue, or "Ten Words." They are the "privileged expression of the natural law," which is written on the hearts of all people.

What are the Beatitudes?

The Beatitudes are the teachings of Jesus that summarize the path to true happiness, the Kingdom of God, which is living in communion and friendship with God, and with Mary and all the Saints. The Beatitudes guide us in living as disciples of Christ by keeping our life focused and centered on God.

What is the New Commandment?

The New Commandment is the commandment of love that Jesus gave his disciples. Jesus said, "I give you a new commandment: love one another. As I have loved you, so you should also love one another" (John 13:34).

What are the Works of Mercy?

The word *mercy* comes from a Hebrew word pointing to God's unconditional love and kindness at work in the world. Human works of mercy are acts of loving kindness by which we reach out to people in their corporal and spiritual needs.

What are the precepts of the Church?

Precepts of the Church are specific responsibilities that concern the moral Christian life united with the liturgy and nourished by it.

Holiness of Life and Grace

What is holiness?

Holiness is the state of living in communion with God. It designates both the presence of God, the Holy One, with us and our faithfulness to him. It is the characteristic of a person who is in right relationship with God, with people, and with creation.

What is grace?

Grace is the gift of God sharing his life and love with us. Categories of grace are sanctifying grace, actual grace, charisms, and sacramental graces.

What is sanctifying grace?

The word *sanctifying* comes from a Latin word meaning "to make holy." Sanctifying grace is a gratuitous gift of God, given by the Holy Spirit, as a remedy for sin and the source of holiness.

What is actual grace?

Actual graces are the God-given divine helps empowering us to live as his adopted daughters and sons.

What are charisms?

Charisms are gifts or graces freely given to individual Christians by the Holy Spirit for the benefit of building up the Church.

What are sacramental graces?

Sacramental graces are the graces of each of the sacraments that help us live out our Christian vocation.

What are the Gifts of the Holy Spirit?

The seven Gifts of the Holy Spirit are graces that strengthen us to live our Baptism, our new life in Christ. They are wisdom, understanding, right judgment (or counsel), courage (or fortitude), knowledge, reverence (or piety), wonder and awe (or fear of the Lord).

What are the Fruits of the Holy Spirit?

The twelve Fruits of the Holy Spirit are visible signs and effects of the Holy Spirit at work in our life. They are charity (love), joy, peace, patience, kindness, goodness, generosity, gentleness, faithfulness, modesty, self-control, and chastity.

The Virtues

What are virtues?

The virtues are spiritual powers or habits or behaviors that help us do what is good. The Catholic Church speaks of Theological Virtues, Moral Virtues, and Cardinal Virtues.

What are the Theological Virtues?

The Theological Virtues are the three virtues of faith, hope, and charity (love). These virtues are "gifts from God infused into the souls of the faithful to make them capable of acting as his children and of attaining eternal life" (CCC 1813).

What are the Moral Virtues?

The Moral Virtues are "firm attitudes, stable dispositions, habitual perfections of intellect and will that govern our actions, order our passions, and guide our conduct according to reason and faith. They make possible ease, self-mastery, and joy in leading a morally good life" (CCC 1804).

What are the Cardinal Virtues?

The Cardinal Virtues are the four Moral Virtues of prudence, justice, fortitude, and temperance. They are called the Cardinal Virtues because all of the Moral Virtues are related to and grouped around them.

What is conscience?

The word *conscience* comes from a Latin word meaning "to be conscious of guilt." Conscience is that part of every human person that helps us judge whether a moral act is in accordance or not in accordance with God's law; our conscience moves us to do good and avoid evil.

Moral Evil and Sin

What is moral evil?

Moral evil is the harm we willingly inflict on one another and on God's good creation.

What is temptation?

Temptation is everything, either within us or outside us, that tries to move us from doing something good that we know we can and should do and to do or say something we know is contrary to the will of God. Temptation is whatever tries to move us away from living a holy life.

What is sin?

Sin is freely and knowingly doing or saying that which is against the will of God and the Law of God. Sin sets itself against God's love and turns our hearts away from his love. The Church speaks of mortal sin, venial sin, and capital sins.

What is mortal sin?

A mortal sin is a serious, deliberate failure in our love and respect for God, our neighbor, creation, and ourselves. It is knowingly and willingly choosing to do something that is gravely contrary to the Law of God. The effect of mortal sin is the loss of sanctifying grace and, if unrepented, mortal sin brings eternal death.

What are venial sins?

Venial sins are sins that are less serious than a mortal sin. They weaken our love for God and for one another and diminish our holiness.

What are Capital Sins?

Capital Sins are sins that are at the root of other sins. The seven Capital Sins are false pride, avarice, envy, anger, gluttony, lust, and sloth.

Christian Prayer

What is prayer?

Prayer is conversation with God. It is talking and listening to him, raising our minds and hearts to God the Father, Son, and Holy Spirit.

What is the prayer of all Christians?

The Lord's Prayer, or Our Father, is the prayer of all Christians. It is the prayer Jesus taught his disciples and gave to the Church. The Lord's Prayer is "a summary of the whole Gospel." Praying the Lord's Prayer "brings us into communion with the Father and his Son, Jesus Christ" and develops "in us the will to become like [Jesus] and to place our trust in the Father as he did."

What are the traditional expressions of prayer?

The traditional expressions of prayer are vocal prayer, the prayer of meditation, and the prayer of contemplation.

What is vocal prayer?

Vocal prayer is spoken prayer; prayer using words said aloud.

What is the prayer of meditation?

Meditation is a form of prayer in which we use our minds, hearts, imaginations, emotions, and desires to understand and follow what the Lord is asking us to do.

What is the prayer of contemplation?

Contemplation is a form of prayer that is simply being with God.

What are the traditional forms of prayer?

The traditional forms of prayer are the prayers of adoration and blessing, the prayer of thanksgiving, the prayer of praise, the prayer of petition, and the prayer of intercession.

What are devotions?

Devotions are part of the prayer life of the Church and of the baptized. They are acts of communal or individual prayer that surround and arise out of the celebration of the liturgy.

Glossary

A-B

Abba *page 37*
The name Jesus used for God the Father that reveals the love and trust that exist between Jesus, God the Son, and God the Father.

actual grace *page 157*
Actual grace is the additional gift of God's presence with us to help us live as children of God and followers of Jesus Christ.

Annunciation *page 29*
The announcement to the Virgin Mary by the angel Gabriel that God had chosen her to be the Mother of Jesus, the Son of God, through the power of the Holy Spirit.

attributes of God *page 37*
Qualities of God that help us understand the mystery of God.

Baptism *page 93*
Baptism is the Sacrament of Christian Initiation in which we are first joined to Jesus Christ, become members of the Church, are reborn as God's adopted children, receive the gift of the Holy Spirit, and by which Original Sin and personal sins are forgiven.

Beatitudes *page 181*
Beatitudes are the sayings or teachings of Jesus that are found in the Sermon on the Mount. They describe both the qualities and the actions of people blessed by God.

C-D

charity *page 108*
Charity is one of the three Theological Virtues. It is the virtue, or habit, we receive from God that enables us to love and serve God and others with unselfish devotion.

charisms *page 65*
Charisms are graces, or gifts, given by the Holy Spirit to build up the Church on Earth for the good of all people and the needs of the world.

chastity *page 203*
The virtue of chastity is the respecting and honoring of our sexuality. Chastity guides us to share our love with others in appropriate ways.

Chrism *page 93*
Chrism is one of the three oils the Church uses in the celebration of the liturgy. It is used in the Sacraments of Baptism, Confirmation, and Holy Orders. Chrism is also used in the consecration of churches and altars.

Christ *page 49*
A title for Jesus that states that he is the Messiah, the One whom God promised to send to save his people.

Church *page 73*
The Body of Christ; the new People of God whom God calls together in Christ by the power of the Holy Spirit.

Confirmation *page 101*
Confirmation is the Sacrament of Christian Initiation that strengthens the graces of Baptism and in which our new life in Christ is sealed by the gift of the Holy Spirit.

conscience *page 165*
Conscience is the gift of God that is part of every person and that guides us to know and judge what is right and wrong.

courage *page 64*
Courage, or fortitude, is one of four Cardinal Virtues and a Gift of the Holy Spirit. It helps us stand up for our faith in Christ and helps us overcome obstacles that might keep us from practicing our faith, and to choose that which is good.

covenant *page 173*

A covenant is a sacred agreement or relationship, sometimes sealed by a ritual or ceremony.

Divine Revelation *page 13*

God making known over time the mystery of himself and his divine plan of creation and Salvation.

E-F-G-H

Eucharist *page 109*

Eucharist is the Sacrament of Christian Initiation in which we are made sharers in the Paschal Mystery of Christ, we receive the Body and Blood of Christ, and we are joined most fully to Christ and to the Church, the Body of Christ.

faith *page 15*

One of the three Theological Virtues. A supernatural gift and power from God inviting us to know and believe in him, and our free response to that invitation.

faithfulness *page 48*

Faithfulness is one of the Fruits of the Holy Spirit. When we are faithful, we live according to God's will. We put into practice the teachings of Jesus, the Scriptures, and the Catholic Church.

generosity *page 92*

Generosity is a Fruit of the Holy Spirit. Practicing generosity helps us serve the Church and the world. With generosity, we share our gifts and our talents with others. We share our material and spiritual blessings.

goodness *page 156*

Goodness is a Fruit of the Holy Spirit. We exhibit goodness when we honor God by avoiding sin and always trying to do what we know is right.

Gospel *page 21*

The Gospel is the Good News of God's love revealed in the life, suffering, Death, Resurrection, and Ascension of Jesus Christ.

Holy Trinity *page 29*

The central belief of the Christian faith; the mystery of One God in Three Divine Persons— God the Father, God the Son, God the Holy Spirit

honesty *page 209*

Honesty is the refusal to lie, steal, or deceive in any way.

hope *page 56*

Hope is the virtue that keeps us from discouragement by placing our trust in Jesus and the promise of eternal life.

humility *page 144*

Humility is the ability to acknowledge that all of our blessings come from God. This virtue enables us to see ourselves and value ourselves and all other people as children of God. It enable us to bless God for all the good in our lives.

I-J-K-L

Inspiration of the Bible *page 21*

The Holy Spirit guiding the human writers of Sacred Scripture to faithfully and accurately communicate God's Word.

integrity *page 208*

This virtue enables a person to be the person God created him or her to be. A person of integrity says and does what he or she knows and believes is the right thing to do and say.

joy *page 36*

Joy shows that we are cooperating with the grace of the Holy Spirit. We recognize that true happiness comes, not from money or possessions, but from knowing, trusting, and loving god. Joy is a Fruit of the Holy Spirit.

justice *page 209*

The Cardinal Virtue of justice is the giving to God and all people what is rightfully due to them.

kindness *page 128*

Sometimes used to translate the biblical word mercy; We live the virtue of kindness by generously treating others as we want to be treated. We are called to be as kind to others as God is to us.

Kingdom of God *page 73*

All people and creation living in communion with God at the end of time when the work of Christ will be completed and he will come again in glory.

knowledge *page 12*

Knowledge is a virtue and a Gift of the Holy Spirit that allows you to choose the right path to God. It encourages you to avoid obstacles that will keep you from God.

liturgy *page 85*

The liturgy is the work of the Church, the People of God, of worshiping God. Through the liturgy, Christ continues the work of Redemption in, with, and through his Church.

Lord *page 49*

A title for Jesus that states that Jesus is truly God.

Lord's Prayer *page 217*

The early Christians called the Our Father the Lord's Prayer because it was given to them by Jesus. The Church teaches us that the Lord's Prayer is a summary of the whole Gospel.

M-N-O

manna *page 193*

Manna is the food miraculously sent to the Israelites during their forty years in the desert.

Mass *page 109*

Mass is the main sacramental celebration of the Church at which we gather to listen to God's Word and share in the Eucharist.

meekness *page 192*

Meekness is the virtue that helps us to maintain our confidence in God when difficulties come into our lives, rather than being overcome by the difficult condition itself.

mercy *page 120*

Mercy is one of the Fruits of the Holy Spirit. A person who acts with mercy has a forgiving and understanding heart.

moral decisions *page 165*

Moral decisions are the good choices we make to live as children of God and followers of Jesus Christ.

obedience *page 172*

Obedience is to freely choose to follow God's ways because of our love for God and our trust in his faithfulness to the Covenant. We know that God only desires what is best for us.

P-Q

Paschal Mystery *page 57*

The Paschal Mystery is the "passing over" of Jesus from life through death into new and glorious life; the Passion, Death, Resurrection, and glorious Ascension of Jesus.

Passover *page 57*

Passover is the Jewish feast celebrating God's sparing of the Hebrew children from death and the passage of his people from slavery to freedom.

peace *page 72*

Peace is one of the signs, or Fruits of the Holy Spirit. As faithful disciples, we cooperate with the grace of the Holy Spirit to create peace throughout the world.

perseverance *page 84*

Perseverance is the virtue by which we hold to our faith, even through trying events or circumstances. To persevere in faith, we must continually nourish faith with the Word of God and the celebration of the Sacraments.

piety *page 216*

Piety is a gift of the Holy Spirit that leads to a devotion to God. It is an expression of a person's deep reverence for God. It flows from one's recognition of the value of a person places on their relationship with God. Piety also is an expression of one's deep respect for one's parents and family.

prudence *page 164*

Prudence is the virtue that helps a person know what is good and choose to do it. It is an important virtue in making Christian decisions.

R–S

reverence *page 20*

Reverence is a virtue and a gift of the Holy Spirit that helps us to respect and honor God, Mary and the Saints, the Church and people as "images of God."

Sacrament of the Anointing of the Sick *page 129*

The Sacrament of the Anointing of the Sick is the Sacrament of Healing that strengthens our faith, hope, and love for God when we are seriously ill, weakened by old age, or dying.

Sacrament of Holy Orders *page 137*

The Sacrament of Holy Orders is the Sacrament through which a baptized man is consecrated to serve the serve the whole Church as a bishop, priest, or deacon.

Sacrament of Matrimony *page 145*

The Sacrament of Matrimony is the Sacrament at the Service of Communion that unites a baptized man and a baptized woman in a lifelong bond, or covenant, of faithful love to serve one another and the whole Church as a sign of Christ's love for the Church.

Sacrament of Penance and Reconciliation *page 121*

In the Sacrament of Penance and Reconciliation, we receive God's forgiveness, through the ministry of the priest, for the sins we commit after Baptism.

Sacraments *page 85*

Sacraments are the seven main liturgical signs of the Church given to the Church by Jesus Christ. They make his saving work present and make us sharers in the life of God, the Holy Trinity.

Sacraments at the Service of Communion *page 137*

The Sacraments at the Service of Communion are the two Sacraments that set aside members of the Church to serve the whole Church, namely, Holy Orders and Matrimony.

Sacraments of Healing *page 121*

There are two Sacraments of Healing. They are the Sacrament of Penance and Reconciliation and the Sacrament of the Anointing of the Sick.

Sacred Tradition *page 65*

Sacred Tradition is the passing on of the teachings of Christ by the Church through the power and guidance of the Holy Spirit.

sanctifying grace *page 157*

Sanctifying grace is the gift of God's life and love given in Baptism that makes us holy and helps us live holy lives.

Sermon on the Mount *page 181*

The Sermon on the Mount includes the teachings of Jesus that are grouped together in chapters 5, 6, and 7 of the Gospel of Matthew.

T–Z

temperance *page 200*

Temperance gives balance in the way we act and speak in a good way. This Cardinal Virtue also enables a person to express their feelings appropriately.

Ten Commandments *page 193*

The Ten Commandments are the laws of the Covenant revealed to Moses and the Israelites on Mount Sinai.

understanding *page 100*

Understanding is a gift of the Holy Spirit that helps us know the meaning of the teaching of the Church. It also helps us be sympathetic to others and sense when someone is hurting or in need of compassion.

wonder and awe *page 28*

This gift of the Holy Spirit encourages us to respect and be in awe of God. The mystery of faith is something that can cause us to marvel, or stand in awe, at God's great love.

Index

Credits